Ickes, William John.
Everyday mind
reading

D0820919

everyday
MIND READING

foreword by
elliot aronson

everyday
MIND READING

understanding what
other people think and feel

william ickes, ph.d.

Prometheus Books

59 John Glenn Drive
Amherst, New York 14228-2197

Published 2003 by Prometheus Books

Inquiries should be addressed to
Prometheus Books
59 John Glenn Drive
Amherst, New York 14228–2197
VOICE: 716–691–0133, ext. 207
FAX: 716–564–2711
WWW.PROMETHEUSBOOKS.COM

07 06 05 04 03   5 4 3 2 1

Library of Congress Cataloging-in-Publication Data

Ickes, William John.
Everyday mind reading : understanding what other people think and feel / William Ickes
  p. cm.
Includes bibliographical references.
ISBN 1–59102–119–7
1. Empathy. I. Title.

BF575.E55I35 2003
155.6—dc22

2003018602

Printed in the United States of America on acid-free paper

To Mary Jo

CONTENTS

foreword

BY ELLIOT ARONSON

It already felt like a long flight—and we had only been off the ground for a little more than an hour. The loquacious middle-aged man sitting next to me seemed intent on preventing me from reading my novel. First he treated me to a superficial but seemingly endless analysis of his take on the crisis in the Middle East. Then, hardly pausing for breath, he launched into the intricate details of his great success at selling real estate in spite of a tightening economy. He then proceeded to take out his wallet and show me snapshots of his wife and kids. Finally, he leaned back, stretched, and yawned. It looked as though he was about to take a nap; I eyed my novel hopefully. No such luck. He turned to me and asked, "And what do *you* do?"

"I'm a psychologist," I said.

His eyes widened, and he shrank back several inches. "Uh, oh. I guess all this time you have been reading my mind!"

It is not the first time a stranger has said something like that to me and it probably won't be the last—unless I go out of my way to conceal my occupation. The irony is that most psychologists are no better (and, I would hope, no worse) than anyone else at this kind of mind reading—at least to the extent that my accidental companion had in mind.

Wait a minute! How in the world do I know what he had in mind? In spite of my initial disclaimer, is it possible that I was accurately reading his mind after all?

Well, yes and no. I made an educated guess. From the look of concern (fear?) that I saw on his face and from the way he framed his statement ("Uh, oh . . ."), I surmised that he feared that there was nothing he could conceal from me. In his mind, I would be able to take one look at him and, like the stage mind reader, complete with tux and turban (hilariously parodied by Johnny Carson as "Carnac the Magnificent"), I would close my eyes for a few seconds, concentrate really hard, and then reveal that he was contemplating divorcing his wife and running off with his secretary—Ralph!

In that "voyeuristic" sense, no one can read minds—not even Carnac. On the other hand, we humans *are* social animals and, as such, it is natural for us to empathize with one another—to look and listen carefully and try to figure out what other folks are thinking and feeling. This is the phenomenon that William Ickes has been studying for most of his professional life. And what he has done in this highly readable book is to explain why empathy is an important human attribute. He goes on to show us that some people have greater empathic ability than others—and that those who are good at it can have a real advantage over those who aren't. For example, one of the studies he cites shows that mothers who can accurately guess their children's thoughts and feelings have children with higher self-esteem than the children of less accurate mothers.

So what are the less accurate mothers supposed to do? Fortunately, Ickes and his colleagues have done some careful research demonstrating that empathic accuracy can be improved through the use of a special kind of feedback training and that the beneficial results of this training emerge quickly. The fact that we can improve empathic ability has important implications that extend beyond mothers and the self-esteem of their children. For starters, imagine a world where physicians, teachers, counselors, and diplomats were able to increase their empathic accuracy. We would all be the beneficiaries.

To his credit, Ickes sees this skill as a double-edged sword and alerts us to the downside of empathic accuracy. Specifically, he notes that there are sure to be some things going on in the minds of other people that, if available to us, would cause us pain or distress and that we would just as soon *not* know about. Moreover, although it is a clear advantage to have a physician or a counselor with a high degree of empathic accuracy, what about people trying to sell us life insurance or a used car? I would just as soon that they couldn't read my mind, thank you. Ickes's caveat notwithstanding, I believe that the advantages of empathic accuracy far outweigh the disadvantages. My guess is that few of us will ever get so good at mind reading as to bring us more pain than insight or to constitute a menace to others by invading their privacy. In short, improving our empathic accuracy is a worthwhile goal.

Although this book can be helpful in enabling us to become better mind readers, it is far more than a mere pie-in-the-sky, self-help book of the kind that is based on untested homilies and unproven folk wisdom. William Ickes is a serious scientist who has been studying this phenomenon for many years. He and I first became acquainted almost thirty-five years ago when he began his graduate studies in the psychology department at the University of Texas where I was a professor. I was immediately impressed with him, in part because, unlike most entering graduate students who are shopping around for a topic of interest, he seemed to have a reasonably clear goal. He wanted to know more about the most fundamental of social psychological questions: How do we come to know one another? And, more specifically, how can we determine the thoughts and feelings of another person?

Finding the answers to these questions is not as easy as it may seem. As a young scientist, Ickes had to develop a new kind of methodology—one that combined the best aspects of the laboratory experiment with the realism of naturalistic observation. One of the special treats of this book is the way the author takes us through the scientific study of everyday mind reading—a path that gives his readers an understanding of how science works as well as providing them with the tools to evaluate the efficacy of his own findings.

Some of the findings in this book square with common sense, but there are a great many surprises as well. Close friends are better at reading each other's minds than the minds of strangers, sure, but what about married couples? Do they get better at it as they continue to live with each other? And is it true that, because of what has been called "women's intuition," women are more empathically accurate than men? Read on and you will find the answers to these and a host of other interesting questions.

It shouldn't take a terrific mind reader to infer that I am feeling very proud of my former student. He has given us a remarkable book. It is an adventure story of the rarest kind: a treatise on the scientific pursuit of an important and elusive idea that reads like an exciting mystery story.

One

A MASTER OF INTRUSIVENESS

Richard Burton was one of the most intrusive people ever born. He was compelled to know everyone's secrets, and he wouldn't let up until he did. It wasn't enough for him to know who you were, what you said, what you did, and how you lived. He had to speak your language, practice your customs, wear your clothes, read your books, ingest your drugs, and make love to your women. It was almost as if he had to climb into your head, poke around in every crevice of your mind, and then look back out at the world through your eyes—thinking your thoughts and feeling your feelings. Indeed, his wife Isabel said as much when she wrote of him that "He saw and knew all the recesses of men's minds and actions."

No, I'm not talking about Richard Burton, the hard-drinking Welsh actor who took a couple of rides on the matrimonial roller coaster with Liz. I'm talking about Sir Richard Francis Burton, the

Fig. 1. Richard Francis Burton at the time of his marriage to Isabel. (Adapted from his wedding portrait by Louis Desanges, 1861)

nineteenth-century Renaissance man who inhaled knowledge and experience the way a spent swimmer inhales air. According to Fawn Brodie, one of his biographers, this Richard Burton was a "soldier, ethnologist, archeologist, poet, translator, and one of the two or three great linguists of his time. He was also an amateur physician, botanist, zoologist, and geologist, and incidentally a celebrated swordsman and superb raconteur."

Burton's exploits were the stuff of legend, and most of them were variations on the same theme: finding out the secret things that other people know. As a spy for the British Army during its conquest of India in the 1840s, he frequented the marketplaces of the Sind disguised as an Arab-Iranian trader, and then conveyed his intelligences to General Charles Napier. A few years later, disguised as a wandering dervish-doctor, he was one of the first non-Moslems to penetrate the sacred shrines of Mecca and Medina, risking the fate of the infidel if his true identity were revealed. Spurred by these successes, he set himself the even riskier goal of being the first European infidel to enter the holy city of Harar in Somaliland. After dropping his Arab disguise and boldly presenting himself at the city gates as an emissary from England, Burton spent several days under close watch in Harar before finally being released as a "dangerous guest." These adventures in intrusiveness set the stage for his epic expedition with John Hanning Speke to search for the headwaters of the Nile.

Burton visited and studied literally dozens of the world's cultures, and in each case made extraordinary efforts to understand how the members of that culture thought and felt. His first step was always to immerse himself in the language, often studying it for periods as long as twelve to fourteen hours a day. In Brodie's words, "He took to languages . . . as other men to liquor, intoxicated by the sense of mastery and the exhilaration of unlocking mysteries." During his earliest years in India, Burton studied for and successfully passed a series of rigorous military language exams in Hindustani, Gujarti, and Marathi. Later, he took up Persian and "went on to Sindi, Punjabi, Telugo, Pashto, Multani, Armenian, and Turkish. . . . Eventually he became one of the three or four great linguists of his time, mastering in the end twenty-nine languages and enough dialects to add up to more than forty." Indeed, he considered it a matter of principle "never to travel where the language is unknown to me."

By adopting the language, dress, and customs of a culture, Burton was able to access its deepest secrets through the minds of its members. Byron Farwell, perhaps the most culturally well-versed of the Burton biographers, described the sheer range of information that Burton, in his disguise as Mirza Abdullah, was able to obtain as a spy in Karachi for the British Army. In addition to learning a great deal about the sexual practices of the Orient, he "made notes on folk tales, religions, magic, native cures, aphrodisiacs and talismans; weapons, armour, soldiers and methods of fighting; tribes, races, castes and trades; weddings, funerals, festivals, and courtship." According to Brodie, he also made detailed reports on the difficult-to-prosecute crimes of wife killing, infanticide, and male and female prostitution. Once Burton had mastered the art of gaining access to private residences in his disguise as a rich Arab-Iranian merchant, he "soon had a store of private histories, domestic scandals, and details of harem life."

Reading the indigenous literature was another key that Burton used to understand how the members of a particular culture thought and felt. He found that poetry and folklore offered one source of insight into a people's passions, values, and beliefs; that philosophical and religious works offered a second source; and that books of erotica offered a third. He read widely in all of these categories, and he managed to translate a surprising amount of what he read. As Brodie said, "One stands in awe of the ease with which he moved from Hindustani for his 'Pilpay's Fables' and *Vikram and*

Vampire—to Portuguese for his *Camoens* and *Lacerda*—to Arabic for the *Arabian Nights* and the *Perfumed Garden*—to Neapolitan Italian for his *Il Pentamerone*—to Sanskrit for his *Kama Sutra* and *Anaga Ranga*, and to Latin for his *Priapeia* and *Catullus*."

Sharing even more directly in the states of consciousness experienced by others, Burton rarely missed an opportunity to sample whatever drugs and intoxicants were locally available. In the Sind, "he smoked opium and drank bhang [a hemp derivative] with the addicts." He also wrote a lengthy military report about "the kinds of wines, liqueurs, 'alcohols' and narcotics used in Sind," in which he "spoke with authority . . . having tried most, if not all, of the intoxicants mentioned." In the West African kingdom of Dahomey, he accepted the invitation of his host, King Gelele, to refresh himself by drinking rum "from brass-mounted skulls of former enemy chiefs." In the American West, he made note of the various colloquial names given to whisky (tarantula juice, red eye, strychnine, etc.), and, having also acquired the phrase "liquoring up," he quickly adopted the custom. Getting liquored up was also a regular feature of his subsequent travels in Argentina, Chile, and Peru.

Lovemaking can provide a particularly intimate form of contact with other minds, and the young Richard Burton took advantage of it. When he and his brother Edward were living with their family in the south of France, they initiated "a series of love affairs with various pairs of sisters." In Pisa, they proposed marriage to two Italian sisters, Caterina and Antonia Pini, while carrying on dalliances with other local girls. Soon after his arrival in India, the newly commissioned Ensign Richard Burton acquired the customary *bubu*—a native mistress. In Portuguese Goa, he courted a pretty and willing young nun, but failed in his plan to "rescue" her when he and his accomplice made a wrong turn within the nunnery of Santa Monaca and carried off the sleeping form of the ugly sub-prioress instead. Outside Karachi, he fell famously in love with a Persian girl whose beauty he immortalized in verse. It was, not surprisingly, the face beneath the veil that intrigued him the most.

If any further evidence of Burton's passionate curiosity is needed, the most dramatic example was provided by his wife, Isabel. Following their marriage, Richard became increasingly aware that the major rival for his wife's affection was the Catholic Church, to which her commitment was devout and unwavering. According to Brodie's account,

> When they were first married, he was nettled by Isabel's going off to confession. His sense of rivalry challenged, he determined to ferret out for himself his wife's innermost thoughts, one of the supreme secrets for this passionately inquisitive man. Foiled by the defenses of a woman schooled from childhood in pretence, he turned to hypnosis. Isabel herself described it:
>
> "Richard was a great mesmerizer. . . . [H]e began with me as soon as we were married; but I did not like it, and used to resist it, but once he had complete control, no passes or contact were necessary; he used simply to say, 'Sleep,' and I did. He could do this at a distance . . . and if he tried to mesmerize anybody else and I was anywhere in the neighbourhood, I absorbed it, and they took nothing. . . . He used to mesmerize me freely, but he never allowed anyone else, nor did I, to mesmerize me. Once mesmerized, he had only to say, 'Talk,' and I used to tell him everything I knew . . ."

Knowing that Burton was interested in all of her secrets, including her sexual feelings, Isabel wanted him to discontinue his practice of hypnotizing other women as well. She seemed to have regarded this practice as equivalent to a seduction, and a bitter quarrel resulted on one occasion when she discovered that he had, without her knowledge and consent, hypnotized the sister-in-law of Lord Amberley, at whose home she and Richard were currently staying.

As time passed, Isabel felt that it was increasingly difficult to keep her husband out of her mind. She believed that he could "read" her thoughts and feelings at any time and from any distance. And she was not the only person who attributed such an uncanny ability to him. According to Farwell, "Burton had an affinity for gypsies," in whose company he found occasional solace. "The *Gypsy Lore Journal* once said of him that 'he had the peculiar eye, which looked you through, glazed over and saw something behind. . . . [He] was the only man, not a gypsy, with that peculiarity.'"

If such accounts can be believed, Richard Burton was as relentlessly inquisitive as a person can be. He was, to put it bluntly, one of the most intrusive people ever born, a master of intrusiveness.

Unlike Burton, I can't claim to read other people's minds with an exceptional degree of skill. My own empathic ability is only slightly above-average—respectable though far from outstanding. But what I *can* claim is this: I can measure how well you, or anyone else of reasonably normal intelligence, can read other people's minds. In other words, I can assess how accurately you can infer the specific content of other people's thoughts and feelings.

My name is William Ickes. I am a research psychologist. And this book is the story of how my colleagues and I came to study what might be called *everyday mind reading*. It is the story of the research that we have already done on this topic, and of what this research has taught us about the psychology of empathic accuracy. To some extent, it is also my story, and I will tell you that part of it as well.

Sources for Chapter 1

Brodie, Fawn M. *The Devil Drives: A Life of Sir Richard Francis Burton.* New York: W. W. Norton, 1984.

Farwell, Byron. *Burton: A Biography of Sir Richard Francis Burton.* London: Penguin Books Ltd., 1990.

Rice, Edward. *Captain Sir Richard Francis Burton.* New York: Harper-Perennial, 1991.

two

AN APPRENTICESHIP

Although it must be obvious, I will state at the outset that I am no Richard Francis Burton. I am, instead, a non-Renaissance man whose accomplishments are pretty much limited to my own chosen field of psychology. Unlike Burton, I have never fought with a sword, spied for my country, or risked my life in exploration. I have also never dined with monkeys, ridden an alligator, evaded assassins, courted a nun, or drunk rum out of a human skull—all of which Burton purportedly did as well.

I can't even claim to be a linguist, being reasonably fluent only in English. (Does Texan count as a second language?) In Montreal, I was chagrined when my smattering of French was barely adequate for placing an order at McDonald's (*"Je voudrais un Big Mac et un café noir sans sucre"*). In Strasbourg, I was even more chagrined when my halting franglais earned me the amused contempt of a smug French waiter and the unwanted *bonhomie* of an American expatriate wino.

As a world traveler and student of other cultures, I'm not even in the running. I have been to fewer than a dozen countries outside the United States. Much of the time I have spent traveling has been in the air. My experiences with ground transportation have been limited mostly to taxis and trains; I have never traveled on horseback or as part of a camel caravan. And any interest I might have in getting to know a new place and its people has typically been sacrificed to the demands of attending conference sessions and giving talks on university-approved budgets that rarely permit any extra time for sightseeing or extended travel.

There is no way around it. In just about every way that counts, I'm as different from Sir Richard Francis Burton as a hound dog is from a hippogriff. There is, however, one respect in which Burton and I are very much alike: in our inordinate interest in the content of other people's thoughts and feelings. Like Burton, I have an intense curiosity about what is going on in other people's minds. Officially, my excuse for this curiosity is that it's my job—I am, after all, a psychologist. Unofficially, however, I have to acknowledge that there is more to it than that. When I look back over my professional life, it is evident that I have been pursuing a decades-long apprenticeship in the study of how, when, and why we are able to "read" other people's thoughts and feelings.

My apprenticeship as a research psychologist began in the fall of 1969, when I started my first semester of graduate study in psychology at the University of Texas. In those days, the social atmosphere in Austin was considerably more interesting than its current slacker stereotype would suggest. Austin, along with points farther west such as Taos and Sante Fe, had become a haven for the migrating hippies who had left San Francisco when the Summer of Love ended and the mean-spirited hard-drug scene began.

When the immigrant hippie culture hit Austin, it collided with the existing mix of cowboy complacency and south-by-south-western gentility. The result was a roiling turbulence that eventually spawned such cultural prototypes as the Cozmic Cowboy, the Damned Hippie Liberal, the Druggy Pundit, and the Slacker Artiste. Socially, the usually placid Austin, like the Comal River further south, was abruptly transformed into a turbid swirl of cross-currents and deep eddies—a culture in which such traditional streams as The University, the Darrell Royal Football Dynasty, and the South Congress Deal Makers were suddenly infused by the fresher or (depending on one's perspective) more polluted streams of Underground Comix, the Armadillo World Headquarters, and the Hippie Hollow Nude Bathing Society.

I liked this turbulent energy. I liked its promise of new beginnings, of new forms emerging to challenge the old. It fit my mood as a person who was about to reinvent himself. I was brash enough to admit to myself the extent of my own ambition. I wanted more than a doctoral degree, a good job, and the chance to do some original research. My long-term goal was nothing less than changing the face of experimental social psychology. I was careful, however, to keep this brash ambition to myself.

By luck, I had landed in the social psychology program at UT in what were probably the glory days of that program. My primary mentors during my four years of graduate school were Robert Wicklund and Elliot Aronson. Bob Wicklund is one of the field's most talented theorists. He not only is adept at constructing elegant social psychological theories of his own but also has a remarkable gift for uncovering the weaknesses in other people's theories. Elliot Aronson is one of social psychology's most creative and accomplished experimentalists. He is also the most charismatic and effective classroom teacher I have ever seen. Looking back, I realize that I could not have had two better mentors and role models during my formal apprenticeship as an experimental social psychologist.

As grateful as I was for their mentorship, however, it wasn't long before the revolutionary in me began to question the limitations of the kind of experimental social psychology that I was being trained to do. I wanted to study people's naturally occurring social behavior—their thoughts, feelings, and actions during their ongoing interactions with others. I quickly learned, however, that it was rare for social psychologists to actually do that kind of research. In general, such research was considered too difficult, too labor intensive, too time consuming, too lacking in experimental control, and too complicated in terms of the unconventional statistical analyses it required.

The kind of laboratory study that most social psychologists did instead was one in which a single research participant was presented with a plausible, but usually fabricated, scenario that allegedly had real social implications. For example, the participant might be led to believe that she was being interviewed for a job on campus. Or the participant might be asked to view and rate photographs of potentially available dating partners. Or the participant might be asked to administer electric shocks to another participant each time he made a mistake on a memory task. Or the participant might be asked to write a persuasive essay that other participants would later read. And so on. In the vast majority of these studies, no participants actually got a job, or got a date, or shocked someone, or influenced someone through the essays they wrote. But if the experimental scenarios were plausible enough, the participants *believed* that such things could and would happen—and presumably based their subsequent behaviors upon these beliefs.

In a typical laboratory experiment of this type, each participant is randomly assigned by the experimenter to one of the study's conditions. Minimally, there is one experimental condition and one control condition, but often there are several different conditions within a particular experiment. Although the participants in all conditions are presented with the same general scenario (for example, rating photographs of potential dating partners), at least one aspect of this general scenario is systematically varied or *manipulated* by the experimenter from one condition to the next. (For example, in one condition of the study the potential dating partners are all physically attractive, whereas in another condition they are all physically unattractive). The researcher is interested in how such manipulated variations in the common scenario will influence the subsequent reactions (thoughts, feelings, motives, and behavior) of the participants in the different conditions of the study.

Consider, however, the participants' own perspective on what is occurring. They have been put into a novel experimental situation and are understandably concerned that they not make fools of themselves by acting inappropriately. For this reason, they are motivated to use whatever cues are available to help them figure out what "role" they should play in the particular variant of the experimental scenario with which they are currently confronted. In this sense, they are like novice actors who are forced to ad lib their part in an established play with an established set of players. The experimental script for each condition has been written beforehand, and the experimenter and any confederates who are involved have already memorized what lines they will say and when they will say them. Only the naive participants are required to figure out for themselves what part they will play in this production, and then to improvise the words and actions that seem most appropriate to this part.

They usually get a lot of prompting, however. In fact, according to this dramaturgical view of the typical social psychology experiment, the participants' reactions to a given scenario are typically "prompted" in a number of ways. The participant is obviously prompted by the "plot line" defined by the prescribed words and actions of the experimenter and any experimental confederates who might be present on the scene. The participant is also prompted, however, by the experimental setting itself and by the various "stage props" (photographs, rating scales, etc.) that are encountered within that setting. There are, in effect, cue cards everywhere.

Why does all of this prompting occur? So that when the participant has reached what amounts to a choice point in the experimental script, the researcher can present a special "variable cue" that constitutes the manipulation of what, in scientific parlance, is called the *independent variable.* This manipulation (for example, presenting photos of either physically attractive or physically unattractive potential dating partners), is strategically placed at the precise point in the script when the variable cue it provides can be expected to channel the participant's subsequent behavior in one direction or another, according to the researcher's hypothesis. The fact that the placement of this variable cue must be strategic and nonarbitrary is important because it implies that the independent variable derives at least part of its meaning from the specific context established by the previous scripted events. In other words, the independent variable will not necessarily be interpreted in the same way or have the same effects on the participants' behavior if it is presented in a different script or at a different point in the same script.

When I first read about this dramaturgical view of the typical social psychology experiment, I found it more than a little disturbing. In particular, it led me to wonder whether the participants' behavior in such experiments could always be interpreted as evidence bearing on the researcher's hypotheses, or whether—in certain cases, at least—it should be interpreted as evidence bearing more on the researcher's skill as a *manipulator.* For there is no doubt that, from the dramaturgical perspective, the researcher is the ultimate manipulator—a combination writer-producer-director-stage-manager who attempts to create an experimental play so tightly constructed that the participants in each condition are virtually compelled to play their parts "correctly."

But if they do play their parts correctly, what can we conclude from that? If the participants in these studies act the way they are predicted to act, does their behavior really provide evidence for the validity of the researcher's hypothesis? Or does it merely attest to the subtlety and effectiveness of the researcher's manipulative skill? And are these two interpretations mutually exclusive, or is it possible that both could be true? These questions were not easy to answer. And, as I would later discover, they would continue to preoccupy me long after I left graduate school.

After completing my Ph.D. in the summer of 1973, I took a faculty position in the psychology department at the University of Wisconsin. I had looked forward to the move as an opportunity to strike out on my own and develop a research direction that no one else had pursued before. But although my research did expand into some new problem areas, I found that, after a year at Wisconsin, I was still doing the kind of traditional laboratory experiments that I had been trained to do. And why not? It was not only the obvious path; it was the path of least resistance. I was good at experimental design, the studies I was doing were interesting and informative, and it was easy to find people to collaborate with.

As time went by, however, I found myself plagued with the nagging sense that I was supposed to be doing a different kind of research. I had no idea yet what kind of research that might be, but I did try to identify the specific source of my discontent. As I did so, it gradually became apparent that the uneasy sense I was having was related to my earlier uneasiness with the image of the researcher-as-manipulator. Further reflection led me to make an even more interesting discovery: at a deeper level than I had looked before, the image of the researcher-as-manipulator was associated in my mind with Maurice Conchis, the title character in John Fowles's novel *The Magus*.

This was a significant association. I had first read *The Magus* while in graduate school, when it was a current favorite of the graduate students in psychology, and I had read it twice more since then. It is a brilliant and multilayered novel, a psychological thriller in which the protagonist's shifting frames of reference blur the distinctions between fantasy and reality, truth and lies, chance and choice, past and present, trust and betrayal, illusion and enlightenment.

The Magus is presented to the reader as a first-person account by its protagonist, Nicholas Urfe, of the strange events in his life that begin when he arrives on the (fictional) Greek island of

Phraxos. Nicholas is drawn to an isolated villa owned by Maurice Conchis, a wealthy older man whose life and purposes keep eluding Nicholas's attempts at analysis. Gradually, Nicholas realizes that Conchis is manipulating him—manipulating his very sense of reality—through an extravagant series of staged events. The central players in these events are two beautiful twin sisters, Lily and Rose, whose identities are elusive and whose motives are unclear. But there are many other players in Conchis's cast, and Nicholas finds himself playing a Pirandellian role in a succession of events that are both real and surreal, hallucinatory and revelatory.

Nothing in *The Magus* is as simple as it first appears, and this is particularly true of its title character, Maurice Conchis. There are times when Conchis is, indeed, a master manipulator—a person who plays god by subjecting mere mortals to test situations of his own devising. There are other times, however, when he chooses instead to simply observe his subjects—eavesdropping on their conversations and filming their private and public actions without their knowledge. As a student of human behavior, Conchis is not only a manipulator, a would-be experimentalist; he is also a close and careful observer of human nature.

It isn't surprising, then, that once I began to examine my mental association of Maurice Conchis with the researcher-as-manipulator, I was soon confronted with the alternative association of Conchis with the researcher-as-observer. And it was this alternative association that was to change the course of my career as a research psychologist. For as sneaky as the practice of "spying" on other people might be, I eventually decided that if it were done within the bounds of appropriate ethical constraints, it would be a viable and even desirable alternative to the established practice of "manipulating" them.

Conchis's strategy for learning what he wanted to know was to balance these two approaches of manipulation and observation. Ironically, however, there was no comparable balance within the field of social psychology, where experimental manipulation was clearly the rule and behavioral observation was rare. The obvious way to achieve such a balance was to do fewer studies that manipulate people into displaying certain kinds of behavior, and to do more studies that get them to reveal themselves through their own spontaneous actions. But it occurred to me, with the benefit of Conchis's example, that there might be another, less obvious way to accomplish the same goal.

Perhaps, like Conchis, I could figure out a way to blend the two approaches, combining some of the best features of experimental laboratory research with some of the best features of more naturalistic observational research. Perhaps a kind of hybrid procedure could be developed—one that would allow the researcher to study participants' behavior within a controlled laboratory setting but that would also allow the participants the freedom to talk and act in a natural, spontaneous way. Ideally, this hybrid procedure would present the participants with few, if any, situational cues that might "prompt" or constrain their behavior. And, if I could get the experimenter to go off for awhile and leave two participants by themselves, it should be possible to unobtrusively eavesdrop on the participants' initial interaction while they were waiting for the experimenter to return.

I spent several months during the first half of 1975 thinking about the features I wanted to include in this new research paradigm. Much of this thinking was done out loud in discussions with my first graduate student, Richard Barnes, with whom I hoped to test the new procedure in a study that we were planning for the fall semester. Over the course of this extended period of thought and discussion, the features in the following "wish list" came to mind:

❖ To study spontaneous, naturally occurring interaction behavior, we had to develop a procedure in which pairs of naïve research participants could interact freely. This consideration led us to rule out the possibility of using a procedure in which a naïve participant "interacted" with an experimenter or an experimental confederate whose words and actions had been predetermined and prescripted.

❖ To observe these interactions within a controlled laboratory setting but allow the participants to relax enough to interact in a spontaneous and relatively unguarded way, we had to make our setting resemble as much as possible a real-life setting where strangers routinely meet and engage in casual conversation. This consideration (along with another *Magus*-inspired precedent that I will describe in the next chapter) suggested that we should use a simple "waiting room" situation in which the research participants would spend several minutes together waiting for what they regarded as the actual experiment to begin.

❖ To minimize any situational cues that might "prompt" or constrain the participants' behavior, we had to minimize the experimenter's contact with the participants until their initial interaction had already taken place. We also had to refrain from instructing the participants to "talk and get to know each other" during the time that the experimenter went off and left them alone.

❖ To study the participants' actual interaction behavior (as opposed to just their impressions of it), we had to obtain a videotaped and audiotaped record of the time they spent waiting together. This recording had to be done unobtrusively and without the participants' prior knowledge to ensure that it would not interfere with the spontaneity and naturalness of their interaction.

To this list of desired features, we added a few others that were needed to address the relevant ethical issues, such as obtaining the participants' written consent to use their data and giving them a complete debriefing at the end of their session in the lab. With these considerations in mind, Rick and I spent much of the summer preparing the laboratory setting and solving the specific procedural problems that our new research paradigm presented. After several weeks of work, everything was finally in place.

But when we had finished developing our new research paradigm, what did we have? Obviously, something rather different from the usual laboratory experiment. I could try to describe it to you in the dry, jargony language of the research psychologist, but it's likely that I would just wind up boring you. It would be better if I could give you the experience of being a "virtual participant" in a study of this type. That is what I have attempted to do in the first part of the next chapter.

Welcome to the waiting room.

SOURCES FOR CHAPTER 2

Fowles, John. *The Magus*. New York: Little, Brown, & Company, 1965.

Ickes, William. "A Basic Paradigm for the Study of Personality, Roles, and Social Behavior." In *Personality, Roles, and Social Behavior.* edited by William Ickes and Eric S. Knowles. New York: Springer-Verlag, 1982, pp. 305-41.

three

THE
WAITING ROOM

You are participating in a psychology experiment. You have arrived for the 10 A.M. session and are surprised to discover that you aren't the only person who has signed up for this time slot. Another participant—an attractive stranger of the opposite sex—is walking beside you down a long hallway as you both follow the experimenter past a row of cubicles and around a corner to a suite of laboratory rooms on the right. Stealing a glance at this attractive stranger by your side, you wonder what kind of experience you will share during the next hour or so.

The experimenter leads you and your coparticipant into a large, windowless, white-walled room. A quick inspection reveals that the room is institutionally furnished. Facing you along the opposing wall, several feet back from the open doorway, is a long, low couch with metal armrests and flat vinyl cushions. In front of the couch is a low wooden coffee table. Its surface is bare except for a pair of identical clipboards, each containing what appear to be some printed rating forms. To the left of the couch is a small square table. It supports a slide projector pointed toward a projection screen that faces the couch from a distance of about ten feet. The slide tray is half-filled and contains thirty or forty color slides whose opaque iridescence can be seen even from across the room.

The experimenter asks you and your coparticipant to take a seat on the couch. You sit down first and don't know whether to feel relieved or disappointed when the other person sits a respectful distance away from you. It's evident that you both feel somewhat awkward in this situation, having to relate to each other as opposite-sex strangers who have not yet been introduced but who must share each other's company through whatever unexpected events the next hour might bring.

As it happens, the first unexpected event occurs within the next few seconds. The experimenter has just explained that you and the other person will have the task of viewing and rating a series of slides. Stepping over to the small table, the experimenter turns on the slide projector to "let it warm up." Suddenly, with a loud pop and an abortive burst of light, the projector bulb burns out. A look of surprise mingled with confusion passes over the experimenter's face. *What to do now?* The look changes to one of mild annoyance.

"I'm going to have to get a new projector bulb," the experimenter says. "I think they have some in the storage room in the main office downstairs. I'll be gone for a few minutes, so just wait here and we'll start the experiment as soon as I return." And, with these words, the experimenter has disappeared out the door and down the hallway, leaving you and the attractive stranger alone together on the couch.

Now the confusion and uncertainty is yours. Should you say something—perhaps introduce yourself? Or should you wait for the other person to speak? A few seconds pass without any words being exchanged. Now you wonder if it might be better to continue to sit quietly and say nothing at all. Perhaps it would compromise the experiment in some way if you and the other person were to talk to each other—particularly if you discussed your impressions of the experiment and what it was intended to test. So saying nothing to the other person might be the safest course to follow . . .

As you sit there in silence, however, it occurs to you that a decision to say nothing also seems to require not making eye contact, which makes the situation even more awkward because it feels rude to act as if the other person isn't even present. And this isn't a person you want to offend—it's someone you're attracted to. So why not go ahead and introduce yourself? Perhaps the attraction is mutual, and something interesting will develop. The experimenter has already been gone for more than a minute; if you're going to make a move, it should probably be now.

Good! The other person just asked *you* a question. It's your turn to respond. What should you say? And how much eye contact should you make? Too little, and you seem uninterested; too much, and you seem to be pushing things. You start talking about which instructors you have for introductory psychology, and then continue by comparing their lecture styles and grading policies. These are safe topics for establishing some common ground, but they keep things on a pretty superficial level. What can you do to steer the conversation in a more intimate direction? And how much time do you have before the experimenter returns?

Not much, as it turns out. There is time for only a few minutes of conversation with your attractive partner before the experimenter comes back into the room carrying a new projector bulb in its little yellow box. It's too bad the experimenter's errand didn't take longer—the conversation was just getting interesting.

The experimenter puts the box down on the small table next to the slide projector, then turns toward the two of you and says, "This might be a good time for me to ask what impressions, if any, you have about the experiment at this point. For example, do you have any specific ideas about what the experiment might be about?"

You look at your coparticipant. Because you were both so

involved in the conversation you were just having, neither of you seems to have given the matter much thought. "Nothing specific," you say. "Just what you told us," your partner chimes in. "Viewing a set of slides and making some kind of judgments about them."

Now another unexpected event occurs. The experimenter informs you that the study isn't really about viewing slides at all. The projector bulb was rigged; it only *appeared* to burn out. And the slide-viewing task? It was just a cover story for the real purpose of the experiment, which (in case you haven't guessed by now) is to study the spontaneous, naturally occurring interaction of two strangers who are left alone together while they are presumably waiting for an experiment to begin. In fact, the first stage of the experiment is now complete. It involved covertly videotaping the interaction between you and your coparticipant during the 6-minute period when the experimenter was out of the room.

You and your partner look at each other, feeling the implications of this information sink in. The experimenter has a videotape record of everything you said and did when you were left alone together. Is there anything on the tape that is likely to prove embarrassing in retrospect? Who is going to see the tape? And why weren't you informed about the taping in advance? Even though you are in a psychology experiment—and therefore expect to be studied in ways that aren't always obvious at the outset—you're not sure that you like the feeling of having been deceived, no matter how clever the deception.

The experimenter asks if either of you were aware of being covertly videotaped. You and your partner look at each other again, shaking your heads. Neither of you had a clue. But although you now feel motivated to discover where the videocamera might be concealed, you are unable to find any sign of one in the "waiting room" where you are seated. Where is it? How did the researchers manage to hide it so effectively? And how could they be justified in using it to spy on you in this way?

As if anticipating these questions, the experimenter shows you where the camera and microphone were hidden. *So that's where they were.* The experimenter then goes on to explain the reason for waiting until now to tell you about the videotaping. In retrospect, this reason seems obvious. If the researchers were to succeed in capturing your spontaneous, naturally occurring interaction behavior, it was important that you and your partner not know in advance that your interaction would be videotaped. Such knowledge could have easily biased your behavior in ways that would make it studied and self-conscious rather than spontaneous and naturalistic.

On the other hand, the experimenter explains, it was also important to safeguard your right to privacy. For that reason, the equipment was set up to record automatically, before the two of you even entered the "waiting room." If either of you has any objection to giving your signed permission for the videotape to be used as data in the study, you can watch while the tape is rewound to its original counter setting and then erased up to its current setting. In that way, you can both be assured that the contents of your interaction will remain your own private concern.

You both decide to sign the consent form, which requests that you further consent to participate in the next phase of the study. The experimenter explains that, in this next phase, you and your partner will be asked to make a record of all the thoughts and feelings you remember having had during the 6-minute interval you spent waiting together. You nod and sign the form as if this is a simple and reasonable request, but privately you're skeptical. How do the researchers expect you to remember your previous thoughts and feelings? It doesn't seem like something that you—or, for that matter, most people—could do very well.

The experimenter collects the signed consent forms and then escorts you and your partner out of the "waiting room" and around the corner to the row of cubicles in the long hallway. You are seated in the first cubicle; your partner is taken to an identical cubicle two doors down.

There is only one chair in this little room, and you are sitting in it. Behind you is the door to the cubicle, and in front of you, mounted to the wall, is a countertop on which you are resting your elbows. Just above the countertop, at your current eye level, is a two-way window. A large television monitor in an adjacent control room faces into the cubicle from the other side of the glass; its screen is dark and blank. Spread out before you on the countertop are a remote start/pause control, a sharpened pencil, and a supply of identical printed forms (see fig. 3.1).

The experimenter comes into the cubicle and gives you the same task instructions your partner has apparently just received. You and your partner will each be viewing separate, identical videotapes of the brief, unstructured interaction in which you both just participated. The interaction will appear on the television monitor, beginning at the point at which the experimenter left you alone together. Your task, like your partner's, is to view the videotaped interaction and use the remote start/pause control to pause the tape each time you remember having had a specific thought or feeling. Then, while the tape is stopped, you are to fill in one of the "slots" in the thought/feeling reporting form.

First, you are to record the exact time when the thought or feeling occurred, by referring to the running time display that appears as an overlay in the upper-left corner of the video image. Second, after you have recorded the time of the "tape stop" in the column on the left, you are to decide whether what you experienced at that point was a thought or a feeling, and then check the appropriate alternative at the left of the wide center column to indicate your judgment. Third, using the alternative you chose—"I was thinking:" or "I was feeling:"—as the start of a sentence, you are to complete the sentence by writing out the specific content of your thought or feeling in the space provided. Fourth, you are to circle the alternative in the right column which best describes the overall emotional tone of your thought or feeling—positive (+), neutral (0), or negative (–).

Once you have finished recording your first thought or feeling,

DATE _____

NUMBER _____

M   F

TIME	THOUGHT OR FEELING	+, 0, -	
	☐ I was thinking: ☐ I was feeling:	+ 0 -	
	☐ I was thinking: ☐ I was feeling:	+ 0 -	
	☐ I was thinking: ☐ I was feeling:	+ 0 -	
	☐ I was thinking: ☐ I was feeling:	+ 0 -	
	☐ I was thinking: ☐ I was feeling:	+ 0 -	
	☐ I was thinking: ☐ I was feeling:	+ 0 -	

Figure 3.1. Thought/feeling reporting form.

you are to restart the videotape using the remote control and watch the interaction until you reach the next point where you remember having had a specific thought or feeling. You should then pause the tape at that point and record the content of your thought/feeling entry, just as you did before, and continue following this procedure until you have reported all of the thoughts and feelings you remember having had during the time you and your partner were left alone together.

The experimenter emphasizes the importance of recording *all* of your thoughts and feelings as accurately and completely as possible. You are assured that your interaction partner will never see your reported thoughts and feelings, which will later be coded and analyzed for research purposes in a way that preserves your anonymity. Although it is important that you record every thought or feeling that you distinctly remember having had during the interaction with your partner, it is equally important that you *not* record any thoughts or feelings that occur to you for the first time while you are viewing the videotape, that is, thoughts or feelings that you think you *should* have had or *could* have had at a particular point.

The experimenter leaves the cubicle and goes to the control room in which your television monitor is located. A few seconds later, an image blooms into color on the screen. It is you and your interaction partner, sitting on the couch in the "waiting room." Your image is partially blocked by that of the experimenter, who is seen standing in front of the couch, filmed from behind. The experimenter's voice is saying ". . . back in a few minutes, so just wait here and we'll start the experiment as soon as I return." The experimenter turns toward the camera, looms momentarily larger while walking to the open doorway, and then walks out of camera range to the right of the screen. You now see the image of yourself and your partner on the couch, looking at the empty doorway through which the experimenter has just passed.

The image of yourself on the television screen glances over at the image of your interaction partner, and now a brief expression flashes across your televised face—a look which you recognize and simultaneously remember as reflecting the confusion you felt at that point. The thought you were having then comes back to mind. Using the remote control, you pause the tape and record this thought on the reporting form: "I was thinking: *should I introduce myself, or should I wait for the other person to talk first?*"

Then you restart the tape and watch as, a few seconds later, your electronic self's gaze becomes more inward-focused. Because you remember having had another thought at that point, you pause the tape again and record this next thought/feeling entry: "I was thinking: *(wondering) if it might be better to sit quietly and say nothing at all.*" You restart the tape and, barely a moment later, this thought is followed by another one: "I was thinking: *(wondering) if it would compromise the experiment if we talked to each other at this point—for example, if we discussed our impressions of the experiment and what it was supposed to test.*" Stopping the tape again, you record this entry on the thought/feeling reporting form.

In these last few pages, I have tried to convey a sense of the kind of experience you might have as a participant in one of our dyadic interaction studies. What you have just read is a fairly accurate depiction, from the perspective of a typical research participant, of how my colleagues and I study the initial interaction between strangers using our *unstructured dyadic interaction paradigm*.

Let me decode that last bit of jargon for you. A *dyad* is a pair of individuals—a two-person group. A *paradigm* is a general procedure for conducting research on a given topic. And the topic in this case, *unstructured dyadic interaction,* is the spontaneous interaction that occurs between two individuals who have not been given the "task" of interacting with each other, but instead have been left on their own to decide whether, in what ways, and to what extent, they will do so.

In the summer of 1975 I developed the first version of the unstructured dyadic interaction paradigm at the University of Wisconsin in collaboration with my first graduate student, Richard Barnes. Rick and I put the procedure together over several weeks that summer, working mostly from my intuitions. What I didn't tell Rick, however, was that my intuitions in this case were guided less by theory than by a literary metaphor.

I suspected that Rick was already having some private doubts about working on the project. Even as a second-year graduate student, he knew that our new research paradigm was a radical departure from the conventional experimental paradigms that are typically used in social psychological research. To his credit, he was willing to put aside whatever doubts he might have had and to join me in what must have seemed a rather quixotic enterprise. So I didn't want to scare him off by telling him that a major source of inspiration for our new paradigm was the metaphor of the *salle d'attente*—the waiting-room—in John Fowles's novel *The Magus*.

I had reread *The Magus* the previous year, and I was surprised at how often the metaphor of the waiting room kept coming back to me. Early in the novel, Nicholas is warned by his predecessor, Mitford, to "Beware of the waiting-room." He is reminded of this allusion several months later when, for the first time, he sees the words SALLE D'ATTENTE on a sign posted outside Conchis's villa. But many more months will pass before Nicholas understands the full import of the sign. With the benefit of hindsight, he sees that it was intended to warn him, as it had warned previous trespassers, that he had ventured into a place in which unexpected events would occur that would force him to confront himself in a way he had never done before.

Similarly, in the dyadic interaction paradigm, the waiting-room metaphor is also used in both a literal and a figurative sense. On the one hand, the room in which our dyad members are covertly videotaped is literally a waiting room—a place in which they are simply passing the time until the experimenter returns. On the other hand, the room is also a testing-ground—a place in which our dyad members can interact (or not) as they choose, while at the same time being observed and videotape-recorded without their knowledge. Accordingly, although our *salle d'attente* is a subtler, less dramatic variant of its counterpart in *The Magus*, it is also a place in which unexpected events occur that will lead the participants to reveal themselves to us as well as to each other.

Consider, from the experimenter's perspective, the many ways in which the participants reveal themselves to us in the dyadic interaction paradigm. While they are seated on the couch in the observation room, we can unobtrusively record on videotape any spontaneous interaction that occurs between them during the 6-minute interval when they are left alone together. If the dyad members subsequently give their signed permission for us to use this videotape record as a data source, our research assistants can later view the videotape and record any of a number of interaction behaviors we might want to study. For example, the videotape record can be coded to determine how close the dyad members sat together on the couch, how much they talked and gestured to each other, how much they looked and smiled at each other, how many questions they asked each other, and so on. Virtually any overt behavior the dyad members display during the time they spend in the "waiting room" can be coded from the videotape and analyzed as data.

But the dyad members don't just reveal their overt behavior to us—they reveal their covert thoughts and feelings as well. Immediately following their interaction, the dyad members are seated in separate cubicles. At this time, they each view a copy of the videotape of the interaction in which they have just participated, and they each create a written, time-logged record of all of the specific thoughts and feelings they distinctly remember having had. (Our thought/feeling reporting form was modeled on one that psychologists John Cacioppo and Richard Petty sent me; their version had been used at Ohio State University in some earlier studies of attitude change.)

The thoughts and feelings we obtained from our research participants were an incredibly rich source of data. We quickly discovered that the contents of these thoughts and feelings could be coded and categorized in any number of ways, either by our research assistants or by the dyad members themselves. For example, the dyad members can code each of their own thought/feeling entries as either a thought (T) or a feeling (F). They can also code the emotional tone of each thought/feeling entry as generally positive (+), neutral (0), or negative (−). Research assistants can later code the same thoughts and feelings on other dimensions—for example, as a thought or feeling that concerns the self (S, the person who reported it), the interaction partner (P), some other person or persons (O), or some environmental object, event, or circumstance (E).

From such data, one can easily compute what percentage of a particular dyad member's thoughts and feelings have been categorized as thoughts (versus feelings), as positive (versus neutral or negative), as self-focused (as opposed to partner-focused), and so on. Similarly, by cross-classifying the thoughts and feelings on more than one dimension, one can easily compute what percentage of a particular dyad member's thoughts and feelings have been categorized as negative self feelings, or as positive partner thoughts, and so on.

Following in a tradition first established by the psychologist Raymond Corsini and later elaborated by the philosopher-psychoanalyst R. D. Laing and his colleagues Herbert Phillipson and A. R. Lee, one can also categorize thoughts and feelings according to whether they represent *direct perspectives* or *metaperspectives*. Direct-perspective thoughts and feelings reveal how one person perceives herself (S → S, "I'm feeling a bit strange today"), an interaction partner (S → P, "He's so conceited"), some other person(s), (S → O, "What a bunch of degenerates!"), or some environmental object, event, or circumstance (S → E, "Is this the right street? Or did I miss the turn?"). Metaperspective thoughts and feelings are more complex; they reveal how one person thinks another person perceives someone or something (S → P → S, "I think he likes me"; S → P → P, "But I think he likes himself even more"; S → P → O, "He's really angry at that kid with the nose ring"; S → P → E, "He was probably relieved when the police arrived").

In general, then, thoughts and feelings can be categorized as follows:

Direct Perspectives		*Metaperspectives*	
S → S	S's perception of S	S → P → S	S's perception of P's perception of S
S → P	S's perception of P	S → P → P	S's perception of P's perception of P
S → O	S's perception of O	S → P → O	S's perception of P's perception of O
S → E	S's perception of E	S → P → E	S's perception of P's perception of E

As Laing and his colleagues have pointed out, metaperspective thoughts and feelings represent instances of attempted mind reading—instances in which one person tries to mentally represent the perception, thought, or feeling of another person. However, because the first person cannot "read" the other's mind directly, the attempted mind reading must always be done indirectly. That is, it must take the form of an *inference* that the first person makes about the second person's current subjective experience.

Beginning in the next chapter, and continuing through the rest of this book, we will explore different aspects of this process of *empathic inference*—a process that can also be called "everyday mind reading." Before we do that, however, I'd like to give you a sense of how our research with the dyadic interaction paradigm developed. As you will see, our first step was to see if we could measure the content of the dyad members' own respective thoughts and feelings in a demonstrably valid way. Our next step was to use this method of thought/feeling assessment to gain insight into the processes occurring in the initial interactions of same-sex and opposite-sex strangers. Our third step was to modify the thought/feeling assessment procedure to permit us to measure and study the dyad members' *empathic accuracy*—the degree to which they could accurately infer the specific content of their interaction partner's thoughts and feelings.

❖   ❖   ❖

When we first used the dyadic interaction paradigm to analyze the behaviors that dyad members display during brief, unstructured interactions, no one seriously questioned whether we had measured these behaviors in a reliable and valid way. After all, the research assistants who served as the raters in our studies had already had years of experience in everyday social interactions. They therefore found it easy to identify when a particular dyad member started talking, or smiling, or gesturing, and so on. But just to be on the safe side—to ensure that the raters' judgments would be optimally reliable—we trained them for hours to use an electronic timing system to record the onset and offset of particular interaction behaviors.

It's not surprising, then, that when different raters coded the same behaviors, they typically achieved very similar (and therefore highly reliable) estimates of the total number of times a particular dyad member spoke, or the total amount of time the same dyad member spent smiling, and so on. And it's also not surprising that none of the reviewers who evaluated our work for publication seriously questioned the validity of these measures—that they really did measure the behaviors of talking, smiling, gesturing, etc.

Things became more complicated, however, when we later expanded the dyadic interaction paradigm to assess the content of the dyad members' reported thoughts and feelings. We thought that the reviewers would take less for granted in this case, and would require us to demonstrate the validity of the resulting thought/feeling content measures. We expected them to argue that it wasn't enough for us to simply claim that what our raters had categorized as negative self thoughts or positive partner feelings really were what we purported them to be; we needed to provide corroborating evidence for such claims. And we believed that the reviewers might even have some cause for expressing this concern, because if our measures of thought/feeling content turned out *not* to be valid, there would be reason to question the validity of any research findings that were based on such measures. Worse yet, there would be reason to question whether the method we were using to assess thought/feeling content was one that should be used at all.

We weren't anxious to see our new method consigned to the Scrap Heap of Scientific Discards, so we (Eric Robertson, William Tooke, Gary Teng, and I) decided to give the reviewers what we thought they might want. In the first of our studies that assessed dyad members' thoughts and feelings as well as their overt behavior, we tested the validity of our thought/feeling content measures in several different ways. This study, which was conducted at the University of Texas at Arlington, examined the initial interactions of 30 pairs of strangers. We captured the strangers' interactions on videotape, got them to make a record of all of their thoughts and feelings, and then asked them to rate various aspects of their interaction at the end of the study.

Our first validity test was based on the simple idea that the more positive thoughts and feelings we have about a new acquaintance, the more we will probably like that person. This expectation was confirmed in the data from our study. We found that the greater the percentage of positive partner-focused thoughts and feelings the dyad members reported having had during their initial, unstructured interactions, the more liking for their partners they later reported on a questionnaire they filled out at the end of the experiment. The correlation between positive thoughts about the partner and rated liking for the partner was encouragingly strong.

Other validity tests were based on the idea that certain personality traits might be reflected in the kinds of thoughts and feelings that people are likely to report having had in initial, unstructured dyadic interactions. For example, we predicted that the dyad members' scores on a personality measure of social anxiety would be correlated with the percentage of negative self-focused thoughts they reported. This prediction was confirmed: the interactants who were socially anxious reported higher percentages of negative self thoughts during their interactions than those who weren't. Similarly, we predicted that the dyad members' scores on a personality measure of private self-consciousness (introspectiveness) would be correlated with the percentage of neutral self-focused thoughts and feelings they reported. This prediction was also confirmed: the more introspective interactants were also those who reported the higher percentages of neutral self thoughts and feelings.

Finally, consistent with stereotypes about the differing social orientations of women and men, the women reported having had more positive, partner-focused thoughts and feelings than the men. In addition, the women reported having had more metaperspective thoughts and feelings that sought to represent their interaction partners' view of things. The behavioral data added further detail to this picture; they showed that the women also engaged in more talking, smiling, and eye contact, and were more likely to turn toward their partners during the interaction. These results all seem to fit the gender-role stereotype that women are more likely than men to act in ways that encourage the development of close relationships with others. And we were happy to find that the thought/feeling data would tell us a story that the behavioral data would support.

Having obtained some solid evidence for the validity of our thought/feeling assessment procedure, we wanted to use this procedure to help us understand what happens when strangers first meet and begin to interact. Our next study focused on same-sex strangers, and it teamed me with my colleagues William Tooke, Linda Stinson, Vickie Lau Baker, and Victor Bissonnette. To give you a quick preview of the findings: If the results of this study were a picture, I would give it the caption *Real Men Don't Get Intimate*.

The overall goal of the study was to compare the initial interactions of male-male versus female-female strangers. Using the dyadic interaction paradigm, we unobtrusively captured the strangers' interaction on videotape, obtained their consent to continue with the experiment, and asked them to independently report the various thoughts and feelings they had had during the interaction while viewing it on videotape. As before, our research assistants later coded each reported thought or feeling as positive (+), neutral (0), or negative (–); as focused on self (S), partner (P), some other person(s) (O), or some aspect of the environment (E); and as representing the perceiver's direct perspective (for example, $S \rightarrow E$) or a metaperspective that represented what the interaction partner might have been thinking or feeling (for example, $S \rightarrow P \rightarrow E$).

Through their data coding, our raters had generated a fairly large set of thought/feeling content measures (percentage of positive thoughts and feelings, partner-focused thoughts and feelings, metaperspective thoughts and feelings, and so on). We wondered if these measures could be used to help us identify *intersubjective themes* that might distinguish the initial interactions of the male strangers from those of the female strangers. The basic questions we were asking are fairly simple ones. How similar are the dyad members in the kinds of thought/feeling content they report? Are the male dyad members similar on a different set of thought/feeling content measures than the female dyads are? If so, do these different sets of thought/feeling content measures suggest different intersubjective themes that might distinguish the initial interactions of male strangers from the initial interactions of female strangers?

To answer these questions, we computed between-partner correlations for each of the thought/feeling content measures (assessing, for example, whether the percentage of positive thoughts and feelings that Partner B reported tended to correspond, or co-vary with, the percentage of positive thoughts and feelings that Partner A reported). We computed these interpartner correlations for the male-male dyads, and then computed the analogous set of correlations for the female-female dyads.

The results were, at first glance, surprising. Our commonsense intuition might be that women are more sensitive than men to the emotional tone of social interactions. We found, however, that the male strangers were similar to each other in the percentages of positive and negative thoughts and feelings they reported, whereas the female strangers were not. In other words, the male strangers appeared to be more attuned to the emotional tenor of their initial interaction with each other, so that if one man reported a high percentage of positive (or negative) thoughts and feelings, his partner did the same. In contrast, the female strangers seemed to be reporting thoughts and feelings whose emotional content was more individualized and less intersubjective, as if their emotions were running on different tracks rather than on the same one.

At first, we were somewhat puzzled by these results. Eventually, however, we arrived at a possible explanation: the greater similarity in the emotional tone of the male strangers' thoughts and feelings might have occurred because they were more motivated than female strangers to closely monitor the emotional tone of their initial interactions. Our tentative hypothesis was that male strangers are more concerned than female strangers about keeping their initial interactions within an acceptable emotional range. Specifically, they are trying to keep these interactions from becoming too positive (that is, too intimate).

There are at least two reasons to believe that "too much" intimacy could be a problem for male strangers. First, it could interfere with the greater concern that men have to establish their level of dominance and status vis-à-vis each other early in their relationship. Second, it could result in attributions of homosexual interest, which men typically find more threatening than women do. Either or both of these reasons could explain why male strangers might be more motivated than female strangers to closely monitor the emotional tone of their interaction in order to keep it within mutually acceptable limits.

This explanation sounds plausible enough, but how could we test it further? What additional evidence would help to confirm our hunch that the male strangers tried to keep their interactions from becoming too intimate, and therefore allowed themselves a narrower range of behavior in this regard? The best evidence would

seem to lie in the nonverbal "intimacy behaviors" of the participants in our study—behaviors such as their levels of smiling, gesturing, and eye contact. If the male strangers displayed lower
average levels and less variability (more constraint) in these behaviors than the female strangers displayed, we would have even better
evidence that the men were more motivated to monitor and control
their intimacy levels.

When we coded and analyzed the dyad members' nonverbal
"intimacy behaviors," this is exactly what we found. The men
smiled, gestured, and made eye contact less often and for shorter
periods of time than the women did, and they were consistently less
variable (that is, more constrained) in their display of these behaviors. Even more convincing, we found the same pattern of results in
a second, replication study. Once again, the men were more similar
than the women in the percentages of positive and negative thoughts
and feelings they reported, and they displayed lower levels of—and
less variability in—their smiling, gesturing, and eye contact.

It is clear that the male strangers in these studies achieved a significant degree of synchrony or correspondence in the affectively
positive or negative content of their thoughts and feelings. What is
even more interesting, however, is that they seem to have done this
entirely through nonverbal channels. When I viewed the videotapes
of these interactions, not once did I see one of these guys turn to the
other and say, "Yuh know, if we're not careful, things might get a
little too intimate here. So let's make damn sure that doesn't
happen." And yet, in spite of not making the issue explicit by
talking about it, the men in these dyads achieved an emotional synchrony in their thought/feeling content that seemed to reflect the
implicit management of their nonverbal intimacy behaviors. In
other words, they displayed an implicit emotional rapport, an
implicit *empathy*, that might be viewed as a precursor of more
explicit empathic inference-making.

Just as we had hoped, our measures of thought/feeling content provided useful insights into the processes occurring in the initial interactions of same-sex strangers. It was perhaps inevitable, therefore, that our next study would focus on the initial interactions of opposite-sex strangers. This study was conducted in collaboration with my colleagues Stella Garcia, Linda Stinson, Victor Bissonnette, and Stephen Briggs. For reasons that will become clearer in a moment, if the results of *this* study were a picture, I would give it the caption *Opening Moves in the Dating Game.*

To some extent, you are already familiar with the study; it was the source of the experimental scenario you read at the beginning of this chapter. There are some important features of the study that I haven't yet told you about, however. First, each of the men and women who participated in the study had completed a lengthy "research survey" questionnaire at the beginning of the semester. One of the scales they filled out was a brief, 9-item measure of their self-reported shyness. Second, the assignment of the men and women to opposite-sex dyads was essentially random. In other words, chance determined which man was paired with which woman in each of the dyads. Third, from the videotapes we made of the resulting interactions, several raters later judged the physical attractiveness of the male and female dyad members. The average of their ratings (which they made on a "Bo Derek" scale from 1 to 10) provided a reasonably good estimate of just how physically attractive or unattractive each participant was.

Another important feature of the study was that we coded a large number of behavioral measures from the videotapes. They included measures of how much and how often the individual dyad members talked, gestured, looked, and smiled. They also included measures of the relative frequency with which each dyad member used different categories of personal pronouns (first-person singular, first-person plural, second person, third person, etc.) during his or her conversation with the partner. To these behavioral measures, we added the various kinds of thought-content measures that we had first coded in our earlier study of same-sex dyads.

Through our analyses of these data, we could determine how the behavior and thoughts and feelings of one or both partners were related to the men's shyness, the men's physical attractiveness, the women's shyness, and the women's physical attractiveness. In particular, we could determine whether our measures of thought/feeling content were useful in helping us to understand the initial interactions of opposite-sex strangers who vary in their levels of shyness and physical attractiveness.

By themselves, the behavioral data offered a fascinating insight into the different ways that men and women respond in an initial interaction with a physically attractive member of the opposite sex. The way the men reacted was both familiar and predictable: the more physically attractive their female partners were, the more the men kept trying to start up a conversation with them—even when the women made only token, noncommittal responses. I don't know if it is fair to say that the men were "hitting on" these attractive women. However, it is interesting to note a related finding: the more physically attractive the women were, the more often the men reported metaperspective thoughts and feelings in which they tried to represent to themselves what their female partners might be thinking and feeling. It is certainly plausible that the men were indeed "hitting on" the attractive women, and that each time their attempt to initiate a conversation sequence failed, the men attempted to psych out their partner's thoughts and feelings in order to come up with yet another conversational gambit to try.

How did the women act who were randomly paired with physically attractive men? They acted in what I think is a wonderfully subtle way. The more attractive their male partners were, the less the women used third-person singular pronouns (he, she, him, her, himself, herself) in their conversation, thereby making fewer references to other individuals who were not currently present. Although the attractive men tended to do this too, the effect was stronger for the women, who appeared to be setting the tone for these "exclusive" conversations in which other people were mentioned rarely, if at all. It is as if the women were creating an *intimate* conversational context—one in which it was implied that there were only two people in the world (me and you), and that everyone else (all the hes and shes of the world) had temporarily ceased to exist.

When this interesting finding turned up in our data, it immediately reminded me of the scene in the film *Ryan's Daughter* when the British soldier (played by Christopher Jones) first walks into the noisy Irish pub in which the young newlywed (played by Sarah Miles) is working. The moment their eyes meet, the rest of the world literally vanishes from the screen. All that is left is the young soldier and the young wife, set against a visual background of pure black and against an auditory background of complete silence. The effect is both strange and powerful: the relationship between the two has immediately become an exclusive one; no one or nothing else exists. In a similar way, the effect of the women's pronoun use in our study is also strange and powerful. By talking to their attractive male partners as if no one else in the world exists, the women could quickly convey the sense that their relationship was an exclusive one.

Clearly, both the women's attractiveness and the men's attractiveness had strong effects on their initial, opposite-sex interactions. But what kinds of effects, if any, did the men's shyness and the women's shyness have? In general, the men's shyness had a pervasive dampening effect on these initial interactions: the shyer the men were, the less they and their female partners talked to each other, looked at each other, and smiled at each other. (The women's shyness had a similar dampening effect, but on most measures it was much weaker than the one for the men.)

The shy men's nonverbal behavior was especially odd. For one thing, they tended to adopt relatively "closed" body postures, sitting with their arms and legs drawn in close to their bodies. For another, they used relatively few hand and arm gestures while speaking, again reflecting a more closed and unexpressive social orientation. Strangest of all, perhaps, they avoided sustained eye contact with their female partners, quickly breaking off any mutual gazes before the women had a chance to do so. The men's shyness appeared to inhibit the women's nonverbal behavior in somewhat similar ways, leading them to gesture less and to initiate eye contact less frequently.

We were intrigued to discover that the men's shyness also had a pervasive effect on the content of their own and their partners' reported thoughts and feelings. The shyer the men were, the more negative self-focused thoughts and feelings and the fewer partner-focused thoughts and feelings they reported. It was as if the shy men were sitting in our "waiting room" in painful self-absorption, so plagued with anxiety and self-criticism that they were unable to devote much time to having thoughts and feelings about their female interaction partners. Even more intriguing, however, was our discovery that the men's shyness had a similar effect on the women's subjective experience: the shyer their male partners were, the more negative self-focused thoughts and feelings and the fewer partner-focused thoughts and feelings the women reported.

These findings suggest that when women first interact with shy men, they experience their partners' shyness as if it were somehow *contagious*. The women who were paired with the shy men in our study seemed to acquire not only certain aspects of the men's inhibited nonverbal styles but a similar state of negative self-absorption as well. But how does this apparent "shyness contagion" come about?

Undoubtedly, the female partners of these shy men are influenced by the entire pattern of behavior that the shy men display. However, if I were asked to speculate on the single factor most responsible for transmitting the men's shy demeanor to the women with whom they were paired, I would place my bet on the men's apparent unwillingness to engage in any extended eye contact with these women. Imagine how it must feel, in your initial interaction with an opposite-sex stranger, to try to establish eye contact with him and discover that he quickly looks away whenever you attempt to do that. You might decide that there is something wrong with him, or you might decide that he thinks that there is something wrong with you. Or you might correctly infer that he is shy, and then become self-conscious because of your concern not to upset or offend him. In any of these scenarios, however, you are likely to be so unnerved by the quality of your current interaction experience that you tend to withdraw into yourself, becoming nonverbally less expressive and subjectively more self-absorbed.

The thought/feeling data from this study did indeed add some interesting insights about the processes that occur in initial, opposite-sex interactions. On the other hand, they left some important questions unanswered. For example, how accurate were the metaperspective thoughts and feelings reported by the men who were paired with attractive female partners? Were they really able to infer what their partners were thinking and feeling with sufficient accuracy that they could come up with just the right conversational opening to try next? Or were they misreading their partners' thoughts and feelings, and therefore failing to realize that the problem wasn't the type of "line" they were using but the fact that their partners had no desire to interact with them?

To take another example, consider the effects of the men's shyness on their own and their partners' interaction behavior. Did the shy men accurately perceive that their female partners were becoming as anxiously self-absorbed as they were themselves? Did the women who were paired with these men understand that when the men broke off eye contact with them, it was because the men were having negative feelings about themselves? Or did the women fail to understand this and decide that the men must be harboring critical and rejecting thoughts and feelings about *them*?

These kinds of questions made us increasingly aware of the limitations of a method that assessed only the *actual thoughts and feelings* reported by each dyad member. To answer such questions, we needed a method that also assessed the *inferred thoughts and feelings* that each dyad member attributed to his or her interaction partner. In other words, it was time to address the problem of measuring mind reading.

Once I had started to think seriously about this problem, the solution seemed obvious. Indeed, its blueprint was already to be found in our thought/feeling assessment procedure. To assess the dyad members' inferences about each other's thoughts and feelings, we would need to have them each view the videotape a second time. On this second viewing, however, we would stop the tape for them at each of the points at which their *partner* had reported having had a specific thought or feeling. At each of these partner-defined "tape stops," each dyad member would attempt to infer the specific thought or feeling that the partner had experienced at that point, and then record this *inferred* thought or feeling on an empathic inference form (see fig. 3.2).

The idea sounds simple, doesn't it? In its basic conception, it was. Remember, however, that this idea came to me nearly a decade after Rick Barnes and I had developed the original version of the unstructured dyadic interaction paradigm in the summer of 1975. More precisely, it occurred to me soon after Eric Robertson, William Tooke, Gary Teng, and I expanded the original paradigm in the fall of 1984 to include an assessment of the dyad members' actual thoughts and feelings. Without all of that history, and all of the work we had done using the earlier incarnations of the dyadic interaction paradigm, it is unlikely that this retrospectively simple idea would have occurred to me. Fortune did indeed favor the prepared mind in this case.

But although this idea took us a huge step closer to being able to study the ability of one person to accurately infer the specific content of another person's thoughts and feelings, there were still a

DATE _____

NUMBER _____

M   F

TIME	THOUGHT OR FEELING	+, 0, -	
	☐ He/she was thinking: ☐ He/she was feeling:	+ 0 -	
	☐ He/she was thinking: ☐ He/she was feeling:	+ 0 -	
	☐ He/she was thinking: ☐ He/she was feeling:	+ 0 -	
	☐ He/she was thinking: ☐ He/she was feeling:	+ 0 -	
	☐ He/she was thinking: ☐ He/she was feeling:	+ 0 -	
	☐ He/she was thinking: ☐ He/she was feeling:	+ 0 -	

Figure 3.2. Empathic inference form

few "messy details" to be worked out along the way. How we addressed and dealt with these messy details is the topic of the next chapter.

SOURCES FOR CHAPTER 3

Fowles, John. *The Magus*. New York: Little, Brown, & Company, 1965.

Garcia, Stella, Linda L. Stinson, William Ickes, Victor Bissonnette, and Stephen R. Briggs. "Shyness and Physical Attractiveness in Mixed-Sex Dyads." *Journal of Personality and Social Psychology* 61(1991): 35–49.

Ickes, William, Eric Robertson, William Tooke, and Gary Teng. "Naturalistic Social Cognition: Methodology, Assessment, and Validation." *Journal of Personality and Social Psychology* 51(1986): 66–82.

Ickes, William, William Tooke, Linda L. Stinson, Vickie Lau Baker, and Victor Bissonnette. "Naturalistic Social Cognition: Intersubjectivity in Same-Sex Dyads. *Journal of Nonverbal Behavior* 12 (1988): 58–84.

Laing, R. D., Herbert Phillipson, and A. R. Lee. *Interpersonal Perception: A Theory and a Method of Research*. New York: Springer, 1966.

four

MEASURING
MIND READING

F ools rush in where angels fear to tread. There's no question about what category I'm in.

The first of the "messy details" I had to confront was that, in the fall of 1985, I knew little, if anything, about the research literature on empathic inference. In fact, I was then only vaguely aware that there actually *was* such a literature. The advantage of being an impetuous fool in this regard was that I didn't take the time to try to locate and read the bulk of this literature, much of which I now realize would probably have just discouraged me. Instead, in collaboration with my colleagues Linda Stinson, Victor Bissonnette, and Stella Garcia, I immediately began work on a study that was intended to demonstrate the viability of measuring empathic accuracy within the framework of the latest incarnation of the dyadic interaction paradigm.

By now you are familiar with most of the procedure. The randomly matched pairs of opposite-sex strangers in this study were covertly videotaped while they were left alone together in the "waiting room." After being informed about the videotaping and the general purpose of the study, they were asked to sign a consent form to indicate their willingness to continue. They were then taken down the hall and seated in separate cubicles, where they independently viewed a copy of the videotape of the unstructured interaction in which they had just participated. During their first pass through the tape, they stopped it at the appropriate points to make a written record of all of the thoughts and feelings they distinctly remembered having during the interaction.

The new part of the procedure involved the assessment of the dyad members' empathic inferences. During a second pass through the videotape, an experimenter stopped the tape for each participant at those points during the interaction at which his or her partner had reported having had a specific thought or feeling. The participants' task at each of these tape stops was to make a written inference about the content of their partner's thought or feeling at that point. They recorded each inference on the kind of thought/feeling inference form depicted on page 56.

Each time the videotape was stopped for them, the participants used the thought/feeling inference form to record the following information. First, using a timer that appeared as an overlay on the videotape, they wrote down the time at which the tape had been stopped (as a check to ensure that all of the tape stops were accurate). Second, they checked a box on the form to indicate whether, in their judgment, their interaction partner had been experiencing a thought or a feeling at that time. Third, they completed the sentence stem that they had just chosen ("He/she was thinking:" or "He/she was feeling:") by writing out their inference about the specific content of the partner's inferred thought or feeling in the space provided. Fourth, they circled one of the codes (+, 0, –) that appeared in the right-hand column of the form to indicate whether, in their judgment, the partner's inferred thought or feeling was generally positive, neutral, or negative in its overall affective tone.

After each thought/feeling inference had been recorded, the participant used the remote control to restart the videotape, which ran until the experimenter paused it when the next tape stop was reached. This procedure was repeated until both dyad members had recorded their inferences about all of their partner's thoughts and feelings.

Now that you have a general idea of the procedure we use to study people's empathic inferences, I can offer you a choice. If your curiosity has been satisfied with the bare-bones summary I have just provided, you might want to skip the middle part of this chapter and pick things up again on page 77. On the other hand, if you want to know exactly how we measure empathic accuracy using the data collected with this procedure, read on. We'll eventually get down to the nuts and bolts of the relevant measurement issues, for those who like to examine things at that level.

During the weeks when the data from our collaborative study were being collected, I finally had some time to think in a more deliberate and less intuitive way about the new empathic accuracy measure that we were attempting to develop. I realized that I knew next to nothing about the relevant research literature, and that I should probably start educating myself. So I went to the library, where I decided to begin by examining the history of the word "empathy" and its use in psychological research.

The first thing I learned came as a surprise. Empathy, I discovered, is not an old concept; it is a new one that has been around for little more than a century. On the other hand, my next discovery came as no surprise. I learned that, from its very inception, "empathy" has been a kind of Rorschach word into which everyone can project his or her own unique meaning. Indeed, the earliest uses of the word "empathy" were all based on the notion of projection.

A German philosopher, Theodor Lipps, first introduced the term *Einfuhlung* (empathy) around 1903 as a central concept in his theory of esthetic experience. Lipps proposed that to fully appreciate a work of art (a painting, a novel, a play, etc.), we must imaginatively project our awareness into the "frame" of that work. In other words, we must imaginatively recenter our consciousness *within* the work of art so that it now becomes our frame of reference and the new "ground" against which our subsequent esthetic experience occurs. This is the kind of experience we refer to colloquially when we describe ourselves as being "really into" a particular film, novel, or piece of music.

From what I can tell, Lipps's concept of empathic projection had a relatively broad impact on the intellectuals of his day. In Europe, for example, it influenced the work of Sigmund Freud, Hermann Rorschach, and Max Scheler, each of whom put his own spin on the concept while adapting it to his particular purpose. Sigmund Freud used the notion of empathic projection to help explain how psychotherapists can achieve a unique understanding of each of their patients. He also warned us, however, of the confusion between self's and other's perspective that can result. Hermann Rorschach made empathic projection the basis of his famous Inkblot Test, arguing that when patients project their awareness into an inkblot, their experience of the inkblot becomes confounded with their own (largely unconscious) needs and motives. And Max Scheler used the *Einfuhlung* concept as a point of departure for an ambitious philosophical analysis—one that sought to distinguish *Einfuhlung* from other psychological states in which the subjective experience of both self and other are involved.

Scheler's analysis, as interpreted by the sociologist Howard Becker, distinguishes at least six of these psychological states. Because there are no conventional English terms for four of the states, Becker followed Scheler's lead in proposing names for them:

1. *Compathy*—emotional solidarity; sharing the same feelings by dint of sharing the same fate or current circumstance with the other. For example, when two parents stand at the grave

of their child, they experience a common sorrow and grief. However, they do not do so indirectly—by means of apprehending each other's sorrow and grief—but directly and simultaneously. They recognize that each person shares the other's grief, but they also recognize that each person's grief is primary and not derived from the other's.

2. *Empathy*—emotional intuition; apprehending or intuiting the other person's feelings by imaginatively adopting the other's perspective.

3. *Mimpathy*—emotional imitation; modeling the other's feelings without sharing them, as in the case of an actor who feigns his character's anger without experiencing it himself, or of a novelist who understands and conveys her character's despair without experiencing it herself.

4. *Sympathy*—emotional participation; apprehending the other's feelings and participating in them, as when one friend rejoices in another's good fortune or is saddened by another's loss.

5. *Transpathy*—emotional contagion; becoming "infected" or infused with the prevailing emotional state of others, such as feeling merry during a party, solemn during a court sentencing, or panicked during a natural disaster.

6. *Unipathy*—emotional identification; "an intensified form or marginal case of transpathy" in which one person is so absorbed by another person's feelings that there is a blurring of the distinction between self and other.

These six states appear to differ along three implicit and partially overlapping dimensions. The first dimension concerns the degree to which the perceiver objectifies (that is, forms an explicit cognitive representation of) the other person's feelings. The second dimension concerns the degree to which the perceiver actually shares the other person's feelings. And the third dimension concerns the degree to which the self/other distinction is maintained.

With regard to the first dimension, the explicit, objective understanding of the other's feelings is most apparent in the case of mimpathy and least apparent in the case of transpathy, with the four other states—compathy, empathy, sympathy, and unipathy—falling somewhere in between. With regard to the second dimension, the degree to which the perceiver actually shares the other person's feelings appears to be greatest in the cases of compathy and unipathy, somewhat less in the cases of transpathy, sympathy, and empathy, and least in the case of mimpathy. With regard to the third dimension, the maintenance of the self/other distinction appears to be greatest in the case of mimpathy, least in the case of unipathy, and intermediate in the cases of empathy, sympathy, compathy and transpathy.

I was impressed by Scheler's distinctions, and found them useful in helping me to understand why the concept of empathy has been the topic of so much debate and disagreement among philosophers, clinical practitioners, and social scientists. Because empathy falls into the middle ground—the "gray area"—of all three of the dimensions described above, it has an inherent ambiguity that invites the kind of definitional debates that have continued unresolved since the term *Einfuhlung* was first introduced nearly a century ago. As Theodor Reik noted in 1948,

> . . . the expression 'empathy' . . . sounds so full of meaning that people willingly overlook its ambiguity. To speak of empathy has on occasion been as senseless as to discuss sitting in a box without distinguishing whether one means a compartment in a theater, the driver's seat or a big case. The word empathy sometimes means one thing, sometimes another, until now it does not mean anything.

Reik's frustration here is obvious, but his final comment is far too cynical. The word "empathy" is not devoid of meaning; it clearly refers to a psychological state in which the subjective experience of both self and other are involved. Reik's more general complaint is valid, however, in pointing out that there are many psychological states that meet this broad definition and that most writers have failed to discriminate them, instead using the word "empathy" as if it were a blanket term designed to cover them all.

Part of the problem seems to be that very few writers during the past seventy years were even aware of Scheler's more subtle distinctions. But perhaps a greater part of the problem is that the concept of empathy is itself such a central one, falling as it does in the more ambiguous, gray-area regions of all three dimensions—emotional objectification, emotional sharing, and distinguishing self from other. Because of its centrality and consequent ambiguity, empathy naturally overlaps with the more peripheral but less ambiguous "neighboring states" of compathy, mimpathy, sympathy, transpathy, and unipathy. Little wonder, then, that it has so often been confused with any and all of them.

Scheler's analysis was useful in helping me distinguish empathy—the intuition of another's subjective experience—from those neighboring psychological states in whose company it is found. On the other hand, Scheler's analysis had relatively little to say about accuracy—about the extent to which one person could *accurately* apprehend, infer, interpret, intuit, or understand what another person was currently thinking or feeling. It seemed to me that if any research psychologists had given serious thought to the accuracy issue, they would most likely be clinical researchers who were interested in whether psychotherapists could accurately infer the specific content of their clients' thoughts and feelings. The logical next step, then, should be to search the clinical research literature to see what light, if any, it might shed on the issue of empathic accuracy.

Unfortunately, I didn't have the time to do any more library research at that point. The usual other demands (teaching, supervising the laboratory research, reviewing journal articles, etc.) had all crowded back into my life, each clamoring for its share of attention. Fortunately, however, professors have a standard ploy for dealing with a situation like this—they try to get one of their graduate students to do the research for them.

In this case, it was (relatively) easy. From a former colleague, Tom Monson, I had inherited an outstanding graduate student named Carol Marangoni who was the perfect candidate in all respects. She was intellectually strong, she was good with theory, she had already completed a master's degree in clinical psychology, and she was looking for an interesting topic for her dissertation research. I therefore felt only slightly Machiavellian, and even less guilty, when I began to steer Carol in the direction of doing a clinically relevant study of empathic accuracy that would complement the study that my other graduate student colleagues and I were already conducting.

Carol, of course, immediately saw right through my intentions, and sarcastically confronted me with them in her colorful, New York Italian style. It was already clear to her that the project would involve an extraordinary expenditure of time and effort, with an awful lot of "having to make things up as I go along." I therefore had to be patient, and continued to push the dissertation idea over the course of several discussions that were peppered with Carol's frequent expostulations and Italianate abuse. This went on until—as I knew it would—the idea finally seized her. Her response was to seize it right back, wrestle it into submission, and make it her own. Days later, Carol was a force sweeping through the stacks of the university library, where she relentlessly tracked down, copied, and read everything that every clinical researcher had ever written that was even remotely related to the topic of empathic accuracy.

From Carol's review of the relevant literature, I began to get an increasingly complete account of what clinical researchers had done with the concept of empathic accuracy. Not much had happened until 1957, when Carl Rogers had called attention to *accurate empathy* as one of the three "necessary and sufficient facilitative core conditions" for therapeutic change (the other two conditions were the therapist's genuineness and nonjudgmental caring for the client). Rogers's conception of empathy, which proved to be highly influential, required that the therapist be able to track, on a moment-to-moment basis, the "changing felt meanings which flow in this other person." In other words, to achieve the kind of empathy that is an essential condition for effecting therapeutic change, the therapist must be able to accurately infer, from one moment to the next, the content of the client's successive thoughts and feelings.

Rogers's concept of accurate empathy seemed to be virtually identical to our own notion of empathic accuracy, the only difference being the greater emphasis that we placed on the word *accuracy*. We wondered, however, if we would find ourselves in the unenviable position of having "reinvented the wheel." Had clinical researchers already figured out a way to measure the kind of empathy that Carl Rogers had described? Or might we, in our own naively impetuous way, have succeeded where others had failed?

The more Carol—and eventually, I—continued to read, the more certain we became that no one else had developed a method for measuring empathic accuracy that met all of the criteria implied by Rogers's definition. The requisite criteria appeared to be these. First, the method should allow one person (in generic terms, *the perceiver*) to generate his or her own inferences about the content of the thoughts and feelings of another person (in generic terms, *the target person*). Second, the method should permit an assessment of the degree to which the perceiver's inferences are accurate in each case—that is, the degree to which the content of the perceiver's inference matches the content of the target person's actual thought or feeling. Third, the method should provide a way to track the perceiver's empathic accuracy over time—across a succession of the target person's thoughts and feelings.

Carol found no evidence in the relevant clinical literature of a method that met all three of these criteria. Most of the available research concerned the empathic accuracy of graduate students in clinical psychology who were in training to become practicing psychotherapists. It focused on the students' ability to accurately infer the thoughts and feelings of clients whom they or someone else had worked with, based on a supervised review of audio- or videotapes made during the therapy sessions. However, the typical criterion for assessing the accuracy of the students' inferences about a given client's thoughts and feelings was not the match between the student's inference and the thought or feeling which the client had actually reported. Instead, it was the match between the student's inference and the supervising psychotherapist's inference of what the client had been thinking or feeling.

The assumption implicit in such a method, of course, is that the only real expert on the client's thoughts and feelings is the supervising psychotherapist; the client's own opinions in this regard are typically discounted as lacking in clinical insight. If one can accept this assumption on faith (and we couldn't), then the senior psychotherapist is, by stipulation, a consummate mind reader who can discern the thoughts and feelings of virtually all clients with exceptional accuracy. The accuracy of the novice therapist's mind-reading ability can therefore be judged with respect to this exemplary standard of comparison. On the other hand, it cannot be judged with respect to the client's own reported thoughts and feelings, because the client's surface thoughts and feelings might mask truer and deeper ones that the client is either unaware of or unable to express.

What bothered us the most about this clinical approach to assessing empathic accuracy is that it put the question of accuracy outside the realm of meaningful scientific investigation. Accuracy, within this methodology, becomes strictly a matter of faith: either you believe in the supervising therapist's omniscience or you don't. If the goal of this method is to train novice therapists to make inferences that are more like the ones experienced therapists make, there might well be some value in this approach. However, if the goal is to train novice therapists to be more accurate in their perceptions of their client's thoughts and feelings, what guarantee is there that their supervisors are themselves accurate in the first place? Absolutely none, as far as we could see. And clearly, this kind of "accuracy" does not satisfy Carl Rogers's criterion that each of the therapist's inferences should match "the changing felt meanings which flow in," and therefore reside in, the clients themselves.

Although Carol and I were not impressed with this traditional approach to assessing empathic accuracy in a clinical context, we were intrigued by a more recent method that psychologist Nathan Kagan and his colleagues had developed. These investigators asked their research participants to view a standard-stimulus videotape that contained excerpts from a number of different therapy sessions involving different clients and therapists. The videotape was paused for the participant (perceiver) at each point at which the client had reported having had a specific thought or feeling. The perceiver's task at each of these points was to read a set of multiple-choice options representing possible thoughts and feelings the client might have reported at that point, and then choose the one which the perceiver believed the client had actually reported. Empathic accuracy was measured as the percentage of correct choices the perceiver made across the entire videotape.

Perhaps Carol and I felt a greater affinity for the Kagan technique because it resembled our own technique in making the content of the clients' own reported thoughts and feelings the criterion against which the accuracy of the perceiver's inferences was assessed. Certainly, we found it rewarding to know that Nathan Kagan and his colleagues shared our preference for this criterion, as had Carl Rogers himself.

On the other hand, Kagan's approach did not allow perceivers to generate their own inferences about the content of the clients' thoughts and feelings, and Carol and I regarded this as a serious limitation. To put it simply, there was no guarantee that perceivers who were good at choosing the client's thought or feeling from a set of multiple-choice alternatives were comparably good at generating the actual content of the thought or feeling on their own. It is certainly possible that perceivers might score similarly well (or poorly) on both tasks, but it is also possible that they might not. Some perceivers might be relatively good at the multiple-choice task but relatively poor at the task of generating the actual content of the client's thought or feeling, whereas for other perceivers the reverse might be true.

Still, Carol and I found much to admire in Nathan Kagan's approach. Of particular interest was its use of a standard-stimulus videotape—a feature that ensured that all perceivers would infer the thoughts and feelings of the same set of target persons. We felt that the greatest advantage of using a standard-stimulus videotape was that empathic accuracy scores could be meaningfully compared *across perceivers*. Because all perceivers viewed and judged the same set of target persons, it would be possible to rank the perceivers—from best to worst—in terms of their success (or failure) at inferring the thoughts and feelings of any or all of the target persons. It would also be possible to determine whether or not the perceivers maintained a similar ranking from one target to the next. If they did, then their ability to accurately infer the thoughts and feelings of one target person would be correlated with their ability to accurately infer the thoughts and feelings of other target persons.

As Carol began to develop the proposal for her dissertation study, she decided to combine our developing method for assessing empathic accuracy with a standard-stimulus procedure of the type that Kagan and his colleagues had used. By then it was clear exactly what our method for assessing empathic accuracy would be. Linda Stinson—who had served as the experimenter in our first empathic accuracy study—had finished collecting all of the data for that study, which we were now ready to code and analyze. While Linda had been running the pairs of opposite-sex strangers through the procedure, Vic Bissonnette and I had been dealing with another one of those "messy details": figuring out how to compute the dyad members' empathic accuracy scores.

The problem broke down like this. There was a man and a woman in each of the dyads of our study. After their interaction together, the man and the woman were seated in separate cubicles. The man made a written record of all of his thoughts and feelings during the interaction, while the woman made a separate written record of hers. Then the man attempted to infer the content of each of the woman's thoughts and feelings, while the woman attempted to infer the content of each of the man's thoughts and feelings. The problem, as Vic and I saw it, was to reliably measure the degree to which the content of the perceiver's inference matched the content of the actual thought or feeling which the target person (the perceiver's interaction partner) had reported.

The solution we came up with reflected our long history of collaborating on customized data-coding software for our dyadic interaction research. We decided to create an interactive software program that the undergraduate raters (research assistants) who were working in our lab could use to rate the accuracy of each of the inferences which a given perceiver had made. Vic and I began by designing the program in a purely conceptual way—discussing what the user interface would look like and what the various subroutines would do. Then Vic, with his superior programming skills, wrote virtually all of the code.

The resulting program, *Content Accuracy*, was the prototype for the similar, but much more sophisticated, programs (*Rate*, programmed by Stephen Trued, and *Read Your Mind*, programmed by Golden Strader) that eventually replaced it. Because there is little to be gained by reviewing the features of the earlier programs, let me bring you up to the present by describing how the current program, *Read Your Mind*, operates.

Read Your Mind was developed and written by Golden Strader, our resident byte wrangler. With the aid of this program, one of our research assistants begins by creating a set of text files. Each text file contains all of the actual thoughts and feelings reported by a given target and the corresponding inferences made by the perceiver(s). Once all of text files for a particular study have been created, the program is ready to be used by the group of undergraduate raters who will be making the empathic accuracy judgments for that study.

When a rater boots up the *Read Your Mind* program, a graphic user interface with pull-down menus appears on the screen. The interface is designed to present each of the target person's actual thoughts or feelings in a rectangular box at the top of the screen and the perceiver's corresponding inferred thought or feeling in a similar box in the middle of the screen. A "prompt box" in the lower-right corner of the screen displays the response options that the rater should use when judging the degree of similarity in the content of each actual-versus-inferred thought/feeling pair. The three response options are 0 (essentially different content), 1 (similar, but not the same, content), and 2 (essentially the same content).

Our raters' task is a relatively simple one. They compare the actual thought or feeling at the top of the screen with the inferred thought or feeling in the middle of the screen, decide how similar the two are, and then input a similarity rating of 0, 1, or 2. A rating of 0 is assigned if there is no apparent similarity in the content of the actual thought/feeling versus the inferred thought/feeling; a rating of 2 is assigned if essentially the same content is evident (though paraphrased or expressed in different words); and a score of 1 is assigned to all of the "gray area" cases in between. Here are some examples from our first empathic accuracy study of cases in which the raters agreed in assigning scores of 0, 1, or 2 when judging the similarity between the content of the actual versus the inferred thought/feeling:

Example 1: A case in which the raters assigned a score of 0 (essentially different content):

He said: I was thinking that I needed to shave.

She inferred: He was feeling tension because there was no conversation between us.

Example 2: A case in which the raters assigned a score of 1 (similar, but not the same, content):

She said: I was thinking I was interested in what he had to say.

He inferred: She was thinking about the story I was telling her.

Example 3: A case in which the raters assigned a score of 2 (essentially the same content);

She said: I was feeling embarrassed because it seems like everyone expects you to have a major.

He inferred: She was feeling embarrassed about not having a major.

The three response alternatives and their associated labels are the same ones Vic and I decided upon when we initiated our studies of empathic accuracy several years ago. Our goal was to provide the raters with only a few, relatively well-defined response options. We didn't want to frustrate them by providing several response options reflecting distinctions that were too subtle and difficult for them to make. In retrospect, perhaps the best decision we made was to instruct the raters to use the rating of 1 (similar, but not the same, content) as their default rating for all of the ambiguous, "gray area" cases. Assigning a 1 whenever there is no compelling basis for assigning either a 0 (essentially different content) or a 2 (essentially the same content) tends to minimize any disagreements among the raters, resulting in a better, more reliable assessment of the perceivers' empathic accuracy scores.

Another messy detail we had to deal with, of course, was how to turn all the resulting 0s, 1s, and 2s into a global measure of the perceiver's empathic accuracy. Essentially, the problem here is one of *aggregation*: Are we justified in combining the raters' individual empathic accuracy ratings, and, if so, how?

The solution to this problem is simple and straightforward, but it requires a number of steps. In the first step, we check to see if the different raters are sufficiently similar in their judgments to justify combining their ratings by averaging them. (By now, the outcome of this step is highly predictable; in the studies we have conducted during the past several years, the level of similarity/agreement in the raters' judgments has always ranged from good to excellent). In the next step, we add together the averaged ratings for all of the thought/feeling inferences the perceiver has made. This step gives us a global measure of the total number of "accuracy points" the perceiver has achieved.

We're not done yet, however. Recall that in our dyadic interaction studies, the partners can report different numbers of thoughts and feelings. For example, the female partner might report 14 thoughts and feelings, whereas the male partner might report only 9. This means, of course, that the male partner will have the opportunity to make 14 inferences about his female partner's thoughts and feelings, whereas the female partner will have the opportunity to make only 9 inferences about the male partner's thoughts and feelings. If we assume, just to keep things simple, that both partners earn an average of one "accuracy point" for each of the inferences they make, then the man will wind up with 14 accuracy points and the woman with only 9—even though, at the level of each particular inference, the man is no more accurate than the woman is.

Obviously, if we want a meaningful way to compare the empathic accuracy of the two dyad members, we will need to convert their total accuracy points to "percent correct" measures. We do this according to the simple formula $p = t / (n \times 2)$, where p is the percent correct, t is the total number of accuracy points, n is the number of inferences made, and 2 is the maximum number of possible accuracy points per inference. Using p to compare the man's and the woman's percentage accuracy, we can see that they are the same. For the man, $p = 14 / (14 \times 2) = .50$, and for the woman $p = 9 / (9 \times 2) = .50$. Because it is usually more convenient to deal with integers than with decimals, our convention is to multiply p by 100 to get P, which is 50 (50% correct) in the examples used here.

Let's review all of these steps, using a slightly more complicated hypothetical example. Two dyad members—Nicky and Alexandra—have attempted to infer each other's thoughts and feelings from a videotape of their interaction. Nicky made inferences about the 7 thoughts and feelings that Alexandra reported, while Alexandra made inferences about the 8 thoughts and feelings that Nicky reported. Five raters then judged the accuracy of each inference, with each rater assigning a score of 0, 1, or 2.

The individual scores that the five raters (R1 through R5) assigned to each of Nicky's 7 inferences look like this:

	R1	R2	R3	R4	R5	Avg.
Nicky's 1st inference	1	0	1	1	1	0.8
Nicky's 2nd inference	2	1	2	2	1	1.6
Nicky's 3rd inference	0	0	0	0	1	0.2
Nicky's 4th inference	2	2	2	2	2	2.0
Nicky's 5th inference	1	2	2	1	1	1.4
Nicky's 6th inference	1	1	1	2	1	1.2
Nicky's 7th inference	1	1	0	1	1	0.8

By adding the average scores for his 7 inferences together, we compute Nicky's total accuracy points as $(0.8 + 1.6 + 0.2 + 2.0 + 1.4 + 1.2 + 0.8) = 8$. Dividing that number by the maximum points that Nicky could have possibly obtained (2 points per inference X 7 inferences = 14 points), we get $(8 / 14) = .5714$. Nicky's percentage accuracy score is 57.14%. Keep in mind, however, that there is nothing sacrosanct or absolute about this particular number: it is merely the best estimate we can get using the data from 5 raters. If we had used 10 raters instead of just 5, we would probably have gotten a very similar number—say 55.87%. And the odds are good that this new number, 55.87%, would be an even more precise measure of Nicky's empathic accuracy in this case, because it was based on the data from a much larger set of raters.

Now let's look at the individual scores that the same five raters (R1 through R5) assigned to each of Alexandra's 8 inferences:

	R1	R2	R3	R4	R5	Avg.
Alex's 1st inference	0	0	0	0	1	0.2
Alex's 2nd inference	1	1	0	1	1	0.8
Alex's 3rd inference	0	0	0	0	1	0.2
Alex's 4th inference	1	2	1	2	1	1.4
Alex's 5th inference	1	2	1	0	1	1.0
Alex's 6th inference	0	0	0	0	0	0.0
Alex's 7th inference	1	1	0	0	1	0.6
Alex's 8th inference	2	1	1	0	0	0.8

By adding the average scores for her 8 inferences together, we compute Alexandra's total accuracy points as $(0.2 + 0.8 + 0.2 + 1.4 + 1.0 + 0.0 + 0.6 + 0.8) = 5$. Dividing that number by the maximum points that Alexandra could have possibly obtained (2 points per inference X 8 inferences = 16 points), we get $(5 / 16) = .3125$. Alexandra's percentage accuracy score is 31.25%. Again, however, remember that this number is our best estimate of her score, based on the data from only 5 raters. By adding more raters, we could expect to get an even more precise estimate.

Perhaps the best reason to use a percent-correct measure to

express empathic accuracy scores is that it is easy to understand. A score of 0 (zero) means that a person was completely inaccurate in inferring the content of another person's thoughts and feelings, whereas scores of 20, 35, or 50 mean that the person was 20%, 35%, or 50% accurate, relative to the total number of accuracy points possible. At the other extreme, a score of 100 would mean that the person was 100% accurate (though perhaps only the Amazing Kreskin and certain psychotherapists would expect to achieve scores like this!).

Another good reason to use a percent-correct measure is that, if adopted as a common convention by researchers, it makes it easy to compare the results of one study with those of other studies. Such comparisons are often difficult to make in psychological research, where the standardization of methods and measures tends to be the exception rather than the rule.

Our collective attitude at this point was like that of an aircraft design team who, having just built the prototype, is anxious to see if it will fly. We had developed a procedure that enabled us to record the inferences that dyad members made about the content of each other's actual thoughts and feelings. We had also developed an interactive computer program that enabled our research assistants, working independently, to rate the degree of empathic accuracy evident in each of the perceivers' thought/feeling inferences. Finally, we had figured out a way to convert the resulting ratings into a global empathic accuracy score for each of the perceivers in the study.

But would this method really succeed in capturing empathic accuracy—the extent to which one person can read another person's mind? Could the sentences that people used to report their own thoughts and feelings and to convey their inferences about someone else's thoughts and feelings really get at the essence of everyday mind reading? At that point, the answers weren't yet available. However, while we waited for our first set of results to come in, I was encouraged to find the following quote by the eminent social psychological theorist, Erving Goffman:

> It can be argued that . . . we are made out of sentences, our innermost self consisting of unvoiced verbal expression. Novelists and cartoonists can get inside the minds of their figures without causing us surprise because that's what our mind is—a thing designed for others to get inside of, a box of sentences.

We had opened up that "box of sentences," but what would we find inside? Scientifically valid insights or a Pandoran pandemonium? Clearly, the real measure of our success would not be found in our solutions to the various measurement problems I have just described. It would be found instead in the results of our first empathic accuracy study. We hoped that our data would help answer a number of specific research questions that we had. When the data were finally analyzed, we found that they did.

Our first question concerned the range and average level of our research participants' "everyday mind reading" ability. Because the dyad members in our study were opposite-sex strangers with no previous history of acquaintanceship, there was probably no reason to expect that any of them would achieve exceptionally high empathic accuracy scores. Still, the question of just how well opposite-sex strangers can read each other's thoughts and feelings is a question of considerable practical interest, as countless would-be daters, "blind" daters, and other first-time daters can attest.

At the risk of disappointing any readers who are telepathy enthusiasts, the data from this study did not reveal any mentalist superstars. The average empathic accuracy score was only 22% on our scale from 0 to 100. The worst of the "amateur mind readers" in our sample scored right at 0%, displaying absolutely no empathic insight whatsoever. On the other hand, the best of these amateur mind readers was still far from perfect, scoring only 55%. Although the average level of empathic accuracy was well above a chance baseline, which we estimated to be around 5%, it is clear that the opposite-sex strangers in our study were only modestly successful in reading each other's thoughts and feelings.

If I should venture to offer any practical advice to daters and would-be daters based on such preliminary findings, my advice would be to relax; it's likely that the person you are with knows only a fraction of what's going on inside your head. (Of course, some people might have the opposite concern; for them, it is the other person's *cluelessness*, not the other's presumed omniscience, that is the problem.)

A second question we considered was whether the perceivers' accuracy in reading an opposite-sex stranger's thoughts and feelings was related to their attempts to figure out what the stranger's personality was like. In other words, are the perceivers who are better at reading their partner's mind also more motivated to try to understand their partner's personality?

To answer this question, we asked our research assistants to compute the percentage of the *perceivers'* thoughts and feelings in which they attributed some enduring trait or characteristic to their interaction partner. Examples of such thoughts and feelings are *This guy is pretty creative*, *She is snobbish*, and *What a weirdo!* When the data were analyzed, we found that the perceivers' empathic accuracy scores were indeed correlated with the percentage of their own thoughts and feelings that attributed an enduring trait or characteristic to their new acquaintance. In other words, as the perceivers' empathic accuracy increased, their percentage of partner attributions increased as well. This finding suggests that the perceivers differed in the strength of their motive to "get to know" their new acquaintance, and that that this motive influenced both their level of empathic accuracy and the extent to which they attempted to make attributions about their partner's more enduring characteristics.

A third question—a set of questions, really—was posed by the cultural stereotype of "women's intuition." Would the women in these opposite-sex dyads have more success reading the men's thoughts and feelings than vice versa? Or would any advantage the women might have in this regard be canceled out by the men being less expressive than the women, and therefore more difficult to "read"?

Our data enabled us to answer the first question but not the second. Contrary to the stereotype of "women's intuition," the women's empathic accuracy scores were only slightly higher than those of their male partners, and this slight difference was insignificant from a statistical standpoint. But as I have already acknowledged, the possibility remained that the women's advantage might have been canceled out by the men being less expressive, and therefore harder to "read." The resulting ambiguity meant that, for the present, we had to regard the validity of the "women's intuition" stereotype as an unresolved issue that subsequent research would have to resolve. (Fortunately, you won't have to be as patient as we were in seeing what form this resolution would take. The relevant evidence and arguments are presented in chapter 6.)

A fourth question we asked of our data was whether we could predict the perceivers' empathic accuracy scores from their scores on a widely used empathy questionnaire. This questionnaire, developed by psychologist Mark Davis, contained items designed to measure four theoretically important components of empathy: *perspective-taking*, *empathic concern*, *fantasy identification*, and *personal distress*. Would the perceivers' scores on any or all of these empathy components correlate with their empathic accuracy scores?

The answer was a definite no. There was not a single reliable correlation between the perceivers' scores on any of these components—their propensity to imagine the perspective of others, feel emotional concern for their plight, identify with fictional characters, and experience emotional distress when others suffer—and the perceivers' empathic accuracy scores. If you think this outcome is surprising, be prepared for further surprises of this type. In chapter 7, we will see that this outcome has occurred repeatedly in studies that have attempted to relate perceivers' scores on various personality measures to their empathic accuracy scores.

A fifth question we considered was whether different aspects of the dyad members' interaction behavior might be related to their success in inferring each other's thoughts and feelings. For example, are opposite-sex strangers who talk to each other a lot able to read each other's minds better than those who don't?

According to the data, they are. But talking to each other a lot is only one part of a larger pattern. We found that our opposite-sex strangers were successful in reading each other's thoughts and feelings to the extent that they talked, looked, and smiled frequently during the time they were left to wait together. But though the amount of conversation they had was clearly important, the focus of their conversation—who they talked about—was important as well. Specifically, their empathic accuracy was highest when they used relatively many first-person singular pronouns but relatively few third-person pronouns in their conversation.

Perhaps you might be thinking that these results are not at all surprising. Opposite-sex strangers who have highly involving initial interactions—ones in which they talk a lot, look at each other frequently, and focus the conversation on themselves rather than others—should acquire a lot of information that is relevant to what each person might be thinking and feeling. In contrast, opposite-sex strangers who have uninvolving initial interactions—ones in which they talk to each other relatively little, look at each other infrequently, and focus the conversation more on others than on themselves—should acquire much less information of this type.

Be forewarned, however. There is more to empathic accuracy than simply listening to what our interaction partners tell us, or seeing what they appear to show us, about their underlying thoughts and feelings. And while these sources of information are undoubtedly important in first encounters, they are generally less important in established relationships, as the research findings reported in the next chapter will reveal.

SOURCES FOR CHAPTER 4

Becker, Howard. "Some Forms of Sympathy: A Phenomenological Analysis." *Journal of Abnormal and Social Psychology* 26 (1931): 58–68.

Becker, Howard. "Empathy, Sympathy, and Scheler." *International Journal of Sociometry and Sociatry* 1 (1956): 1–22.

Goffman, Erving. *Frame Analysis.* New York: Harper & Row, 1974.

Ickes, William, Linda L. Stinson, Victor Bissonnette, and Stella Garcia. "Naturalistic Social Cognition: Empathic Accuracy in Mixed-Sex Dyads." *Journal of Personality and Social Psychology* 59 (1990): 730–42.

Kagan, Nathan. *Interpersonal Process Recall.* East Lansing: Michigan State University Press, 1977.

Marangoni, Carol, Stella Garcia, William Ickes, and Gary Teng. "Empathic Accuracy in a Clinically Relevant Setting." *Journal of Personality and Social Psychology* 68 (1995): 854–69.

Reik, Theodor. *Listening with the Third Ear: The Inner Experience of a Psychoanalyst*. New York: Farrar, Strauss, 1948.

Rogers, Carl. "The Necessary and Sufficient Conditions of Therapeutic Personality Change." *Journal of Consulting Psychology* 21 (1957): 95–103.

Scheler, Max. *The Nature of Sympathy*. Translated by Peter Heath with an introduction by Werner Stark. London: Routledge & Kegan Paul, 1954. Reprint, Hamden, Conn.: Archon Books, 1970.

Stinson, Linda L., and William Ickes. "Empathic Accuracy in the Interactions of Male Friends versus Male Strangers." *Journal of Personality and Social Psychology* 62 (1992): 787–97.

five

GETTING TO
KNOW YOU

The French philosopher Jean-Paul Sartre took a pessimistic view when it came to dealing with strangers. According to Sartre: once a stranger, always a stranger. "The Other is on principle inapprehensible; he flees me when I seek him and possesses me when I flee him."

The Spanish philosopher José Ortega y Gasset took a more optimistic view, believing that today's stranger can become tomorrow's friend: ". . . as I continue to have dealings with him, good or bad, [the] Other becomes more definite to me and I increasingly distinguish him from the other *Others* whom I know less well. . . . The Other becomes close to me and unmistakable to me. He is not just some or any other, indistinguishable from the rest—he is the Other as unique."

The contrast between these two views is sharply drawn in the following quote from Dame Edna Everage (the alter ego of actor

Barry Humphries). Dame Edna leans toward Sartre's more cynical perspective: "My mother used to say that there are no strangers, only friends you haven't met yet. She's now in a maximum security twilight home in Australia."

Call us naïve, but we were willing to bet on the merits of Ortega's position. Now that we had figured out a way to measure people's "everyday mind reading" ability, we wanted to see if we could establish evidence for the validity of this measure. So we made a simple prediction that we expected to be confirmed if our measure of empathic accuracy were indeed a valid one. We predicted that, in general, friends would be more accurate than strangers in "reading" the content of each other's thoughts and feelings.

As an experimental hypothesis, this one was not overly impressive. It was derived from common sense rather than from a formal theory; it was intuitive rather than counterintuitive; and it was obvious rather than subtle. But we had to start somewhere in order to validate our empathic accuracy measure, and this seemed like as good a place as any to begin. So Linda Stinson and I decided to test for the predicted "acquaintanceship effect" in a study that compared 24 pairs of male friends with 24 pairs of male strangers. Our goal was not only to see if the friends were indeed more accurate than the strangers in "reading" the content of each others' thoughts and feelings, but to try to understand *why* this might be the case.

The male friends in each session had known each other for at least a year, whereas the male strangers were randomly paired and were meeting each other for the first time. The dyad members were seated by the experimenter in the observation room, where their subsequent interaction was unobtrusively recorded on videotape during the six minutes the experimenter left them alone together. After they had been debriefed and had agreed to participate in the rest of the study, they were escorted to their individual cubicles. There, they each viewed the tape of their interaction, made a record of their own thoughts and feelings, and then viewed the tape again to make inferences about all of their partner's thoughts and feelings.

When the empathic accuracy data were later analyzed, we found—perhaps to no one's surprise—that the male friends were indeed more accurate than the male strangers in inferring the content of each other's thoughts and feelings. In fact, the average empathic accuracy score of the friends (36%) was 50 percent greater than the average empathic accuracy score of the strangers (24%). According to our statistical analysis, this was a substantial difference that was unlikely to have occurred by chance. Still, the mind-reading ability of the participants in this study was not particularly impressive. The friends did do better than the strangers, but even the friends' performance was a long way from a theoretically perfect score of 100%.

Finding that the friends outperformed the strangers was important, however, because it increased our confidence in the validity of our empathic accuracy measure. But now the corollary question loomed even larger: *why* did the friends do better? Although the answer might seem obvious, we discovered that we could think of three different explanations for why this difference had occurred. These explanations were all sufficiently plausible that any of them—either singly or in combination—could conceivably account for our newly obtained "acquaintanceship effect." What were these explanations? Let's consider each of them in turn.

The first explanation was that the amount of *immediate information* exchanged during these 6-minute interactions was greater for the friends than for the strangers. In other words, the friends might have talked to each other more, looked at each other more, asked each other more questions, and so on, thereby conveying more information about the current content of their respective thoughts and feelings. In contrast, the strangers might have talked less and exchanged fewer nonverbal behaviors, thereby conveying less information of this type.

The second explanation was based on the possibility that the friends had more similar personalities than the strangers did, and therefore benefited from a greater level of *personality-based rap-*

port. If birds of a feather really do flock together, then people whose personalities are similar may be more likely to develop friendships than people whose personalities are not. If we further assume that people with similar personalities find it easier to establish rapport with each other and understand each other's thoughts and feelings, then the empathic advantage should go to the friends.

The third explanation was the one that probably seems the most obvious: the friends had already gotten to know each other fairly well, whereas the strangers had just begun to get acquainted. According to this explanation, it was the large amount of *previous information* obtained by the friends that accounted for their higher level of empathic accuracy. Note that this explanation does not depend upon the friends exchanging a larger amount of information right now, in their current interaction. Instead, it merely assumes that the friends have already exchanged a large amount of previous information that the strangers have not.

All of these explanations sound reasonably plausible, so which of them should we believe? All of them? Two of them? Or just one of them? Go ahead and make your own prediction. Which one(s) would you bet on?

If you decided to bet on the first explanation, the news is both good and bad. The good news is that Linda Stinson and I found substantial evidence that the male friends in our study really did share a greater amount of immediate information than the male strangers did. In general, the friends talked and gestured to each other more, looked and smiled at each other more, and even sat closer together on the couch. Accordingly, there is no doubt that they exchanged more verbal and nonverbal information than the strangers did. The bad news, however, is that the overall difference in the amount of immediate information exchanged did not account for the friends' greater level of empathic accuracy. When the data were reanalyzed to control for this difference, the friends' empathic advantage was still clearly evident.

If you decided to bet on the second explanation, the news is again both good and bad. Linda and I did find a bit of evidence that the friends' personalities were more similar than the strangers' were. However, this greater similarity applied to only one of fourteen personality traits that we examined in our study—the trait of sociability. The male friends' sociability scores were strongly correlated, so that each friend tended to match the other in reporting a similarly high, moderate, or low level of this trait, whereas the male strangers' sociability scores weren't correlated at all (which makes sense given the random pairing of the strangers). Although this finding seemed to offer a glimmer of hope for the personality-based rapport explanation, this glimmer faded to black when we conducted the appropriate follow-up analysis. When the data were reanalyzed to control for the degree of personality similarity between the interaction partners, the results showed that our acquaintanceship effect in empathic accuracy could not be attributed to the fact that the pairs of friends were more similar in their levels of sociability than the pairs of strangers were.

If you placed a bet on the third explanation, you can feel good about trusting your intuition in this case. Linda and I found evidence that our acquaintanceship effect was indeed related to the different amounts of previous information that the friends and the strangers had acquired about each other. We reasoned that, because most strangers are not familiar with the details of each others' lives, their limitations would be particularly apparent when they tried to infer each other's thoughts and feelings about events occurring at another place or time. For this category of thoughts and feelings, strangers should make relatively poor empathic inferences because they wouldn't have enough previous knowledge about each other to figure out what events the other might be thinking about that were located not "here and now" but at some other place or time. On the other hand, friends should make relatively good inferences about such thoughts and feelings because their extensive prior knowledge about each other should help them to discern exactly where in space and time the other's thoughts have just led him.

And this is essentially what we found. The empathic accuracy of the strangers suffered to the extent that their interaction partners reported a high percentage of "other place, other time" thoughts and feelings. In contrast, the empathic accuracy of the friends benefited to the extent that their partners reported a high percentage of such thoughts and feelings. The worlds into which the strangers could withdraw were singular and subjective, and their interaction partners were unable to follow them there. But the worlds into which the friends could withdraw were communal and intersubjective, and where one friend went, the other could follow.

There is a famous fictional example of how, in its most dramatic form, this process might work. It appears in the first modern detective story, "Murders in the Rue Morgue," by Edgar Allan Poe. The story's protagonist, C. Auguste Dupin, and his unnamed friend (the narrator of the story), have been walking in silence down a long dirty street near the Palais Royal, each lost in his own thoughts. After fifteen minutes, Dupin makes a concurring remark to his companion about Chantilly, a diminutive stage performer and the very person about whom his friend was, in fact, just thinking.

Astonished at how well Dupin has read his mind, his friend requests, and subsequently receives, an explanation. Dupin, it seems, had combined his extensive knowledge of his friend's previous experiences with a close observation of his current behavior to track his friend's thoughts over the course of the entire fifteen minutes. The chain of thoughts led from a fruit-seller who had rudely brushed past them in the street to a pile of loose paving stones that suggested the word "stereotomy." This word in turn brought to mind the theories of Epicurus, whose ideas about nebular cosmogony then reminded Dupin's friend of the constellation Orion, a name which had the day before been linked with a newspaper article about the little actor Chantilly.

At least seven different steps were required to get Dupin to this final empathic inference, and Poe would have us believe that Dupin did not make a single misstep along the way. Fiction is not fact, however, and empathic accuracy in the real world is almost never the product of such an elaborate concatenation of cognitive contingencies. Instead, it is typically more implicit than explicit, more intuitive than deliberative, and more immediate than delayed. And even in those cases when an explicit inference *is* made, it seldom involves more than one or two successive associations. For example, when one friend falls silent the moment the name "Aspen" comes up in the conversation, the other friend might remember Aspen as the site of a recent romantic breakup and then quickly write down the empathic inference, "He was thinking about the last time he saw Jennifer."

The essential conclusion, of course, is that in real life, just as in fictional life, friends achieve greater empathic accuracy than strangers do because the friends have an intersubjective history of "knowing" each other that strangers lack. In retrospect, this conclusion might appear to be entirely obvious and commonsensical. Whatever explanation(s) you were willing to bet on before, it might now appear—with the benefit of hindsight—that the only really plausible one is the third: the one based on the differences in the amount of *previous information* that friends versus strangers have acquired about each other.

This isn't the end of the story, however. There is something more to add, another feature of the data worth considering. Although differences in the amount of *immediate information* did not account for the significant difference in empathic accuracy between the friends and the strangers, they did play an important, though somewhat unexpected, role in our results. For when we analyzed the data separately for the friends and the strangers in our study, we found that the strangers' empathic accuracy was strongly correlated with the total amount of verbal and nonverbal behavior they had exchanged during their 6-minute interactions. In contrast, the friends' empathic accuracy was essentially uncorrelated with the total amount of their verbal and nonverbal behavior. The puzzling question raised by these findings is why the total amount of immediate information predicted the empathic accuracy of the strangers but not of the friends, even though the friends exchanged substantially more of this immediate information than the strangers did.

To answer this question, let's pause a moment and review the pattern of results. Essentially, we found that although the friends exchanged a greater amount of immediate information than the strangers did, this difference did not account for the friends' higher level of empathic accuracy. Instead, the friends' greater accuracy was accounted for by the greater amount of *previous information* about each other that the friends had acquired. Does this mean, then, that differences in the amount of *immediate information* were of no consequence whatever? No, it doesn't, because the data also revealed that differences in the amount of immediate information *did* account for why different pairs of strangers—but not different pairs of friends—were more or less successful in their attempt to "read" each other's thoughts and feelings.

If the pattern of results still sounds confusing, then consider this: What the data seem to be telling us is that the strangers and the friends relied on different sources of information when they tried to infer their interaction partners' thoughts and feelings. For the strangers, the amount of verbal and nonverbal information conveyed in their immediate interaction was the only strong predictor of their empathic accuracy scores *because no other information was available to them.* Lacking any previously acquired information about each other, the strangers had no option but to base their empathic inferences entirely on what their partners said and did during the 6-minute period they were left alone together. For the friends, however, another option *was* available: to base their empathic inferences less on the partner's immediate behavior than on whatever items of previously acquired information seemed most relevant in a given instance.

Although this interpretation of the data is a bit more complicated than we might have expected, it is the only explanation that does a good job of accounting for the entire pattern of results. We are now able to see that both immediate information and previously acquired information play important roles in empathic inference. However, the immediate information plays a more important role for strangers than it does for friends, whereas the previously acquired information plays a more important role for friends than it does for strangers. This insight is essential, and it helps us to solve the study's greatest puzzle: that the friends exchanged more immediate information than the strangers did, but that this difference in the amount of immediate information did not account for the acquaintanceship effect in empathic accuracy.

Why didn't the immediate information benefit the friends as much as—or even more than—it did the strangers? The answer may be that the immediate information didn't really add that much to what the friends already knew about each other. Because the friends had known each other for at least a year, they had already acquired an extensive body of knowledge about each other. For them, the immediate information may have had relatively limited value apart from the cues it provided about what particular items of previous information they should recall in order to more accurately infer their partner's current thought or feeling. For the strangers, however, the immediate information was essentially all they had to work with. Our conclusion, then, is that the friends' empathic advantage derived primarily from those items of "shared" knowledge and experience which they had already acquired in abundance, but which the strangers were only just beginning to acquire.

Edgar Allan Poe was apparently well aware of this dynamic. References to the friends' shared knowledge and experience figure prominently in Monsieur Dupin's account of his empathic *tour de force*:

> "I knew that you could not say to yourself 'stereotomy' without being brought to think of atomies, and thus of the theories of Epicurus; and since, when we discussed this subject not very long ago, I mentioned to you how singularly, yet with how little notice, the vague guesses of that noble Greek had met with confirmation in the late nebular cosmogony, I felt that you could not avoid casting your eyes upward to the great *nebula* in Orion, and I certainly expected that you would do so. You did look up, and I was now assured that I had correctly followed your steps. But in that bitter *tirade* upon Chantilly, which appeared in yesterday's '*Musee*,' the satirist, making some disgraceful allusions to the cobbler's change of name, quoted a Latin line about which we have often conversed. . . . I had told you that this [line] was in reference to Orion . . . [and] I was aware that you could not have forgotten it. It was clear, therefore, that you would not fail to combine the two ideas of Orion and Chantilly. That you did combine them I saw by the character of the smile which passed over your lips."

If shared knowledge and experience are so important to the development of empathic accuracy, then even strangers should be more accurate to the extent that they establish "common ground" in their initial interaction. This hypothesis was proposed by Tiffany Graham, another of my student colleagues in the Social Interaction Lab at the University of Texas at Arlington. She found some interesting support for it in a study she conducted for her master's thesis.

Tiffany's study was very similar to the one that Linda Stinson and I had done. An important difference, however, was that Tiffany videotaped pairs of female friends and female strangers in addition to pairs of male friends and male strangers. She was therefore able to determine if female friends had the same empathic advantage over female strangers that male friends had over male strangers. She found that they did. As in our earlier study, the average empathic accuracy score of the friends was about 50% greater than that of the strangers, and the magnitude of this difference was approximately the same for the female pairs as it was for the male pairs. These results indicate that the acquaintanceship effect is just as evident in women's relationships as it is in men's.

But Tiffany did more than simply replicate our acquaintance-ship effect. She also showed that shared knowledge can contribute to the empathic accuracy of strangers in the same way it does to the empathic accuracy of friends. She reasoned that strangers would fail to infer each other's thoughts and feelings about events occur-ring in another time or place if those events were not part of the common ground that had already been established in their conver-sation. If those events had been discussed, however, the strangers should succeed in inferring their partners' event-relevant thoughts and feelings to the extent that the appropriate common ground had been established.

To test this idea, Tiffany asked raters to review the tapes to determine instances in which, through their previous conversation, the partners had established enough common ground that they could plausibly infer the other's specific thought or feeling. Once these ratings had been made, Tiffany used them to compute the pro-portion of each dyad member's actual thoughts and feelings that met her criterion of interest: thoughts and feelings about events in another time or place for which the appropriate common-ground knowledge was already available. She then correlated this propor-tion with the empathic accuracy scores obtained by each dyad member's interaction partner (remember that their partners were the perceivers who inferred these thoughts and feelings). The resulting correlation offered strong support for Tiffany's hypoth-esis. The more that the strangers had communicated the relevant common-ground information to each other, the more accurately they inferred each other's thoughts and feelings about events occurring in another time or place.

The same process, of course, should apply to friends as well. Ironically, however, it is actually more difficult to study this process in friends than it is in strangers. The reason for this difficulty has been identified in research conducted by Sally Planalp and her colleagues. They found that friends are much less likely than strangers to make explicit conversational references to their common ground, merely assuming it instead. This complication makes it very difficult to get an accurate measure of the proportion of friends' thoughts and feelings about events in another time or place for which appropriate common-ground knowledge has already been established.

Such complications aside, the lesson to be learned from Tiffany's study is that shared knowledge contributes to empathic accuracy in strangers' relationships just as it does in friends' relationships. The difference is that the friends have already acquired much more of it. As Tiffany concluded:

It appears that friends are able to accurately infer each other's thoughts and feelings . . . [better] than strangers because of the extensive "common ground" established throughout the history of their relationship. . . . [S]trangers are able to accurately infer each other's thoughts and feelings only to the extent they can establish common ground within the context of the immediate interaction. In a sense, they are emulating the same processes friends employ with one another over a much longer period of time. . . . By doing so, they improve their empathic accuracy relative to strangers who establish less common ground, but because they are dealing with a smaller store of information, they still do not match the friends' empathic accuracy scores.

How does empathic accuracy typically develop over time between same-sex acquaintances? To get a rough idea, I asked Joanna Hutchison to pool the data from Tiffany Graham's study with those from a subsequent study by Paul Gesn. Both studies had examined empathic accuracy in male-male and female-female pairs of varying levels of acquaintanceship.

Joanna began by "standardizing" the empathic accuracy scores for the male and female pairs within each study, to convert them to a common scale of measurement. She then combined the data from both studies into a single, large data set. Within this larger data set, she grouped the data into five categories representing different lengths of acquaintanceship: 0 months (strangers), 1–2 months, 3–8 months, 9–36 months, and 37 or more months. Finally, she computed the average empathic accuracy score for each of these five categories and plotted the results.

The resulting graph (fig. 5.1) gave us our first look at how empathic accuracy might develop over time in same-sex relationships. It suggests that empathic accuracy increases the most during the first few months of acquaintanceship, with nearly 85% of the total increase occurring during the first 6-8 months. After that, however, the increase is slight and extremely gradual, being stretched out over the next 7 or 8 years (84-96 months). The reader should keep in mind, however, that these average changes all occur within the low end (under 30) of the 0 to 100 empathic accuracy scale.

Some qualifications are warranted when interpreting these data. For one thing, the data are cross-sectional rather than longitudinal (that is, different sets of relationships are compared for each point on the length of relationship axis, rather than comparing the same set of relationships over time). For another, the data are limited to the relationships of college students and their same-sex acquaintances. Even with these limitations, however, the findings suggest an intuitively plausible time course for the development of empathic accuracy in the same-sex relationships of young adults. Whether a similar or very different time course applies to other

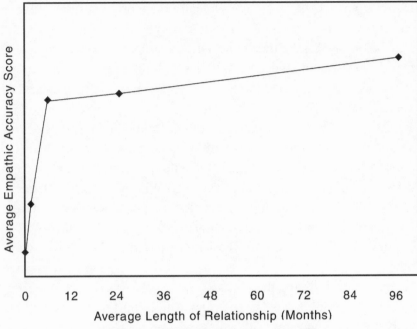

Average Empathic Accuracy Score

Average Length of Relationship (Months)

Figure 5.1. Empathic accuracy for different lengths of relationships.

kinds of relationships (romantic relationships, business relationships, and so on) remains to be seen.

When we talk about the effect of acquaintanceship on empathic accuracy, it is easy to fall into the trap of assuming that "acquaintanceship" can be reduced to the simple passage of time. Equating the degree of acquaintanceship with the length of the relationship may be a convenient fiction, but it is a fiction nonetheless. Even a moment's reflection should be enough to convince us that the mere passage of time doesn't guarantee the kind of in-depth knowledge of others that enables us to accurately infer how they think and feel. If it did, then none of us would have any next-door neighbors who are still strangers to us after many years of living side-by-side with them.

But if a lengthy relationship itself is not sufficient to guarantee the knowledge on which empathic accuracy is based, then what kind of knowledge *is* sufficient? Is it enough to know the other person "from the outside," the way a curious but noninvolved neighbor might? Suppose that you live down the block from me, and that over the course of several years, I learn a variety of facts about you. These facts include such items of information as your name, age, occupation, marital status, family background, religion, income level, political affiliation, hobbies and interests, vacation spots, and the kinds of music and movies you prefer. This background knowledge that I have acquired about you "from the outside" might help me develop a better stereotype of the kind of person and neighbor you are, but how much would it help me infer the specific content of your thoughts and feelings?

Paul Gesn, another of my graduate students, attempted to answer this and some related questions in a study that he conducted as part of his master's thesis research. Paul (who goes by his nickname, Randy) recruited a moderately large sample of same-sex friends or acquaintances to participate in his study. He took care to ensure that the length of their relationships varied greatly, ranging from the relationships of near-strangers who had only recently met to those of best friends who had known each other for years.

When each pair of friends or acquaintances arrived at our lab, Randy seated the participants in separate rooms and asked them to independently respond to a set of paper-and-pencil questionnaires. The items on these questionnaires enabled Randy to find out three things about the partners' relationship: how long they had known each other, how close they felt to each other, and how much background knowledge they had acquired about each other. After estimating how long they had known each other and rating the degree of closeness in their relationship, the participants had to answer a series of questions about both themselves and their partner that required specific information about the person's age, ethnicity, religion, family members, pets, dating partners, work experience, career goals, travels, and leisure-time interests.

After collecting these data, Randy brought the participants back together again and introduced them to another experimenter, who asked them to participate in a second study that would require them to view and rate a set of photographic slides. This supposed "second study" was just a cover story—a ruse for seating the participants side-by-side on the couch in our control room so that we could unobtrusively videotape their spontaneous interaction. In fact, when the 6-minute tape of their interaction was complete, the reason for this deception was explained to them. Then, if they gave their signed consent, they were seated in individual cubicles where they used the videotape to first record all of their own thoughts and feelings and then make inferences about each of the thoughts and feelings their partner had reported.

Randy analyzed the resulting data to see if he could determine what had the single greatest influence on the participants' empathic accuracy. Was it the length of their relationship? The degree of closeness in their relationship? Or the amount of background knowledge they had acquired about each other? Obviously, these three influences cannot be easily separated, so Randy used special statistical analyses that were well-suited for this purpose. Not surprisingly, he found that longer relationships were characterized by both greater closeness and greater mutual knowledge of the other's background. However, he also found that greater closeness was more important than greater background knowledge in predicting which of the longer-term relationships would be characterized by high levels of mutual understanding.

Randy drew two basic conclusions from these findings. First, he concluded that the length of relationship is indeed important to the "acquaintanceship" effect, but only in the sense that it takes time for empathically relevant knowledge to be acquired. Second, he concluded that the most empathically relevant knowledge is *intimate knowledge*—the type of knowledge acquired by experiencing the other person's thoughts and feelings as they are expressed in a close, personal relationship. Although knowing people "from the outside" by acquiring relevant background knowledge may be useful in helping us stereotype them, knowing people "from the inside" contributes more directly to our success in reading their minds.

Social psychologists are often criticized for "proving in their laboratories things that we already know." Based on what I have told you so far in this chapter, you might have decided that this criticism applies to much of our work on empathic accuracy. There is no point denying the validity of this criticism in cases where it applies. It is important to note, however, that the advantages of being able to prove things we already know are not inconsequential. Such rigorous, formalized proofs are as valuable to the scientist as they are to the mathematician. In most cases, they help to strengthen our confidence that the method we are using yields valid results, and this increased confidence becomes especially important when the same method leads us to discover things that we *don't* already know.

One of the things that my colleagues and I didn't already know was this: What is the *least* amount of time it would take to get to know a stranger well enough to read her thoughts and feelings as accurately as a typical friend might? Weeks? Days? Hours?

How about 30 minutes? That's the approximate length of time that certain participants in Carol Marangoni's dissertation study needed to attain levels of empathic accuracy for a total stranger that were comparable to those achieved by the friends in the study that Linda Stinson and I conducted. Carol's study examined the issue of whether a perceiver's accuracy in reading a stranger's thoughts and feelings can, under optimal conditions, improve substantially over a very short period of time. She found that it could.

As noted in chapter 4, Carol's study combined our method for assessing empathic accuracy with the kind of standard stimulus procedure that Nathan Kagan and his colleagues had previously used in their psychotherapy research. Her intent was to videotape a set of psychotherapy sessions, each involving a different female client interacting with the same male therapist, and then persuade each client to view her videotaped session immediately afterward and make a complete record of all of the feelings she distinctly remembered having had. Some time later, using edited versions of the psychotherapy session tapes as her experimental stimuli, Carol planned to show the tapes to undergraduate research participants who would be asked to infer the content of the specific thoughts and feelings that each of the clients had reported. In effect, Carol would be giving her undergraduate perceivers a chance to play amateur therapist and demonstrate their ability to accurately read each client's thoughts and feelings.

After discussing and debating the various options, we eventually decided that Carol should conduct an *analogue study* in which the undergraduate perceivers would infer the thoughts and feelings of "normal" clients in simulated, rather than actual, psychotherapy sessions. We hoped that this decision would enable us to avoid certain problems that might result from using videotapes of "disturbed" clients in actual psychotherapy sessions. It was possible, for example, that clients with serious psychological disorders might exhibit less insight and more confusion about their thoughts and feelings than normal clients would. Beyond that, there were risks associated with recruiting psychologically disturbed individuals to participate in a self-disclosure experience whose potential impact on their own lives and therapeutic outcomes was, at best, unclear.

The decision to use videotapes of normal rather than disturbed clients also made sense in terms of the specific goals of Carol's study. Carol wanted to test the prediction that, over the course of a single psychotherapy session, perceivers could significantly improve their ability to infer the thoughts and feelings of clients they had never seen before. She also wanted to test an interesting corollary prediction: that even more improvement could result from giving certain perceivers immediate, veridical feedback about the clients' actual thoughts and feelings. To give these hypotheses a fair test, it was essential that the clients who appeared on the videotapes be able to provide accurate reports about their thoughts and feelings, because any inaccuracy on their part would compromise the validity of the perceivers' empathic accuracy scores.

For a number of reasons, then, we decided that the clients in the videotapes should be articulate, psychologically healthy individuals with good insight into their own thoughts and feelings. We also decided that the clients should be women, on the assumption that women would be more willing than men to disclose personally meaningful thoughts and feelings, and would do so in a more expressive way. It was now up to Carol to figure out how to recruit the women, arrange for them each to participate in a simulated psychotherapy session, and then ask them to make a complete written record of all of the thoughts and feelings they remembered having had during that session.

With the assistance of our colleague, Stella Garcia, Carol eventually solved all these problems; and, within several weeks, Carol and Stella had taped a set of psychotherapy sessions ranging from 30 to 55 minutes in length. In each session, a different female client discussed an actual problem in her life with a licensed male therapist who had been trained in the Rogerian, "client-centered" tradition.

Although the sessions were simulated with respect to being videotaped for possible use in our subsequent research, they were genuine in nearly every other respect. Each of the women sought the therapist's help in dealing with issues that were of real concern to them. The sessions were videotaped "live" from beginning to end without any prior rehearsal, and the genuineness and spontaneity of the sessions was evident in the clients' range of emotional expression (for example, one woman wept openly as she discussed her recent divorce). The male therapist, who appeared with his back turned to the camera on each tape, used a nondirective approach, helping the client to clarify and explore the implications of her own statements while refraining from giving advice.

Immediately after each of the therapy sessions had been video-taped, Carol took the client upstairs to our laboratory and, for the first time, revealed that we planned to use the tapes as stimulus materials in research designed to test the empathic accuracy of undergraduate perceivers. She explained how, in order to do that, we had to rely on each client to create an accurate record of all the thoughts and feelings she remembered having had during her therapy session. Carol then asked the client to view the videotape of her just-completed therapy session and pause it throughout the session to record all of the thoughts and feelings she remembered. All of the clients agreed to help in this way, and they all signed a consent form allowing us to use their videotape and the accompanying thought/feeling record in our subsequent empathic accuracy research. In return, we agreed to keep the clients' identities confidential, and we allowed them to veto the use of any segments they would prefer to have edited out of their tapes.

From the resulting collection of videotapes and their accompanying thoughts and feelings, Carol chose three tapes to edit and use as the stimulus materials. The clients who appeared in them were all white, college-educated, 24–32-year-old women from middle to upper-middle class backgrounds. Client A discussed the circumstances leading up to her divorce and the effects the divorce had had upon her life. Client B discussed her ambivalent feelings about the current state of her marriage and how difficult they were to resolve. Client C discussed the difficulties she experienced while trying to juggle her two major roles of wife and career woman. Carol edited the tapes of their sessions to create shorter versions that ranged from 26 to 36 minutes in length. Her goal was to preserve the continuity of each tape while limiting it to exactly 30 segments in which the client had reported a specific thought or feeling.

Each stimulus tape could be divided into three phases without disrupting the natural flow of events. Because there were 30 segments on each tape in which the client had expressed a thought or feeling, we treated the first 8 segments as a *baseline phase*, the next 14 points as an *intervention phase*, and the last 8 segments as a *final test phase*. The intervention phase was important because it was the part of the tape that Carol used to provide feedback to half of the undergraduate perceivers in her dissertation study.

For the benefit of the perceivers in her feedback condition, the three tapes were further edited so that the client's actual thoughts and feelings were spliced into the tapes following the points at which the perceivers attempted to infer them. This editing ensured that each time a perceiver in the feedback condition finished writing down a particular thought/feeling inference, what would appear on the screen when the tape was started up again was a 20-second presentation, in sentence form, of the text of the client's actual thought or feeling. On the other hand, this feedback information was *not* spliced into the set of tapes viewed by the perceivers in the no-feedback (control) condition. They would merely see the client-therapist interaction continue from the point at which the tape had been stopped.

Once these two sets of tapes had been prepared, Carol was ready to conduct her dissertation study. In marathon sessions that were nearly four hours in length, her undergraduate perceivers viewed all three tapes and wrote down their inferences about the 30 thoughts and feelings reported by each client. The perceivers who had been randomly assigned to the feedback condition got immediate feedback about the client's actual thought or feeling during the middle portion (14 intervention trials) of each tape, whereas the perceivers who had been randomly assigned to the no-feedback condition got no feedback of this type. Because the sessions were so long and demanding, Carol gave the participants the opportunity to get a free snack and take a 5-minute personal break between each tape.

Carol had been correct in her prediction that the project would require an enormous amount of work. I was definitely not her favorite person by the time all of her data had been collected, coded, double-checked for accuracy, and analyzed. Her mood seemed to brighten, however, as the results of the study came in. The data were interesting—and were almost, but not quite, what she had expected.

For starters, Carol's first hypothesis was supported. As she had predicted, the "amateur psychotherapists" in her study inferred the clients' thoughts and feelings at the end of each tape (final test phase) more accurately than the ones at the beginning of each tape (baseline phase). This was a large effect, representing an average increase in empathic accuracy from 25% for the first 8 thoughts and feelings on each tape to 35% for the last 8 thoughts and feelings. Moreover, the implication of this finding is important. It suggests that if total strangers are willing to talk freely and openly about themselves, eavesdropping observers can—in about half an hour—learn to "read" these strangers' thoughts and feelings with a level of accuracy comparable to that of friends who have known each other for at least a year.

Even more intriguing, however, was our discovery that Carol's second hypothesis was supported as well. The results showed that, by giving some perceivers immediate feedback about the clients' actual thoughts and feelings, we had indeed given an additional boost to their empathic accuracy. The perceivers who received such feedback during the middle portion of the tapes made more accurate inferences during the final portion of the tapes than did perceivers who did not. And this improvement based on immediate feedback occurred *in addition to* the improvement based on acquaintanceship alone, thereby pushing the perceivers' empathic accuracy to an even higher level.

This was an exciting finding for a number of reasons. First, it was a novel finding that, to our knowledge, had never been documented before. Second, it indicated that empathic understanding is a trainable skill, and that providing immediate feedback about a target person's actual thoughts and feelings can be an effective component of empathy training. Third, it suggested that this particular form of empathy training might be highly efficient, in that relatively few feedback trials were required to produce a significant increase in empathic accuracy scores.

We were pleased to find that, just as Carol had predicted, both short-term acquaintanceship and the availability of feedback increased empathic accuracy. Looking more closely at the data, however, we discovered that these effects were noticeably weaker for the tape of Client B's therapy session than for the tapes of Client A's and Client C's sessions. The reason for this difference could be traced to a third major finding from Carol's study—the finding that perceivers were, in general, much less accurate when they inferred the thoughts and feelings of Client B than when they inferred the thoughts and feelings of Clients A and C.

Client B, if you remember, was the ambivalent one. She was struggling to resolve her contradictory feelings about the current state of her marriage, and her comments to the therapist were all variations on this same ambivalent theme. In one statement she would express a positive feeling about the relationship, whereas in the next she would express a doubt or reservation. Her ambivalence was evident throughout the session and remained unresolved at its end. It is little wonder, then, that our undergraduate perceivers found her exceptionally hard to read.

Indeed, the conflicting contents of Client B's thoughts and feelings were so difficult to track that the perceivers' empathic accuracy scores improved only slightly from the beginning of her tape to its end. In contrast, the perceivers found it easier to gain a better understanding of the thoughts and feelings of Clients A and C, who both gave more internally consistent accounts of their problems. Client A provided a coherent, chronological summary of the events that led up to and followed her divorce, and Client C reviewed in sequence the various problems that resulted from the competing demands of her roles in the workplace and at home.

The most obvious implication of this difference in the *readability* of the three clients is that some people are harder to get to know than others. For people who are as difficult to read as Client B, a half-hour spent eavesdropping on their conversation with a therapist might still not help to clarify much the contents of their private thoughts and feelings. It is important to recognize, however, that this isn't just a problem of the target person lacking insight about these thoughts and feelings or being less than articulate in expressing them. Those elements can, of course, contribute to lower readability, but they weren't apparent in Client B's case. On the contrary, Client B was everything that we felt an ideal client should be: mature, intelligent, articulate, and insightful. But she also had a complex, ambivalent inner life that was difficult to apprehend based on only a short, and somewhat voyeuristic, acquaintance.

In fact, Client B's thoughts and feelings were so difficult to read that even the perceivers who got feedback during the middle portion of her tape didn't benefit much from it. When Client B's actual thoughts and feelings appeared on the screen, the perceivers in the feedback condition were probably confused by the succession of conflicting sentiments they read. On the other hand, the same perceivers benefited greatly from the feedback they received during the middle portions of the tapes for Clients A and C. When Client A's and Client C's thoughts and feelings appeared on the screen, the same perceivers were probably reassured to find that their developing view of each client and her problem was increasingly consistent with the successive perceptions and emotions that the client herself expressed.

Although the acquaintanceship and feedback effects were weaker for Client B than for Clients A and C, both effects were statistically reliable when averaged over the data for all three clients. These results confirmed Carol's hunch that even nonprofessional perceivers could, under optimal conditions, quickly learn to read the thoughts and feelings of total strangers with a level of accuracy comparable to that of friends. Of course, to achieve such optimal conditions, you must have bright, articulate target persons who are willing to talk openly about themselves and to provide immediate feedback about their actual thoughts and feelings. Even in such optimal conditions, however, some strangers will be harder to read, and will therefore take longer to get to know, than others.

There are rules, and then there are exceptions. So far, all of the evidence has shown that greater acquaintanceship leads to greater empathic accuracy. And this general rule seems to apply whether we are talking about the short-term "acquaintanceship" of eavesdropping on a client's psychotherapy session or the longer-term acquaintanceship of two people who become friends. But are there any exceptions to the rule that increased acquaintanceship leads to increased accuracy? Specifically, are there any cases in which people actually become *less* accurate in reading each other's thoughts and feelings the longer they have been together?

The answer is yes. One such case has been identified by researchers, and it is not one that many people would have predicted. But an emerging pattern of data now suggests that, for married couples in Western cultures such as New Zealand and the United States, empathic accuracy actually declines over the course of the marriage. That's right: it *declines*.

How could that happen? Are we talking about one or both partners developing Alzheimer's disease or some other cognitive impairment that reduces their empathic ability? No, we're not. Long-term cognitive impairment would certainly count as another exception to the rule that empathic accuracy increases as acquaintanceship increases, but serious impairment of this type is relatively infrequent. What we *are* talking about here is something that is both more common and more likely to affect partners in the first two decades of their marriage: an increasing divergence in their viewpoints and their current concerns that gradually undermines their intersubjectivity and empathic accuracy.

Three New Zealand psychologists—Geoff Thomas, Garth Fletcher, and Craig Lange—found compelling evidence for this long-term decline in empathic accuracy in their study of over 80 married couples. All of the couples, who had been married for an average of over 15 years, lived in the Canterbury region of New Zealand. Thomas and his colleagues invited the members of each couple to their laboratory at the University of Canterbury, where they were asked to discuss certain relationship problems while being overtly videotaped. After the taping had ended, the partners reviewed the tape and recorded all of the actual thoughts and feelings they remembered having had. Then, on a second pass through the tape, they attempted to infer each other's thoughts and feelings at those points in the tape at which the partner had reported them.

Surprisingly, Thomas, Fletcher, and Lange found that empathic accuracy decreased as the length of the marriage increased. In other words, the longer-married couples inferred each other's thoughts and feelings less accurately than the more recently married couples did. What kept this finding from remaining an unaccountable paradox was the researchers' subsequent discovery that this relationship seemed to reflect the degree to which the individual partners' thoughts and feelings were similar or different across time. Recently married partners tended to report more similar thoughts and feelings at different points in their interaction, whereas longer-married partners tended to report more different ones. In other words, the recently married partners seemed to maintain a greater synchrony or "shared focus" in the content of their thoughts and feelings, whereas the longer-married partners seemed to follow more separate and idiosyncratic trains of thought.

A striking literary example of this phenomenon is found in Don DeLillo's novel, *Underworld*. DeLillo takes us into the bedroom of a middle-aged American couple, Nick and Marian Shay. There, he allows us to eavesdrop on the following conversation about plumbing (Marian's concern) and travel plans (Nick's concern). Instead of maintaining a shared cognitive focus throughout their conversation, Marian and Nick begin on very different tracks and only gradually arrive at the same place:

"What's-his-name Terry was here. The heavyset one."

"Been years since I looked at a real map. It's a sort of Robert Louis Stevenson thing to do. We have maps of highways and motels. Our maps have rest stops and wheelchair symbols."

"Just tell me what his name is."

"For what? The faucet?"

"Day before yesterday or yesterday. Today's been so long I don't know anymore. No, the showerhead."

"The hell's wrong with the showerhead? Our maps have pancake houses."

"What's-his-name with the orange pickup."

"Which shower are we talking about?"

"Terry, right?"

She turned a page. She used a book pillow to read when she was in bed. . . .

"I'm going Tuesday. I tell you that?"

"This is, what, Moscow? Or Boston. Too soon for Moscow. Which is the heavyset one? I get them completely."

"I need to get these shoes resoled before I go. Remind me to do that tomorrow."

"I have this thing on my leg."

"It's not Boston," I said.

"It's not Boston."

"It's Portland."

"It's Portland."

To help them develop a more complete account of their findings, the New Zealand psychologists turned to the work of marriage and family researchers who had used cross-sectional and longitudinal survey studies to identify the long-term changes that typically occur in the marriages of North American couples. It was evident that the marriage and family researchers were already quite familiar with the long-term decline in "shared focus" and mutual understanding that had emerged in the New Zealanders' laboratory study. Indeed, researchers Clifford Swensen, Ron Eskew, and Karen Kohlhepp had given a more complete description of this decline in an article they had published in 1981:

> Over the course of a marriage, a husband and wife develop in different directions and at different rates. The pressure of the different duties of each leads to different activities and experiences for each and a subsequent change in attitudes, interests, values, and feelings. The pressure of jobs, children, and other concerns external to the marriage relationship prevent a husband and wife from maintaining intimate contact with each other. They become increasingly estranged from each other. This growing barrier between them reduces the total amount of interaction between them. This suggests that the longer a couple is married, the less well they can know each other, the less accurately they can predict each other's feelings, attitudes, likes, and dislikes.

According to Swensen and his colleagues, longer-married partners do not simply experience a reduced understanding of each other. They also experience a qualitatively different kind of understanding, one that is based more on a stereotyped view of the other than on a genuine "sharing" of the other's thoughts and feelings through intimate contact:

> [Longer-married partners] must continue to maintain a form of relationship, and each maintains a conception of the person that the other is. In the absence of accurate intimate communication, this conception is more the result of the subcultural specification of the roles that they play than it is a function of accurate knowledge they have of each other. Their image of each other becomes increasingly inaccurate and stereotypic.

Thomas, Fletcher, and Lange made a similar, though not identical, argument. They proposed that, during the first years of marriage, the partners tend to be highly motivated to learn to read each other's thoughts and feelings in order to better adapt to each other and to make their new relationship succeed. As time passes, however, the partners begin to feel confident (and even *over*confident) that they already understand each other well. In consequence, they tend to become complacent. Their motivation to actively monitor each other's words and actions generally declines; they spend increasingly more time thinking about their own idiosyncratic concerns; and they are increasingly less able to maintain a shared cognitive focus that helps them track the content of each other's successive thoughts and feelings. The long-term effect is that their overall level of empathic accuracy tends to decline the longer they have been married.

How early in a marriage does this decline in empathic accuracy begin? Although the answer obviously varies from one couple to the next, there is evidence suggesting that, for many couples, this decline may begin before they have completed even the first year of their marriage.

In a study conducted in North Carolina, psychologists Shelley Kilpatrick, Caryl Rusbult, and Victor Bissonnette tracked a large sample of recently married couples across the first three years of their relationships. Some of these couples were tested on two occasions in the researchers' laboratory at the University of North Carolina at Chapel Hill—first when they had been married for approximately six months, and then again when they had been married for 18 months to two years. As in the New Zealand study, the couples in the North Carolina study were videotaped while they discussed current problems in their relationships. Then, working with separate copies of the videotape, the partners independently recorded all of their own thoughts and feelings before attempting to infer all of their partner's thoughts and feelings at the appropriate "tape stops."

Two aspects of this study's findings are of particular interest. First, Kilpatrick and her colleagues found that the couples' empathic accuracy tended to be lower after 18–24 months of marriage than it was after just six months. Although this short-term decline was not significant in a statistical sense, it appeared to be the first stage of the more extended decline that the New Zealand researchers had identified in their study of long-term married couples. Second, Kilpatrick and her colleagues found that, in the early months of their marriages, the partners' level of empathic accuracy was strongly correlated with their level of commitment to the relationship, their willingness to accommodate each other's bad behavior, and their level of marital satisfaction. In short, the better the partners could read each other's thoughts and feelings, the more committed, accommodating, and satisfied they were. However, when the same couples were tested again toward the end of their second year of marriage, only the last of these three correlations was still significant.

What is going on here? In general, the results of the North Carolina study suggest that empathic accuracy plays a large role in helping couples' relationships work effectively during the early months of their marriage. By the time these marriages reach the two-year mark, however, the positive effects of empathic accuracy are much less apparent. But why should this be true? What changes could be taking place during the first two years of marriage that might cause empathic accuracy to play a diminishing role over time?

Kilpatrick and her colleagues offered an interesting, though speculative, answer to these questions. They proposed that empathic accuracy might have its greatest effect on positive relationship outcomes early in the course of close relationships because this is a time when the partners' attitudes, values, and behaviors are still relatively unpredictable and difficult to anticipate and accommodate. Accordingly, partners who can successfully infer each other's thoughts and feelings will achieve better relationship outcomes during this early period of adjustment than will couples who cannot.

With the passage of time, however, the positive effects of empathic accuracy on relationship outcomes may decrease for certain couples. According to Kilpatrick, Rusbult, and Bissonnette, these are the couples whose members have learned each other's idiosyncratic cognitive, emotional, and behavioral predilections and have developed habits that automatically accommodate them. Once these habits are in place, the partners who have developed them will automatically anticipate and accommodate each other's needs without having to rely on their empathic accuracy to prompt them to do so. On the other hand, for the (presumably smaller) subset of couples who do not develop such habits—either because of a continuing ignorance of each other's predilections or an unwillingness to accommodate them—empathic accuracy should continue to play an important role in promoting positive relationship outcomes.

In summary, the process of getting to know another person is a bit more complicated than it might first appear. Friends are better at reading each other's minds than strangers are, but this isn't because the friends share more information when they interact together (although they do), nor is it because the friends have more similar personalities (although they might). Neither is the friends' empathic advantage over strangers attributable merely to the greater length of the friends' relationship: length-of-relationship is important only in the sense that it takes time for empathically relevant knowledge to be acquired.

What kind of knowledge is most relevant to the task of inferring another person's thoughts and feelings? From what our research findings tell us, it is not just the background knowledge that constitutes the facts of another person's life—facts that include the person's age, gender, family background, occupation, political affiliation, and so on. More important is the *intimate knowledge* that is acquired by experiencing the other person's thoughts and feelings as they are expressed in a close, personal relationship. This intimate knowledge is "shared" or intersubjective; it constitutes a common ground that is increasingly implicit and taken-for-granted. Although such intimate knowledge is usually acquired over the course of months, the process of getting to know another person can be greatly accelerated in certain high-disclosure situations such as psychotherapy.

For same-sex acquaintances and friends, empathic accuracy appears to develop fairly rapidly during the first six months and then increase very gradually after that. However, for married couples—who typically experience a much higher level of intimate, day-to-day contact than do same-sex friends—empathic accuracy seems to peak during the first or second year of marriage and then tends to decline. Perhaps this early peak and subsequent decline in mutual mind reading will prove to be more characteristic of cultures in which a long period of acquaintanceship and courtship precedes marriage than of cultures in which marriages are arranged.

Sources for Chapter 5

DeLillo, Don. *Underworld.* New York: Scribner, 1997.

Gesn, Paul R. "Shared Knowledge between Same-Sex Friends: Measurement and Validation." Master's thesis, University of Texas at Arlington, 1995.

Graham, Tiffany. "Gender, Relationship, and Target Differences in Empathic Accuracy." Master's thesis, University of Texas at Arlington, 1994.

Kilpatrick, Shelley D., Caryl E. Rusbult, and Victor Bissonnette. "Empathic Accuracy and Accommodative Behavior among Newly Married Couples." *Personal Relationships* 9 (2002): 369–93.

Marangoni, Carol, Stella Garcia, William Ickes, and Gary Teng. "Empathic Accuracy in a Clinically Relevant Setting. *Journal of Personality and Social Psychology* 68 (1995): 854–69.

Poe, Edgar Allan. *18 Best Stories by Edgar Allan Poe*. New York: Dell, 1983.

Stinson, Linda L., and William Ickes. "Empathic Accuracy in the Interactions of Male Friends versus Male Strangers." *Journal of Personality and Social Psychology* 62 (1992): 787–97.

Swensen, Clifford H., Ron W. Eskew, and Karen A. Kohlhepp. "Stage of Family Life Cycle, Ego Development, and the Marriage Relationship." *Journal of Marriage and the Family* 43 (1981): 841–53.

Thomas, Geoff, Garth J. O. Fletcher, and Craig Lange. "On-line Empathic Accuracy in Marital Interaction." *Journal of Personality and Social Psychology* 72 (1997): 839–50.

Six

WHERE IS WOMEN'S INTUITION?

As we have seen, the process by which two people get to know each other is more complicated than conventional wisdom would suggest. But that, of course, is the major pitfall of conventional wisdom: it offers just enough insight to convince us that we can understand in a simple, straightforward way something that later proves to be more complex. So if conventional wisdom offers an overly simplified and occasionally misleading view of the acquaintanceship process, we should be skeptical enough to wonder if it offers an overly simplified and misleading view of other aspects of everyday mind reading as well.

Consider, for example, the stereotype of "women's intuition." Nearly everyone who lives in a Western culture (and in most Eastern cultures too, I suspect) is familiar with this stereotype. It asserts that women are more empathically accurate than men— better able to infer the specific content of other people's thoughts and feelings. And you don't have to take my word for it that this stereotype exists. Survey data reviewed by psychologist Anthony Manstead reveal that both male and female respondents agree that women have more emotional insight than men and are more "sensitive to the feelings of others." And a study by psychologists Nancy Briton and Judith Hall further documents these beliefs.

Indeed, the stereotype regarding women's intuition is one that I, and probably all of my friends, grew up believing in. The graduate and undergraduate students who work with me grew up believing in it too. It is a fundamental part of the catechism of our gender-role socialization—as fundamental as the beliefs that men have deeper voices than women, or that women are less aggressive than men. It is one of the most widely accepted cultural truisms around. It is simply beyond dispute. Or is it?

The fact is, in the first set of empathic accuracy studies we conducted, my colleagues and I failed to find any support for the women's intuition stereotype. We had looked for such support in seven relevant studies, and in each case the expected advantage of female over male perceivers simply didn't emerge. According to the stereotype, women are supposed to be better than men at inferring other people's thoughts and feelings. So the question we were left with was both frustrating and perplexing: *Why aren't the data showing us this?*

In attempting to answer this question, we didn't intentionally set out to discredit the stereotype of "women's intuition." That was something that just happened, and we were as surprised as anyone at first. It was only much later, looking back, that the pattern seemed so unmistakably clear. And by then we had no choice. We were forced to deal with the next question, "Where *is* women's intuition?"

In our very first empathic accuracy study, we failed to find any support for the women's intuition stereotype. This was the study, described in chapter 4, of the initial interactions of male and female strangers—the study that I conducted in collaboration with Linda Stinson, Victor Bissonnette, and Stella Garcia. After we had video-taped the initial, unstructured interactions of these strangers, we seated the man and the woman in separate cubicles and asked them to list their own thoughts and feelings and then infer their partner's thoughts and feelings with the help of the videotape. When our raters later judged the empathic accuracy of the male and female partners' inferences about each other's thoughts and feelings, we found that the women were only slightly more accurate than the men. This difference wasn't even close to being significant in statistical terms.

Were we surprised by this outcome? Yes and no. On the one hand, we *were* somewhat surprised because we believed implicitly in the validity of the women's intuition stereotype. (We were also aware of some other data that appeared to support the stereotype, but we'll consider those findings later.) On the other hand, our surprise was tempered by the knowledge that clear-cut evidence for the stereotype might not be found in a study that involved only opposite-sex dyads. The problem with an opposite-sex dyads study was this: although the women in the dyads might be better everyday mind readers than their male partners, the women might also be faced with a more difficult mind-reading task than the men because the women might have less "readable" interaction partners.

Let's examine this problem more closely. If the women in our first study really were the more accurate perceivers but their male partners were less expressive and therefore less "readable" than the women were themselves, then we might not be able to see much evidence for the women's intuition stereotype. Essentially, the situation would be one in which the better perceivers (presumably, the women) were paired with the harder-to-read partners (presumably, the men), whereas the poorer perceivers (the men) were paired with the easier-to-read partners (the women). In this kind of situation, the effect of the women's superior mind reading would be offset or "canceled out" by the effect of having partners who were more difficult to read. If such offsetting effects occurred, the results might look exactly like what we found: the women would be slightly, but not significantly, more accurate than the men.

Suppose, however, that the dyad members were of the same sex rather than the opposite sex. In other words, suppose that the empathic accuracy scores of female strangers were compared with those of male strangers. By the logic just described, the situation would now be one in which the better perceivers (presumably women) would be paired with the easier-to-read partners (other women), whereas the poorer perceivers (presumably men) would be paired with the harder-to-read partners (other men). In this same-sex dyad situation, we should have a strong basis for predicting that the women would achieve higher empathic accuracy scores than the men because the women are doubly advantaged (better perceivers, easier-to-read targets) whereas the men are doubly disadvantaged (poorer perceivers, harder-to-read targets).

As you might have anticipated, this same-sex dyads comparison has an important drawback of its own: if we find the expected gender difference, we won't know to what extent it reflects the superior empathic ability of female perceivers or the superior "readability" of female targets. On the other hand, this comparison has an even more important advantage: if we again *failed* to find the expected gender difference, we would have even stronger evidence against the validity of the women's intuition stereotype.

This reasoning played an important role in what we did next. We decided to conduct a study of same-sex dyads as a follow-up to our study of opposite-sex dyads. By comparing the average level of empathic accuracy in the female-female dyads with the average level in the male-male dyads, we should be able to determine if the women would be significantly better mind readers than the men when they also had the easier mind-reading task. If, however, this outcome *didn't* occur—if the women failed to outperform the men in the same-sex dyads study—we felt there would be a compelling reason to question the validity of the women's intuition stereotype.

Linda Stinson, who had served as the experimenter in our first empathic accuracy study, fulfilled the same role in the second. Using the same procedure she had used before, she videotaped the initial, unstructured interactions of 30 pairs of male strangers and 30 pairs of female strangers. Each partner attempted to infer the other partner's thoughts and feelings, and the resulting inferences were later used for rating and computing the dyad members' empathic accuracy scores.

When these data were subsequently analyzed, the results revealed no gender difference in empathic accuracy. None. The average empathic accuracy scores were virtually identical for the male-male and female-female dyads in this study, and the extremely tiny difference that was found actually favored the male, rather than the female, perceivers. Obviously, if there was any evidence for the superiority of women's intuition, it wasn't to be found in the results of this study.

But would it be found if we could combine the data from *both* studies before analyzing them? By pooling the data from the opposite-sex dyads study with the data from the same-sex dyads study before analyzing them, we could create a data set in which all four gender pairings were represented: female perceivers reading the minds of female targets, female perceivers reading male targets, male perceivers reading female targets, and male perceivers reading male targets. Then, by analyzing these combined or pooled data, we could separate two kinds of influences on empathic accuracy scores: how these scores were influenced by the gender of the perceiver, and how the same scores were influenced by the gender of the target. We would also have a much larger sample of data to work with, making our statistical tests more sensitive in detecting such influences if they were, in fact, operating.

Because the opposite-sex dyads study and the same-sex dyads study had both been run in the same lab, with the same experimenter (Linda Stinson), and using the same procedures and the same instructions, I thought the data from the two studies could be meaningfully combined and reanalyzed in this way. So I asked Tiffany Graham to do the combined analysis and let me know what she found. The answer, which came back a few days later, was . . . nothing. The gender of the perceiver had no significant influence on the dyad members' empathic accuracy scores, and the gender of the target had no significant influence on them either. Nor did any of the unique gender pairings (female perceivers with female targets, female perceivers with male targets, male perceivers with female targets, male perceivers with male targets) differ significantly from any other unique pairing in the average empathic accuracy scores they displayed.

In summary, the data from this combined analysis offered no evidence for any kind of gender or gender-composition influence on empathic accuracy. Instead, these "null results" actually tended to discredit two widely held stereotypes relating gender to everyday mind reading. First, they cast doubt on the stereotype that women are more accurate mind readers then men (the women's intuition stereotype). Second, they cast doubt on the stereotype that male targets are more difficult to "read" than female targets are (the inexpressive male stereotype). If either or both of these stereotypes were valid, we clearly weren't finding any evidence for them in the two dyadic interaction studies that we had conducted so far.

In fact, we soon discovered that our failure to find a significant empathic advantage for female, as opposed to male, perceivers was not limited to these two dyadic interaction studies. Carol Marangoni found no significant difference between the empathic accuracy of the female and the male perceivers who attempted to infer the thoughts and feelings of the female clients in her psychotherapy tapes. Similarly, Geoff Thomas, Garth Fletcher, and Craig Lange found no significant difference between the empathic accuracy of the wives and the husbands who participated in their study of New Zealand married couples. Victor Bissonnette, Shelley Kilpatrick, and Caryl Rusbult found no such difference in their study of North Carolina newlyweds. Jeff Simpson, Tami Blackstone, and I found no such difference in our study of over 80 heterosexual dating couples. And Melanie Hancock and I found no such difference in our study comparing the empathic accuracy of men and women who were tested in same-sex, four-member groups.

Where was the empathic advantage that we commonly refer to as "women's intuition?" It wasn't evident in the interactions of opposite-sex strangers, or in the interactions of heterosexual dating partners, or even in the interactions of recently married or longer-married dating partners. It wasn't evident in comparisons of female-female dyads with male-male dyads or of all-female groups with all-male groups. It wasn't evident in Texas, in North Carolina, or even in New Zealand. Was it nothing more than a cultural myth? A fictitious bit of folklore that was ripe for scientific debunking?

That's exactly what I thought it was, after seven studies in a row had failed to produce any significant evidence for the women's intuition stereotype. It was just another cultural myth. A stubborn myth, a persistent myth—but a myth nonetheless. So accept it as a myth, not as reality. And don't continue to use it as another excuse for maligning men; we're not the insensitive oafs that the myth has made us out to be.

That's what I thought.

But then a very strange thing happened . . .

In each of the next three studies conducted in our lab, we found a significant gender difference in empathic accuracy. In each of these studies, empathic accuracy was reliably greater for the female perceivers than for the male perceivers, consistent with the women's intuition stereotype. Support for the stereotype had been conspicuously absent in the results of seven previous studies, but now—all at once—here it was.

This outcome was simply baffling. In science, a given effect or phenomenon doesn't simply lie dormant throughout an extended series of studies, and then suddenly emerge in full bloom across a second series of studies. Scientific phenomena aren't, in themselves, that capricious.

Nor do scientists have much tolerance for such apparent capriciousness. Just as nature abhors a vacuum, so do scientists abhor an elusive and inconsistent finding. On the contrary, we like our findings to be orderly, predictable, and replicable. We can't live comfortably with a finding that is here today and gone tomorrow—or, in the case of our gender difference in empathic accuracy—absent yesterday but here today. When faced with such a finding, we have essentially two options: we can shake our head in disgust and leave the inconsistency as a puzzle for someone else to solve, or we can try to solve the puzzle on our own.

For the scientist, solving the puzzle usually amounts to identifying at least one important procedural or methodological difference between the two sets of studies—the set of studies in which the finding *is* evident, and the set of studies in which the finding *is not* evident. Essentially, this process begins by asking the question, "What's different about these two sets of studies—other than their results?" If any such methodological difference can be identified, the next step is to determine whether this difference could plausibly account for the inconsistency that we have observed in the results of the studies. If the answer is yes, we can proceed to the final step and test to see whether systematically changing this feature of the method really does determine whether we obtain, or fail to obtain, the finding of interest.

My graduate students and I already knew one obvious difference between our first and our second set of studies. The studies that showed no female advantage in empathic accuracy had all been conducted before the fall semester of 1994. In contrast, the studies that showed this advantage had all been conducted since that time. The problem with focusing on this temporal difference, however, was that it didn't provide a scientifically plausible reason for the presence or absence of the "women's intuition effect."

Oh, sure, we could concoct a ludicrous, pseudoscientific "explanation" based on the temporal difference if we just wanted to kid around. We could argue, for example, that in the late 1970s a burst of cosmic radiation caused a worldwide mutation in a sex-linked gene, so that all girl babies born after 1978 have a special "women's intuition" gene that all girl babies born prior to that year do not. Then, after our own laughter and the laughter of our geneticist colleagues had subsided, we could make a serious effort to identify the real reason why the female advantage in empathic accuracy was found in our later studies but not in the earlier ones.

I gave Tiffany Graham the assignment of making such a serious effort. The specific charge I gave her was this: Compare the two sets of studies to see if, apart from when these studies were conducted, there was any consistent difference in the method we used—any systematic change that we made between the first set of studies and the next. If you can find any systematic difference like this, we will evaluate it to see whether it could plausibly account for our inconsistent pattern of results.

Tiffany didn't waste any time getting started on this task. And, less than a day later, she came back with our answer. It wasn't the kind of answer that we had expected, however. We had thought that the two sets of studies might differ with respect to which graduate students had served as the experimenters, or with respect to the type of experimental design that was used. But neither of those features was consistently associated with the presence versus absence of the "women's intuition effect." Instead, the only feature of the method that differed systematically across the two sets of studies was the

DATE _____

NUMBER _____

M   F

TIME	THOUGHT OR FEELING	+, 0, -	
	☐ He/she was thinking: ☐ He/she was feeling:	+ 0 -	
	☐ He/she was thinking: ☐ He/she was feeling:	+ 0 -	
	☐ He/she was thinking: ☐ He/she was feeling:	+ 0 -	
	☐ He/she was thinking: ☐ He/she was feeling:	+ 0 -	
	☐ He/she was thinking: ☐ He/she was feeling:	+ 0 -	
	☐ He/she was thinking: ☐ He/she was feeling:	+ 0 -	

Figure 6.1. Original empathic inference form
(no self-ratings of accuracy).

type of empathic inference form our participants used to record their inferences about the target person's thoughts and feelings.

In the first seven studies (the ones in which a significant gender difference in empathic accuracy was never found), our participants

DATE _____

NUMBER _____

M   F

TIME	THOUGHT OR FEELING	How accurate do you think you were?
	☐ He/she was thinking: ☐ He/she was feeling:	0 - not at all 1 - slightly 2 - moderately 3 - very
	☐ He/she was thinking: ☐ He/she was feeling:	0 - not at all 1 - slightly 2 - moderately 3 - very
	☐ He/she was thinking: ☐ He/she was feeling:	0 - not at all 1 - slightly 2 - moderately 3 - very
	☐ He/she was thinking: ☐ He/she was feeling:	0 - not at all 1 - slightly 2 - moderately 3 - very
	☐ He/she was thinking: ☐ He/she was feeling:	0 - not at all 1 - slightly 2 - moderately 3 - very
	☐ He/she was thinking: ☐ He/she was feeling:	0 - not at all 1 - slightly 2 - moderately 3 - very

Figure 6.2. Revised empathic inference form
(with self-ratings of accuracy).

used an empathic inference form that did not require them to estimate how accurate they had been in inferring each of the target
person's thoughts and feelings (see fig. 6.1). Instead, the form
required the participants to rate the overall emotional tone of each

inferred thought or feeling as either positive (+), neutral (0), or negative (–). However, in the next three studies (the ones in which a significant gender difference in empathic accuracy was always found), our participants used an empathic inference form that *did* require them to estimate their accuracy in inferring each of the target person's thoughts and feelings (see fig. 6.2).

In preparation for a study we conducted during the fall semester of 1994, we had made this change in the empathic inference form to learn something about people's *metaknowledge* of their own empathic accuracy: whether they could tell us which of their inferences were accurate and which of them weren't. Unbeknownst to us, however, changing the empathic inference form in this way seemed to have produced another, quite unanticipated outcome. The new empathic inference form consistently evoked a significant gender difference in the participants' empathic accuracy scores—a significant advantage for female perceivers that we had never seen when the earlier version of the form had been used.

We were frankly somewhat surprised. What we had regarded as a relatively inconsequential change in the final column of our empathic inference form now appeared to be a very big deal. In fact, it appeared to be the crucial methodological difference that determined whether a significant female advantage in everyday mind reading would, or would not, be found. But why? Why should changing the empathic inference form in this way evoke a significant gender difference in empathic accuracy that was never found in studies in which the previous inference form was used?

By putting in some hours at the library, Tiffany came up with a plausible answer to this question as well. She found the answer in an article published in 1983 by the developmental psychologists Nancy Eisenberg and Randy Lennon. A few years before we started doing our work on empathic accuracy, Eisenberg and Lennon had searched the research literature looking for evidence of gender differences in many other measures of empathic responding. The studies they located were very diverse. Some studies focused on the empathic responses of babies (for example, do babies cry when they hear another infant cry?). Other studies focused on the empathic responses of children (for example, can children identify the emotional states implied by the facial expressions of people in photographs?). And still other studies focused on the empathic responses of adults (for example, do adults respond physiologically to another person's distress?).

After reviewing the results of these studies, Eisenberg and Lennon concluded that reliable gender differences in empathic responding occurred only in certain situations. Significant gender differences were commonly found in situations that provided clear and unambiguous cues to the participants that something related to empathy was being studied. On the other hand, significant gender differences were rarely, if ever, found in situations that did not provide such cues. As Eisenberg and Lennon expressed it:

> The sex difference in empathy is most evident when it's obvious [that some empathically relevant] trait or behavior is being assessed. Thus, when individuals have been asked to rate themselves on behaviors or reactions clearly related to the concept of empathy, females have scored much higher than males.... [However,] when the purpose of the assessment situation was not clear, females have still tended to score higher on empathy, but the sex difference is much smaller. Finally, when the measure of empathy has been even more unobtrusive, for example, when physiological measures or facial/gestural measures have been the indices of empathy, females have not exhibited more empathy than males.

From this pattern of data, Eisenberg and Lennon drew the logical conclusion: when women describe themselves as being more empathic than men or when women display more empathic behavior than men, they typically do so in response to strong cues indicating that they are *supposed to be empathic in the current situation*. In other words, gender differences in empathic responding are clearly evident only to the extent that situational cues are present that "remind" women of gender-role expectations that they *should* be more empathic than men. When such situational cues are completely absent, women rarely if ever display greater empathy than men.

Eisenberg and Lennon noted that they were not alone in drawing this conclusion. They cited the results of an earlier investigation by another developmental psychologist, Phyllis Berman. Berman had searched a different body of research literature looking for evidence of gender differences in children's and adults' responsiveness to the young (to infants, baby animals, and very young children). When Berman summarized the results of these studies in an article published in 1980, she too concluded that gender differences were stronger to the extent that situational cues reminded girls and women of their relevant gender-role obligations (in this case, to be responsive to the young).

When Tiffany and I discussed the conclusions that had been drawn by Berman and by Eisenberg and Lennon, their implications for our own work were obvious. It was immediately apparent that the interpretation proposed by these earlier writers could be applied to our empathic accuracy data as well. According to this interpretation, the empathic inference form that was used in our first seven studies (fig. 6.1) did not "remind" the participants that an empathy-relevant behavior (empathic accuracy) was being assessed. However, the empathic inference form that was used in our next three studies (fig. 6.2) *did* provide such a reminder, because it required the participants to rate how empathically accurate they were following each and every one of their thought/feeling inferences. In doing so, it not only reminded the participants that they were being evaluated on an empathy-relevant dimension, but it also reminded them of the gender-role expectation that women are supposed to display greater empathic accuracy than men.

If this interpretation were correct, it would mean that the apparently inconsequential change we made in the empathic inference form was of much greater consequence than we had previously imagined. For, with the benefit of hindsight, it was now evident that this change should have had the effect of reminding women that they were supposed to do better than men on our empathic inference task, and should therefore have motivated the women to try harder than men to maximize their performance. According to this account, a higher average level of empathic motivation—*not* a higher average level of empathic ability—was responsible for the women displaying significantly greater empathic accuracy than the men in our more recent set of studies.

Could this motivational interpretation provide the key to understanding what would otherwise appear to be a rather confusing pattern of results? Tiffany and I were determined to find out.

The first thing we wanted to know was whether we could "turn on" or "turn off" the gender difference in empathic accuracy simply by changing the empathic inference form. Because two new studies were currently being conducted in our lab that used the new inference form, we expected to find a reliable gender difference in both of these studies. And we did. The gender difference was significant in both studies, and in both cases it favored the female over the male perceivers.

Given this outcome, we felt confident that we could "turn on" the gender difference by using the new empathic inference form. But could we do the reverse? Could we "turn off" the gender difference by using the old empathic inference form instead? To answer this question, we decided to use the old inference form in the *next* two studies that we ran. When the results of these studies became available, we found—as expected—that there was no reliable gender difference in either of them.

That just about nailed it down. The odds were vanishingly small (less than 1 in 1,000) that the specific pattern of results we predicted and found in our last four studies could have occurred simply by chance. And the odds were microscopic that the consistent pattern of results we found across the entire set of 14 studies could have occurred simply by chance. The implication was clear: by changing the empathic inference form, we could predict—and apparently control—whether a significant gender difference in empathic accuracy would be present or absent in a given study.

There was one more thing that we wanted to know, however. We wanted to assure ourselves that the effect of using the new inference form was to increase the women's empathic accuracy while leaving the men's accuracy unchanged. We therefore made some relevant cross-study comparisons, and these also produced the expected results. Consistent with our motivational interpretation, using the new inference form appeared to selectively enhance the women's performance while leaving the men's performance unchanged.

What conclusions can we draw from these results? And, more specifically, what are their implications with respect to the validity or the invalidity of the women's intuition stereotype?

First, we can conclude that significant gender differences in empathic accuracy are not always found. Instead of being the rule and occurring in the vast majority of cases, they may even be the exceptions, occurring only when certain conditions are met. According to the available data, one such condition is the presence of situational cues that remind female perceivers that they are expected to be highly empathic.

Second, we can conclude that—in terms of group averages—the average woman probably does not have more empathic ability than the average man. Individuals of both genders do, of course, differ substantially in their level of empathic ability. Some men and women are good at everyday mind reading, other men and women are in the average range, and still other men and women are glaringly deficient in this regard. But, apart from these *individual differences* within each gender, there does not appear to be a reliable group-level difference indicating that the average woman has more empathic ability than the average man. Accordingly, to the extent that the stereotype of women's intuition implies such an ability-based difference in empathic accuracy, the stereotype appears to be false.

Third, we can conclude that the stereotype of women's intuition should probably be reinterpreted, rather than abandoned completely. Although women, on average, do not appear to have more empathic *ability* than men, there is compelling evidence that women will display greater accuracy than men when their empathic *motivation* is engaged by situational cues that remind them that they, as women, are expected to excel at empathy-related tasks. The available data therefore suggest that we should reinterpret, rather than deny the existence of, the gender difference implied by the stereotype of women's intuition. We should acknowledge the reality of this difference, but see it as deriving primarily from a difference in women and men's motivation rather than from a difference in their empathic ability.

In fact, it is very difficult to argue that a difference in women's and men's *ability* could adequately account for the pattern of results I have just described. This difficulty became evident to me when, in anticipating how critics might react to our motivational interpretation, I tried to play devil's advocate by constructing an alternative, "differential ability" interpretation. The following comments about this alternative interpretation are taken from an article that I wrote in collaboration with Randy Gesn and Tiffany Graham:

> One might argue that, as a group, women really do have more empathic ability than men do, but that women are only motivated to display their greater ability when situational cues remind them that, according to their gender-role stereotype, they are supposed to excel in this domain. The plausibility of this alternative explanation can be questioned, however, because it would require us to

assume that whenever such situational cues are not available, women either (a) work less hard than men do on empathic accuracy tasks, thus performing no better than men despite their superior ability, or (b) work below their superior potential for some other unspecified reason(s).

For a number of reasons, my colleagues and I found this alternative interpretation to be less compelling than the motivational interpretation that we, along with Eisenberg and Lennon, have proposed. Here are our reasons for feeling this way:

First, any interpretation of our empathic accuracy data that presumes a gender-based difference in empathic ability is likely to be less parsimonious (less simple and straightforward) than our motivational interpretation. Why? Because it requires the additional assumption that women, more often than men, perform *below* their potential on empathic accuracy tasks. Unless this additional assumption is made, anyone who wants to argue that women have greater empathic ability than men would be hard-pressed to explain why, in the nine studies using the old empathic inference form, the women never once reliably outperformed the men. And if you make this additional assumption, how do you justify it? Why *should* women, more than men, so often perform below their potential as everyday mind readers?

Second, the differential-ability interpretation must also deal with another sticky question that is closely related to the preceding one. According to a second widely held cultural stereotype (i.e., the stereotype of the self-absorbed, socially insensitive male), it is men, not women, who generally perform below their potential on empathic accuracy tasks. So, if you want to salvage the differential-ability interpretation by arguing that it is women, rather than men, who more often perform below their true potential on empathic accuracy tasks, then you also have to explain how—and why—the unflattering stereotype about men is simply wrong. This is an ironic position for advocates of the superiority of women's intuition to be placed in, but the available data may leave them no other choice.

Third, a differential-ability interpretation of the data is also less parsimonious than the motivational interpretation in a much broader sense. To state the matter simply, a differential-ability interpretation cannot readily account for all three sets of findings that I have described—the pattern of findings that emerged in our own empathic accuracy studies, and the two patterns of findings that were previously identified by Berman and by Eisenberg and Lennon. In contrast, the motivational interpretation *can* account for all three sets of findings. It does so by proposing that gender differences in empathy and related behaviors are only evident to the extent that gender-role expectations remind women that they are supposed to be highly empathic, responsive to the needs of the young, and so on.

In the final analysis, it seems unlikely that anyone could propose an adequate interpretation of our empathic accuracy data that is based solely on the assumption of differential ability. For a differential-ability interpretation to successfully account for our entire pattern of our data, it would probably have to invoke the assumption of differential motivation as well. How else could one explain why female perceivers should not always perform better than male perceivers, given their presumably superior level of ability? And if *some* kind of motivational account is required, why not prefer the simpler and more straightforward one—especially if it can be generalized more easily to related sets of findings?

By now it should be clear to you why, despite our initial belief in the women's intuition stereotype, my colleagues and I came to question its validity after the results of our first seven empathic accuracy studies became available. It should also be clear to you why, after years of further research, we now acknowledge some apparent evidence for the stereotype, but interpret this evidence as reflecting a difference between the genders in their empathic motivation rather than in their empathic ability. Our beliefs about women's intuition have obviously changed dramatically over the past several years. Consequently, we no longer believe in the usual interpretation of the women's intuition stereotype: that women, in general, have greater empathic ability than men.

Wait a minute, you might be thinking. Not so fast. The data show that, in the absence of something that uniquely motivates women, female perceivers and male perceivers do not differ significantly in their average empathic accuracy scores. So, with respect to the empathic accuracy measure, it does seem that the average woman may not have better mind-reading ability than the average man. But aren't there other data out there that could be used to make a case for the superiority of women's intuition? Aren't there other kinds of accuracy tasks, or other kinds of psychological measures, on which women do achieve higher average scores than men?

If you were thinking along these lines, I can only say . . . good for you. There is indeed another side to this story that I haven't presented yet, and it is time to take a look at it now.

One obvious way to rebut our current position regarding the presumed superiority of women's intuition is to use one of our own early findings to argue against us. If you've got a good memory, you might recall that such a finding was briefly mentioned in chapter 3. In the study that I and my colleagues Eric Robertson, William Tooke, and Gary Teng conducted to validate our newly developed method for assessing dyad members' own reported thoughts and feelings, we found that the women in the study reported more metaperspective thoughts and feelings than the men. Again, metaperspective thoughts and feeling express how one person thinks that *another* person thinks or feels ($S \rightarrow P \rightarrow S$, "I think she likes me"; $S \rightarrow P \rightarrow P$, "But I think she likes herself even more," and so on). If there is evidence in at least one study that women report having more metaperspective thoughts and feelings than men, doesn't that finding guarantee that women must also be the superior everyday mind readers?

The answer is no—it doesn't. First, the result in question was a single, isolated finding that we have so far been unable to replicate. This failure to replicate should give us reason to doubt both the strength and the generality of the result. Second, even if the finding could be replicated, there is no guarantee that greater metaperspective-taking will always translate into greater empathic accuracy. Although it may do so in some cases, there may be other cases in which greater metaperspective-taking reflects the struggle to compensate for a chronically *low* level of empathic accuracy. In fact, we found no reliable correlation in our study between the percentage of metaperspective thoughts and feelings the perceivers reported and the same perceivers' accuracy in inferring the specific content of their partner's thoughts and feelings.

Okay, so we can't find convincing evidence for the superiority of women's intuition in the research that my colleagues and I have conducted. But how about in other people's research? Is convincing evidence for the superiority of women's intuition to be found there?

My answer to this question is bound to disappoint. Maybe, maybe not.

In my opinion, the best potential candidate for a gender difference in an empathic ability can be found in the work of psychologist Judith Hall. For over two decades, she has reviewed the results of studies that assess people's accuracy in decoding other people's emotional states from nonverbal cues such as facial expressions, body movements, and voice tone. After examining the results of dozens of studies on this topic, Hall has reported that women outperform men in nearly 80% of these studies. Although this basic finding seems to argue for the superiority of women's intuition, she has been appropriately cautious in drawing such a conclusion, for reasons that include the following.

First, the gender differences obtained in the studies Hall examined were not always statistically significant. And although statistically significant differences favoring female over male perceivers did occur more often than chance would predict, the average size of the effect across all studies was actually fairly small. Of course, gender differences on psychological measures tend to be small in general, and the gender difference in decoding other people's emotions from their nonverbal behavior is more reliable than most. Still, we are talking about a relatively subtle effect—one that was characterized as "slight" by psychologist Arthur Jenness as early as 1932.

Second, although it is generally assumed that this difference is one of ability rather than motivation, the assumption of an ability-based gender difference in nonverbal decoding has yet to be tested, let alone validated. In theory, all studies of the type included in Judith Hall's reviews could be reexamined. They could be categorized according to whether or not situational cues were present in each study that could have differentially motivated the empathic inferences of the women and the men. Then the average effect sizes in the two sets of studies could be compared to determine if significant gender differences in nonverbal decoding would be found in the first set of studies (motivating cues present) but not in the second set (motivating cues absent).

In practice, classifying all of the relevant studies in this way would be a difficult and time-consuming thing to do. And establishing the reliability of this classification would be necessary because of the highly subjective judgments this task would require. Still, work of this type might prove to be essential if one wants to determine whether women are superior to men in their *ability,* rather than their *motivation,* to decode other people's emotional states from their nonverbal behavior.

Third, even if such work helped us to decide whether the gender difference in nonverbal decoding was one of empathic ability rather than empathic motivation, we still couldn't be sure whether the difference should be attributed to gender per se or to some other attribute(s) with which gender is associated. As Hall has expressed it, "Because we do not experimentally manipulate gender, we have to deal with many variables that may be correlated (confounded) with gender, such as personality, socialization, and physical characteristics."

But let us assume, just for the sake of argument, that the slight-but-real gender difference in nonverbal decoding reflects a genuine difference in the ability—rather than the motivation—of female and male perceivers. How might we account for such an ability difference, if it exists?

One potential explanation—widely promoted by psychologist Nancy Henley in her 1977 book, *Body Politics*—is based on the idea that women in many cultures, including ours, have less social power than men and may therefore act like subordinate, even oppressed, individuals. According to this *subordination hypothesis,* women must closely monitor the words and actions of the more powerful (generally male) members of the culture in order to "please and appease" them on the one hand and to subtly manipulate them on the other hand. Judith Hall, though herself a major critic of the subordination hypothesis, has offered one of the most cogent summaries of it:

> The oppressed status of women might make sensitivity to non-verbal communication particularly important if it allows them to read better the wishes of more powerful others. A person who has less than optimal social power may learn to act on and employ subtle cues in order to effect more social control.

Although the subordination hypothesis generated a lot of interest at the time it was first proposed, there is currently more evidence against the hypothesis than in favor of it. Judith Hall and her colleagues Amy Halberstadt and Christopher O'Brien have taken an in-depth look at this body of evidence. After summarizing the results of a number of relevant studies, including their own, Hall and her colleagues concluded that measures of subordinate status such as low dominance, low ambition, and low socioeconomic status tend to be *negatively*, rather than positively, correlated with measures of nonverbal decoding. In other words, it is the people with more status and power, not those with less, who tend to be more accurate in decoding other people's emotional states from their nonverbal behavior. This result is consistent with psychologist Daniel Goleman's claim that people's ability to accurately interpret other people's emotional states is a major element in their social and occupational success.

A second potential explanation for the gender difference in non-verbal decoding is based on the idea that women are more socially accommodating than men. At first glance, this explanation seems to resemble, and perhaps just recapitulate, the subordination hypothesis. The important difference, however, is that the *accommodation hypothesis* offers a more positive view of the women's greater tendency to accommodate others. According to the accommodation hypothesis, this tendency does not derive from women's subordinate status. Instead, it derives from women's early social experiences, which are assumed to differ in at least two important ways from men's.

First, girls learn to accommodate each other within same-sex groups in order to maintain stable friendships in which status differences are minimized. In contrast, boys tend to compete for rank and status within their same-sex groups and make fewer efforts to accommodate others. Second, because girls learn that mutual accommodation often involves mutual face-saving, they become increasingly knowledgeable about which nonverbal cues to attend to and which ones to tactfully ignore. In consequence, they may become increasingly more accurate than boys at reading the intended emotional cues that other people want them to read. On the other hand, girls may become increasingly less accurate than boys at reading the "leaky," unintended emotional cues that other people would prefer to keep to themselves.

From what I have seen so far, the research support for the accommodation hypothesis can be characterized as promising but not yet conclusive. Some of the best support comes from the collaborative work of psychologists Robert Rosenthal, Bella DePaulo, and their colleagues. Ross Buck has aptly summarized this work in his book *The Communication of Emotion*:

> Rosenthal and DePaulo (1979a, 1979b) present evidence that, as nonverbal cues become less controlled and more leaky, women progressively lose their advantage over men in their nonverbal [decoding] scores. They hypothesize that women learn not to "eavesdrop" on the leaky nonverbal cues of others, that they in effect see only what the other wishes them to see. In this sense, Rosenthal and DePaulo suggest that women are more "polite" and accommodating in their interactions with others. . . . [These researchers and their colleagues] have found evidence consistent with a social learning interpretation of the sex difference in accommodation. As young girls grow older, they progressively lose more of their advantage over males on leaky channels, while they gain more of an advantage on less leaky channels.

Even more direct support for the accommodation hypothesis can be found in Judith Hall's 1998 survey of the personal characteristics that have been found to correlate with accuracy in nonverbal decoding. Among the strongest correlates of nonverbal decoding accuracy are those attributes that convey the image of a highly accommodating person: a person who is well-socialized, highly communal, and publicly self-aware; a person who displayed an easy childhood temperament, who is responsive to instruction, and who is seen by others as being dependable, nonmanipulative, warm, sensitive, and having a strong desire for reassurance; a person who is tolerant, skilled in role-playing, and flexible in dealing with changing circumstances. Taken together, these findings suggest a strong link between having an accommodating, other-oriented personality and being accurate in decoding other people's emotional states from their nonverbal behavior.

A third potential explanation of the gender difference in nonverbal decoding was considered by Judith Hall in her 1978 review article. She noted, but did not advocate, an *evolutionary hypothesis* that is based on the idea that "females are 'wired' from birth to be especially sensitive to nonverbal cues or to be especially quick learners of such cues. This [idea] would make evolutionary sense, because nonverbal sensitivity on a mother's part might enable her to detect distress in her youngsters or threatening signals from other adults, thus enhancing the survival chances of her offspring."

According to the evolutionary hypothesis, there really *are* sex-linked genes that confer greater empathic ability upon girls than upon boys. But these "more-empathic genes" did not emerge in the nonsensical way I joked about earlier (a burst of cosmic radiation in the late 1970s that caused a worldwide mutation of a sex-linked gene). Instead, they emerged as natural mutations that, over an enormous stretch of time, were increasingly represented in successive generations at the expense of "less-empathic genes" because the women who possessed the "more-empathic genes" could better preserve the lives and reproductive fitness of their children.

The evolutionary account seems plausible, but some of its implications would be difficult to test. One implication is that women should be more adept than men at using nonverbal cues to decode the emotional states of infants and small children. To derive this implication, we must make the additional assumption that men performed relatively little child care over the course of our species' evolutionary history, and were therefore not subject to the same evolutionary pressure as their female partners were to accurately "read" children's emotional states. Even if this assumption is granted, however, we are still faced with the problem of knowing when male and female perceivers are or are not accurate when they attempt to perform such a task. Obviously, preverbal children can't tell us what their current emotional states really are. So devising a valid experimental test of the gender difference in this case would be as difficult as figuring out what the emotions of our tiny "targets" were in the first place.

And there are further complications. If the expected gender difference were found, would it apply only to men's and women's ability to decode the emotional states of their own children or would it apply to their ability to decode the emotions of children in general? From an evolutionary standpoint, the "more-empathic genes" that have the best chance of increasing in subsequent generations should be those which increase accuracy in decoding the emotions of one's own offspring and those of one's close kin. If this is so, then the size of the expected gender difference should theoretically decrease as the degree of genetic relatedness between the perceivers and the "target" child decreases.

A different problem might be encountered if we tried to test the complementary hypothesis that women are better than men in decoding nonverbal behaviors that signal threats to children— either to one's own children or to children in general. From an evolutionary standpoint, the promulgation of one's genes might be best served by being hypersensitive to both actual and feigned threats, not just to actual ones. But being hypersensitive to feigned threats would represent an *inaccurate*, rather than an accurate, decoding of the "threatener's" nonverbal behavior, so tests of this hypothesis might not be definitive either.

Perhaps the best strategy would be to use the evolutionary account to predict a *pattern* of gender differences in empathic inference that would not be predicted by any other account. For example, because of greater uncertainty about their paternity, men should be more sensitive than women in detecting thoughts and feelings of sexual disloyalty in their romantic partners. If men prove to be the more accurate perceivers in this type of situation, whereas women prove to be the more accurate perceivers in the types of situations described above, the overall pattern of results could selectively favor an evolutionary interpretation of the data.

So where is women's intuition? Do women have more empathic *ability* than men? And, if so, is this difference limited to the ability to decode other people's emotions from their nonverbal behaviors?

The issue of whether or not there is a real gender difference in an empathic ability such as nonverbal decoding cannot be resolved here. If there *is* such a difference, it may indeed prove to be limited to nonverbal decoding ability, because it clearly does not extend to the ability to infer the specific content of other people's successive thoughts and feelings. But before we could accept even this more qualified view of the empathic advantage implied by the women's intuition stereotype, we must again consider the alternative view: that this advantage is based upon a difference in empathic motivation rather than a difference in empathic ability.

With regard to the subordination hypothesis, a subordinate person's greater motivation to "please and appease" a person of superior rank or power could, in itself, plausibly account for the subordinate's greater empathic sensitivity. The subordinate's greater motivation to accurately read the other person might, over time, lead to the development of greater empathic ability as well. The important point, however, is that the motivational difference could, by itself, be a sufficient cause of greater empathic sensitivity on the part of subordinate individuals. Of course, because the available data provide no consistent evidence that subordinate individuals really *are* more empathic than individuals with greater rank and power, the point may be moot in this case. It still has some value, however, in illustrating that, in terms of the original subordination hypothesis, a motivational interpretation is no less plausible than one based upon ability.

With regard to the accommodation hypothesis, it is also easy to construct a motivational account as a plausible alternative to one based upon ability. Highly accommodating people should, in general, be more motivated than less-accommodating people to attend to others' nonverbal cues and to work harder at using these cues to accurately infer other people's thoughts, feelings, motives, and needs. Of course, the long-term learning that results from this chronic motivational difference could eventually result in a greater ability difference as well. But it isn't really necessary to assume such a corresponding ability difference, because the motivational difference could itself be sufficient to explain why the more accommodating women outperform the less accommodating men on nonverbal decoding tasks.

Finally, with regard to the evolutionary hypothesis, we can plausibly assume that women are more motivated than men to accurately decode their infants' needs and emotions from nonverbal cues. This assumption follows directly from the concept of *differential parental investment*—the idea that women have a greater genetic stake in their children's welfare than men do because of basic biological differences between the sexes. (In particular, women are reproductively viable for fewer years than men and must devote nine months of each of those years to a single pregnancy, whereas men are capable of impregnating women at any time preceding the onset of impotence). On the other hand, because of their greater concern about paternity, men should be more motivated than women to accurately decode signs of sexual infidelity in their partner's nonverbal behavior. Once again, such motivational differences could, in themselves, be sufficient to account for the predicted gender differences in nonverbal decoding.

The bottom line is that there is currently no compelling reason to prefer one interpretation over the other. The overall gender difference in performance on nonverbal decoding tasks could derive from an ability difference, from a motivational difference, or from some combination of the two.

A different conclusion applies, of course, to the pattern of results obtained using our measure of empathic accuracy. When it comes to inferring the specific content of other people's thoughts and feelings, the ability of the average woman does not appear to exceed that of the average man. And on those occasions when the women's performance *is* reliably better than the men's, there are good reasons to believe that the women are simply more highly motivated.

In fact, the results of two more recent empathic accuracy studies suggest that motivation, like money, changes everything. In the first of these studies, conducted at the University of Ghent, Ann Buysse and I found a motivational exception to the general finding that women do not outperform men when the old empathic inference form (fig. 6.1) is used. In the second of these studies, conducted at the University of Oregon, Kristi Klein and Sara Hodges found a motivational exception to the other general finding—the finding that women typically *do* outperform men when a situational cue reminds them that an empathy-relevant behavior is being assessed.

In the study that Ann Buysse conducted at the University of Ghent, two dating couples were recruited to participate in each session. The male and female members of both couples were asked to engage in two discussions of the same assigned topic: once with their own opposite-sex dating partner and once with the opposite-sex partner from the other dating couple. In half of these laboratory sessions, the assigned discussion topic was practicing safer sex; in the remaining sessions, the assigned topic was favorite leisure-time activities.

The resulting discussions were all captured on videotape. Following the taping, the four participants were given the opportunity to view the tape and request to have it stopped at each of the points at which they remembered having had a specific thought or feeling. The four participants individually recorded their own thoughts and feelings on reporting forms like the one depicted in figure 3.1 (see chapter 3). Then the tape was played back for them a second time, and was paused at the appropriate "tape stops" so that each participant could write down his or her inferences about each of the other participants' thoughts and feelings.

When Ann later computed and analyzed the participants' empathic accuracy scores, she found that they were significantly greater for the female dating partners than for the male dating partners. At first, this outcome seemed surprising. After all, we had used the old empathic inference forms (see fig. 6.1) in this study, and had never once found a significant gender difference in the nine previous studies in which this form had been used. But when we asked ourselves the obvious question ("What's so different about *this* study?"), there seemed to be two obvious answers. (Okay, three obvious answers if you count the fact that the study was conducted in Belgium, but that fact didn't seem to bear on the results). First, in all of the sessions, two heterosexual dating couples were present —a unique feature of the study that might have heightened the participants' awareness of their gender as a variable of possible interest to us. Second, in half of the sessions, all of the opposite-sex discussions concerned the topic of practicing safer sex—a topic that women should have a greater stake in than men because of its implications for possible pregnancy.

In retrospect, it seemed likely that these features—both unique to Ann's study—may have combined to "remind" the women that it was particularly important for them to accurately infer their partners' thoughts and feelings, especially when the topic was practicing safer sex. If this interpretation is correct, it means that using the old empathic inference form does not guarantee a finding of no gender difference in empathic accuracy. If there are other features of the situation that can motivate women to a greater extent than men, then a motivation-based gender difference in empathic accuracy will still emerge.

But suppose that the situation is one in which women are already more motivated than men. What would happen in this situation if a powerful incentive were offered to both men and women to maximize their empathic accuracy? This was the question that Kristi Klein and Sara Hodges sought to answer in a series of two experiments. In the first experiment, male and female perceivers viewed a short, videotaped interview in which a female college student talked about an academic problem she had recently experienced (a low math score on the Graduate Record Exam). After they had viewed this videotape once from beginning to end, the perceivers were informed that they would be asked to view it a second time for the purpose of making inferences about each of the thoughts and feelings the student had reported. Before doing so, however, half of the participants were asked to fill out a questionnaire that assessed their sympathy for the student, whereas the other half were asked to fill out a "filler" (i.e., control) questionnaire that did not refer to an empathy-relevant behavior.

Klein and Hodges found, as expected, that the female perceivers displayed significantly greater empathic accuracy than the male perceivers when they had completed the sympathy questionnaire before starting to work on the empathic inference task. There was no apparent gender difference, however, when the female and male perceivers had initially completed the filler questionnaire instead. Klein and Hodges interpreted these findings as providing additional evidence that researchers can "turn on" a motivation-based gender difference in empathic accuracy by means of a situational cue that reminds women that they are supposed to outperform men on empathy-relevant tasks.

The results of the researchers' second experiment were even more interesting, however. In the second experiment, essentially the same procedures were used, with the important exception that some of the male and female perceivers were randomly assigned to a new monetary payment condition. These perceivers were told that they could earn a cash reward for making accurate inferences about the thoughts and feelings of the student who appeared in the videotape. Specifically, they were informed that they would earn up to two dollars for each empathic inference they made, depending upon its accuracy. At that point, all participants made a single "practice inference" and those in the monetary payment condition received a cash payment according to the accuracy of this inference. Then all of the participants filled out the sympathy questionnaire before inferring the rest of the student's thoughts and feelings during the videotaped interview.

Klein and Hodges predicted that the cash incentive would strongly motivate the performance of both the male and the female perceivers in the monetary payment condition, thereby eliminating the gender difference that they expected to find again in the condition in which no monetary reward was mentioned. And this pattern of results is exactly what their data revealed. Although the women again outperformed the men in the no-payment condition, the women and men both displayed a similar, and substantially greater, level of empathic accuracy in the monetary-payment condition.

It appears, then, that if you can motivate men sufficiently, they can overcome and eliminate the performance gap that occurs when a different kind of motivating cue has selectively enhanced the women's empathic accuracy. These results led Klein and Hodges to draw the following conclusion:

> In sum, motivation seems to be a key component in the process of empathizing with another person. The gender difference that was found in our studies seems to be adequately explained by differential motivation between men and women under different circumstances. We believe that this is an encouraging finding, suggesting that greater empathic accuracy can be achieved by virtually anyone who is given the proper motivation.

The bottom line? The empathic advantage implied by the women's intuition stereotype appears to derive primarily from women's greater empathic motivation, and not from a higher level of empathic ability. If you want to motivate men to be as empathic as women, you can— as Klein and Hodges suggested—simply offer to pay them for it!

SOURCES FOR CHAPTER 6

Berman, Phyllis W. "Are Women More Responsive than Men to the Young? A Review of Developmental and Situational Variables." *Psychological Bulletin* 88 (1980): 668–95.

Briton, Nancy J., and Judith A. Hall. "Beliefs about Female and Male Nonverbal Communication." *Sex Roles* 32 (1995): 79–90.

Buck, Ross. *The Communication of Emotion.* New York: Guilford Press, 1984.

Buysse, Ann, and William Ickes. "Topic-Relevant Cognition and Empathic Accuracy in Laboratory Discussions of Safer Sex." *Psychology and Health* 14 (1999): 351–66.

Eisenberg, Nancy, and Randy Lennon. "Sex Differences in Empathy and Related Capacities." *Psychological Bulletin* 94 (1983): 100–31.

Goleman, Daniel. *Emotional Intelligence: Why It Can Matter More than IQ.* New York: Bantam Books, 1995.

Graham, Tiffany, and William Ickes. "When Women's Intuition Isn't Greater than Men's." In *Empathic Accuracy*, edited by William Ickes. New York: Guilford Press, 1997, pp. 117–43.

Hall, Judith A. "Gender Effects in Decoding Nonverbal Cues." *Psychological Bulletin,* 85 (1978): 845–57.

———. "On Explaining Gender Differences: The Case of Nonverbal Communication. In *Review of Personality and Social Psychology: Vol. 7: Sex and Gender,* edited by Phillip Shaver and Clyde Hendrick. Newbury Park, Calif.: Sage, 1987, pp. 177–200.

———. "How Big Are Nonverbal Sex Differences? The Case of Smiling and Sensitivity to Nonverbal Cues." In *Sex Differences and Similarities in Communication*, edited by Daniel J. Canary and Kathryn Dindia. Mahwah, N.J.: Erlbaum, 1998, pp. 155–77.

Hall, Judith A., and Amy G. Halberstadt. "Subordination and Nonverbal Sensitivity: A Hypothesis in Search of Support." In Mary R. Walsh (Ed.), *Women, Men, and Gender: Ongoing Debates.* New Haven, Conn.: Yale University Press, 1997, pp. 120–33.

Hall, Judith A., Amy G. Halberstadt, and Christopher E. O'Brien. "Subordination" and Nonverbal Sensitivity: A Study and Synthesis of Findings Based on Trait Measures. *Sex Roles* 37 (1997): 295–317.

Ickes, William, Paul R. Gesn, and Tiffany Graham. "Gender Differences in Empathic Accuracy: Differential Motivation or Differential Ability? *Personal Relationships* 7 (2000): 95–109.

Klein, Kristi J.K., and Sara D. Hodges. "Gender Differences, Motivation, and Empathic Accuracy: When it Pays to Understand." *Personality and Social Psychology Bulletin* 27 (2001): 720–30.

Manstead, Anthony. "Gender Differences in Emotion." In *Handbook of Individual Differences: Biological Perspectives*, edited by Anthony Gale and Michael W. Eysenck. Oxford, England: Wiley, 1992.

Rosenthal, Robert, and Bella M. DePaulo. "Sex Differences in Accommodation in Nonverbal Communication." In *Skill in Nonverbal Communication: Individual Differences*, edited by Robert Rosenthal. Cambridge, Mass.: Oelgeschlager, Gunn, & Hain,1979, pp. 68–103.

———. "Sex Differences in Eavesdropping on Nonverbal Cues." *Journal of Personality and Social Psychology*, 37 (1979): 273–85.

Seven

EMPATHS WANTED, INQUIRE WITHIN

W ho are the highly empathic people? This is the question that we consider next.

The conventional answer to this question—that the highly empathic people are women rather than men—is no longer one we can blindly accept. If we have learned anything from our study of the women's intuition stereotype, we have learned that you can't make valid judgments about people's levels of empathic ability simply by knowing their gender. Although women's empathic motivation appears to be more easily engaged than men's, there is presently no compelling evidence that the average woman has more empathic ability than the average man does.

On the other hand, there *is* compelling evidence that the individuals within each gender vary substantially in their overall levels of empathic ability. Remember the study described in chapter 5, in which male and female college students were given the opportunity to act like amateur therapists by inferring the thoughts and feelings of three female clients from the videotapes of their individual psychotherapy sessions? Although the "average" woman was not more empathically accurate than the "average" man, the men and women who participated as the perceivers (amateur therapists) in this study displayed substantial individual differences in their ability to read the female clients' thoughts and feelings.

Some men and women were relatively good at reading the clients' thoughts and feelings; other men and women displayed more average levels of empathic accuracy; and still other men and women displayed poor levels of empathic accuracy. What was particularly striking about these individual differences in performance was their consistency across the three clients. Perceivers who were good at "reading" Client A tended to be comparably good at reading Clients B and C. By the same token, perceivers who were average at reading Client A tended to be average at reading Clients B and C, and perceivers who were poor at reading one client tended to be comparably poor at reading the others.

This evidence for *cross-target consistency* in everyday mind reading is essential if we want to argue that there are stable individual differences in empathic ability. According to conventional wisdom, of course, there really *are* such differences. People are assumed to differ in their underlying levels of empathic ability, and these ability differences are assumed to determine the general success or failure of their everyday mind-reading attempts. In this sense, empathic ability is analogous to the ability to speak a complex language such as Russian. Just as we expect skilled speakers of Russian to be consistently fluent across different conversation partners, so we expect empathically skilled perceivers to be consistently good at reading the minds of different interaction partners. And just as we expect unskilled speakers of Russian to be consistently fumble-mouthed with their conversation partners, so we expect empathically challenged perceivers to be consistently poor at reading other people's thoughts and feelings.

The accumulating research evidence clearly supports our commonsense belief that individuals differ in their overall level of empathic ability. Several studies have now shown that perceivers' empathic accuracy scores tend to be relatively consistent from one target person to the next, and the most straightforward interpretation of this cross-target consistency is that it reflects stable individual differences in the perceivers' overall empathic ability. On the other hand, because the level of cross-target consistency is moderate rather than high, we can infer that other influences—apart from the perceivers' overall empathic ability—are operating as well. As we have seen in chapters 4 and 5, these additional influences include the overall "readability" of the particular target person, the degree of acquaintance between the perceiver and the target, and the degree to which the perceiver receives corrective feedback about the target's actual thoughts and feelings.

If a person's gender is not a reliable indicator of his or her level of empathic ability, do any other reliable indicators exist? The answer to this question is yes. First, and most obvious, a person's age is a reliable indicator of his or her empathic ability, at least during the period from infancy through middle to late childhood. Second, and only somewhat less obvious, the individual differences associated with autism and related disorders are also reliable predictors of people's empathic ability.

With regard to age-related differences, every developmental psychologist—along with just about everyone else on the planet—already knows that human infants are incredibly inept mind readers. (Why else would they so rudely scream their demands at us during the earliest hours of the morning?) By the age of three, however, most children have begun to grasp the basic facts that other people's thoughts and feelings can differ from theirs, and that these differences can derive from corresponding differences in what these other people are in a position to know or to perceive. Being able to infer the *specific content* of other people's thoughts and feelings is a much more difficult achievement, however, with some children appearing to be precocious in this regard and other children appearing to be deficient in varying degrees. Still, the vast majority of us show a dramatic increase in our everyday mind reading ability during the period from infancy through middle to late childhood, though substantial individual differences are evident as well.

Where do the individual differences come from? It appears that in their most obvious and debilitating form, they are associated with a condition called autism. Simon Baron-Cohen, a British psychologist who is an expert on the topic, has described this condition in the following way:

> Autism is considered the most severe of all the childhood psychiatric conditions. Fortunately, it occurs only rarely, affecting between approximately 4 and 15 children per 10,000. It occurs in every country in which it has been looked for, and across social classes. The key symptoms are that social and communication development are clearly abnormal in the first few years of life, and the child's play is characterized by a lack of the usual flexibility, imagination, and pretense. The condition may be associated with many biological abnormalities, such as epilepsy, mental handicap, and a variety of brain pathologies. It also appears that in many cases there is a genetic basis to the condition, since the risk of autism or related problems in identical twins or biologically related siblings is substantially higher than would be expected if autism just struck "by chance." At present, autism is unfortunately a lifelong disorder . . . [though] it sometimes appears to alleviate a little with age, as the child receives the benefits of a range of educational and therapeutic interventions and learns various strategies for adapting to the social world.

Baron-Cohen has argued that severely autistic people are afflicted with *mindblindness*—an inability to read other people's minds and a corresponding inability to even imagine what it is like to be able to do that. From the perspective of a severely autistic individual, other people don't seem to be "persons" at all. They are not dealt with as if they were sentient, self-aware beings who live in an intersubjective social world and who have their own unique inner lives of sensations, thoughts, feelings, memories, motives, desires, and beliefs. Instead, they are treated as if they were little more than noisy, animate objects that have to be dealt with like similar objects in the physical world.

To illustrate what the "social" lives of severely autistic people are like, Baron-Cohen cited the following examples, which he took from clinical descriptions published by Leo Kanner in 1943 and from his own more recent observations:

He seems almost to draw into his shell and live within himself . . .

When a hand was held out to him so that he could not possibly ignore it, he played with it briefly as if it were a detached object . . .

He did not respond to being called, and he did not look at his mother when she spoke to him . . .

He never looked up at people's faces. When he had any dealings with persons at all, he treated them, or rather parts of them, as if they were objects. . . . He allowed his mother's hand to dress him, paying not the slightest attention to her . . .

. . . on a crowded beach he would walk straight toward his goal, irrespective of whether this involved walking over newspapers, hands, feet, or torsos, much to the discomfiture of their owners. . . . It was as if he did not distinguish people from things, or at least did not concern himself about the distinction . . .

As these examples reveal, severely autistic or "mindblind" individuals are not like the rest of us. Each of them lives in an isolated world of their own inner experience. The inner experiences of other people are either beyond their ken or are seemingly irrelevant. And it is important to note that autism is not simply another name for mental retardation. When a team of Israeli researchers compared the mind-reading skills of individuals with autism, individuals with mental retardation, and normally developing individuals, they found that the mind-reading deficit was significantly more profound in autistic individuals than in those with mental retardation, although the mentally retarded individuals also performed less well than their normally developing counterparts.

There is little doubt that we can readily identify people at the extreme low end of the empathic ability dimension. As Baron-Cohen has noted, their mindblindness will be just as obvious to us as the physical blindness of people who lack the ability to see. Much less obvious to us, however, are the more subtle differences in empathic ability that extend across the so-called "normal range." These differences can be so difficult to detect that it may often require an extended period of interaction with a new acquaintance before we can confidently ascribe a high, moderate, or low level of empathic ability to that person.

The slow, patient assessment of other people's empathic skills may be very much the rule in everyday life, but it is a rule that several generations of research psychologists have rebelled against and attempted to circumvent. Research psychologists, like their counterparts in many other fields, are a pretty impatient bunch of people. Our collective mindset is essentially this: *we want our answers and we want them now.*

So when the practice of psychotherapy began to flourish in the early decades of the twentieth century, it wasn't long before psychologists with research interests in clinical and personality psychology started to wonder if there might be a quick and efficient way to identify highly empathic individuals. If such a method could be devised, it could be used to help select the most empathic individuals for graduate training in psychiatry, clinical psychology, counseling psychology, and similar helping professions. Within a relatively short time, many other researchers—communication researchers, marriage and family researchers, industrial and organizational psychologists, and other applied psychologists—had begun to think along very similar lines.

It soon became apparent to researchers in all of these areas that the ability to accurately read other people's minds was a quintessential social skill—perhaps even *the* quintessential social skill. And as the consensus within the scientific community developed on this point, the goal of developing a quick, efficient way to assess individual differences in empathic ability became a kind of Holy Grail, especially for many clinical and applied psychologists.

There appeared to be three general approaches that could be used to achieve this goal. The first approach was the easiest—you could simply ask people, by having them fill out a paper-and-pencil questionnaire, to tell you how empathic they are. A second approach required more time and effort—you could administer similar questionnaires to knowledgeable informants (family, friends, coworkers, classmates, and so on) and ask *them* to rate how empathic your people are. The third approach required even more time and effort—you could develop a performance-based task that would enable you to measure the overall accuracy of people's empathic inferences. If you did the job right, you could assume that the people who score high on the task have more empathic ability than those who score low.

Not surprisingly, the first of these three approaches was by far the most popular. After all, the Holy Grail that most researchers were seeking was a quick and efficient way to assess individual differences in empathic ability, not a laborious and time-consuming one. So beginning in the 1940s and continuing through to the present, literally dozens of scales and questionnaires were developed that were purported by their authors to measure empathy-related dimensions such as emotional intelligence, empathy, empathic concern, perspective-taking, social intelligence, social intuition, and social sensitivity.

Almost without exception, these scales and questionnaires satisfy the need for a measure that is quick and efficient. They are easy to administer, they take little time to complete, and their scoring can typically be done by a computer rather than by hand. There is a basic problem with every one of them, however, and you might have seen it coming: *What if you can't trust the answers people give you?*

Some people, for example, might not know how empathic they are. If you ask these people to complete your questionnaire, they will do their best to accommodate you, but their answers might be little more than guesswork. Other people might believe that, however empathic they might be, they are not as empathic as they would like to be, or as they would like to appear to be. If you ask these people to complete your questionnaire, they will also do their best to accommodate you, but their answers might be little more than manifestations of their own wishful thinking.

It all comes down to this. The only way to know for certain if your questionnaire really measures differences in empathic ability is to correlate people's total scores on your empathy questionnaire with their total scores on one or more performance-based tasks that measure this ability more directly. If the questionnaire scores successfully predict people's performance scores on the empathic ability tasks, then you might be able to dispense with the ability tasks in the future and just collect the questionnaire data instead. However, if the questionnaire scores consistently fail to predict people's performance on the empathic ability tasks, there is reason to worry that your questionnaire isn't measuring what you think it is. You just might be fooling yourself.

There is an interesting irony in this state of affairs. The many researchers who chose the first approach to measuring empathic ability—the development of empathy-relevant questionnaires— eventually found themselves dependent on the work of the relatively few researchers who chose the third approach—the development of performance-based measures. For, sooner or later, the questionnaire researchers were confronted with the need to demonstrate the validity of their paper-and-pencil scales, and the most convincing way to do that was to demonstrate that the scores people got on these scales could predict the same people's performance on empathic ability tasks. The results of the quick-and-easy method simply couldn't be taken at face value; they had to be validated against the results of the more difficult and time-consuming one.

By the time my students and I came on the scene in the 1980s, we found that researchers had already created dozens of empathy-relevant questionnaire measures and about a half-dozen performance-based measures of nonverbal decoding ability. On the other hand, apart from the multiple-choice method that was developed in the 1970s by Nathan Kagan and his colleagues (see chapter 4), we were unable to find another performance-based measure of the ability to accurately infer the specific content of other people's successive thoughts and feelings. Our empathic accuracy measure was one of the first—and we had developed it before Carol Maragoni brought the Kagan technique to our attention.

Naturally, we were curious to see if people's scores on empathy-relevant questionnaires could be used to predict their empathic accuracy scores in the different studies we were conducting. Accordingly, in our very first empathic accuracy study, we asked all of the opposite-sex strangers who participated to complete two questionnaires of this type. One was a popular empathy scale developed by psychologist Mark Davis. The other was a "mind reading" scale that I had developed.

When we examined their content, some of the items on Mark Davis's scale certainly looked like ones that should predict individual differences in empathic ability. For example, Davis's scale included items such as these: "I sometimes try to understand my friends better by imagining how things look from their perspective," and "I sometimes find it difficult to see things from the 'other guy's' point of view" (a reverse-scored item). By the same token, when I wrote the items to be included in my mind reading scale, I deliberately tried to make their content very straightforward and explicit. For example, my scale contained items such as these: "During the pauses in a conversation, I seem to know exactly what another person is thinking or feeling," "I can tell, just by looking at a person, what he or she is thinking or feeling," and "I don't have much insight into other people's thoughts and feelings" (a reverse-scored item).

If evaluated on no other basis than the content of their items, these scales seemed promising as potential predictors of our research participants' empathic accuracy scores. As it happened, however, this promise was not fulfilled. When, in our first empathic accuracy study, we correlated the dyad members' scores on these scales with the scores that reflected their accuracy in inferring each other's thoughts and feelings, we found no significant correlations. There was no evidence that the dyad members' judgments of their own empathic ability on these paper-and-pencil scales could be used to predict how accurately they inferred the specific content of each other's thoughts and feelings during their videotaped interactions.

And, as the results of future studies were to prove, this was not an isolated or unusual case. Questionnaire measures of empathy-related dimensions such as emotional contagion, emotional concern, mind reading, and perspective taking consistently failed to predict our participants' empathic accuracy scores in one study after another. In fact, the farther we got into our program of research, the harder we tried to find *any* empathy-relevant scale or questionnaire that could successfully predict our participants' empathic accuracy scores, either in dyadic interaction studies or in studies using the psychotherapy tapes as our standard stimulus materials. The bottom line, however, was that these attempts were repeatedly unsuccessful.

As if things weren't already bad enough from a predictive standpoint, we soon discovered that they were bad from a postdictive standpoint as well. We made this discovery when Carol Marangoni analyzed the data from her dissertation study, the first study to use her set of psychotherapy tapes as the stimulus materials. After the participants had inferred the thoughts and feelings of all three clients, Carol asked the participants to make retrospective ratings of how accurate they thought they had been in inferring each of the respective clients' thoughts and feelings. In other words, instead of *pre*dicting their overall accuracy in each case, they were asked to *post*dict it.

Carol even took the precaution of showing the participants a brief videoclip of each client before asking the participant to make the postdictive rating of his or her accuracy in inferring that particular client's thoughts and feelings. But, as far as we could tell, this precaution did not seem to help the participants make accurate, postdictive judgments about their relative levels of empathic accuracy in each case. The participants' retrospective ratings of their accuracy for each client were simply not correlated with the levels of empathic accuracy they had actually achieved.

At this point, it occurred to me that many perceivers—perhaps even most of them—might have no idea what their levels of empathic ability really are. If this were true, such perceivers would be unable to provide valid ratings of this ability when a psychologist asks them to do so. Instead, they would provide invalid ratings that would fail to either predict or postdict the same perceivers' empathic accuracy scores. The essential problem, in other words, is that most perceivers might not have the self-insight or *metaknowledge* that is necessary to judge their own level of empathic ability.

The more I thought about it, the more sense this interpretation made. It struck me that empathic accuracy is a rather nebulous skill that is much harder to judge than a more concrete skill such as bowling ability. To appreciate this difference, consider the fact that bowlers receive a lot of diagnostic feedback about their bowling ability and that much of this feedback is in numerical form. Bowlers can literally see how many pins fall each time they roll the ball, and they can gauge their overall performance against the absolute standard of a perfect 300-point game. They can also evaluate their performance in more relative terms—comparing it, for example, to the scores of their fellow bowlers or to their own "average" score. Finally, bowlers can keep track of how their performance varies from one game to the next and can even chart the general trend of their performance across time.

In contrast, perceivers in their everyday lives typically receive only occasional and haphazard feedback about the accuracy of their empathic inferences. Such feedback—when it is available—is often ambiguous or even misleading. In addition, perceivers cannot evaluate their mind-reading performance against an absolute standard, and they may find it very difficult to make even relative comparisons of the types described above. The fact that their interaction partners nod and smile a lot may help to convince them that they truly understand these partners. However, their perception of understanding may be an illusion to the extent that their partners' behavior cannot be taken at face value.

There are a number of reasons, then, why people should have relatively poor "metaknowledge" of their own empathic ability. In an article published in 1993, I summarized these and other possible reasons as follows:

- ❖ To avoid violating privacy norms, perceivers in their everyday social encounters rarely seek explicit feedback about their accuracy at inferring other people's thoughts and feelings.
- ❖ Such feedback, when it is provided, rarely concerns the perceiver's *relative* level of empathic accuracy (i.e., the perceiver's rank order in comparison to other perceivers).

* The verbal and nonverbal feedback that perceivers *do* receive from targets may be misleading (i.e., to be polite and avoid giving offense, targets may provide head nods and other signs of agreement or acknowledgment even when the perceiver has failed to understand them).

* Targets may also mask—or simply fail to display—the cues that signal that they are currently experiencing a covert thought or feeling.

* Perceivers may eventually achieve some insight regarding the degree to which they "understand" their few closest friends and intimates, but mistakenly believe that this level of ability generalizes to other targets as well.

* To the degree that perceivers are egocentric or have systematic biases in the attributions they make about how other people regard them (they are narcissistic, paranoid, etc.), both their empathic accuracy and their metaknowledge of this ability may be impaired.

For the reasons just noted, it might—in retrospect, at least—have been naïve for us to assume that people could give us valid assessments of their overall level of empathic ability. When people fill out questionnaire measures of empathic ability, they are essentially telling us how they think they compare to other people in this regard. Are they only average in their empathic ability, or do they think that their level of ability is much higher, somewhat higher, somewhat lower, or much lower than that of the "average" person?

If people aren't in a good position to make such a judgment, we shouldn't be too surprised. I suspect that, in the course of their day-to-day lives, most perceivers get relatively little useful feedback about how their overall level of empathic ability compares with that of other people. If that is true, then the kind of metaknowledge they would need in order to tell us how they actually rank in comparison to others might not be the kind of metaknowledge that they typically attain.

But what about other, less-demanding forms of metaknowledge regarding one's own empathic ability? Could most perceivers, for example, tell us which people they understand well, and which ones they understand poorly? Or, within the context of a single social interaction, could they tell us which of the target person's thoughts and feelings they can accurately infer and which of these thoughts and feelings they cannot infer at all? Perhaps most perceivers have good metaknowledge in these respects, even if they can't provide valid assessments of how their overall level of empathic ability compares with that of other perceivers.

I think there is reason to assume that, if we simply categorized other people as being our intimates, friends, acquaintances, or strangers, we could make reasonably valid predictions about which people we are likely to understand well, not so well, or not at all. As the research findings in chapter 5 have revealed, we can generally read the thoughts and feelings of our friends and intimates more accurately than those of recent acquaintances or total strangers.

On the other hand, it is sobering to recall that the perceivers in Carol Marangoni's dissertation study couldn't make accurate *post-dictions* about which of the three female clients they understood the best, the second-best, or the worst. Given this finding, I suspect that most perceivers lack the metaknowledge to judge their relative empathic accuracy within a set of recent acquaintances or strangers, even if they have the metaknowledge to make the simpler and more basic distinction between people they have gotten to know well (friends and intimates) and people they barely know at all (recent acquaintances and strangers).

But what about the other type of metaknowledge noted above? Can perceivers accurately judge *which* of a particular target person's thoughts and feelings they can—or cannot—accurately infer? I think the answer may depend on the particular target person who is involved. If the target person is a close friend or an intimate partner, then the answer should be yes. When this person is someone we already know very well, we should be able to judge—with a reasonable degree of metaknowledge—which of the person's thoughts and feelings we can accurately infer and which of them we can infer less accurately or not at all. However, when this person is a recent acquaintance or a total stranger, the answer should be no. Our metaknowledge in this case should be relatively poor, and our judgments of how our empathic accuracy varies from one inference to another should be correspondingly flawed.

Because the relevant research hasn't been conducted yet, I don't know whether I'm right or wrong in my assumption that perceivers will display relatively good metaknowledge in judging which thoughts and feelings of a friend or intimate they can—or cannot—accurately infer. On the other hand, the results of at least one study suggest that perceivers will display poor metaknowledge in judging which thoughts and feelings of strangers or recent acquaintances they can—or cannot—accurately infer.

This study was the basis of a master's thesis written by David Mortimer, another of my graduate students. Using two of Carol Marangoni's psychotherapy tapes as his stimulus materials, David asked the college students who served as the perceivers in his study to attempt to infer the clients' actual thought or feeling at each of the appropriate "stop points" on the videotapes. However, to assess the perceivers' inference-by-inference metaknowledge of their own empathic accuracy, he also asked the perceivers to rate the perceived accuracy of each thought-feeling inference immediately after writing down the content of that inference in the form of a sentence. These perceived-accuracy ratings, which were made on the type of empathic inference form depicted in figure 6.2, could range from 0 (not at all accurate) to 3 (very accurate).

By themselves, these rating data weren't sufficient to tell us about the level of inference-by-inference metaknowledge displayed by each perceiver. However, if David were to correlate the perceiver's actual empathic scores for the various thought/feeling inferences with the perceiver's self-ratings of accuracy for the same set of inferences, the resulting correlation would reveal the degree to which the perceiver was sensitive to the variation in his or her actual empathic accuracy from one inference to the next. If this correlation were substantial, then the perceiver could be credited with having a genuine metaknowledge of the inference-by-inference variation in his or her empathic accuracy. However, if this correlation were trivial (likely to have occurred by chance), then the perceiver could not be credited with having this kind of metaknowledge.

When all of the data for the study had been collected, David's undergraduate research assistants judged the actual accuracy with which each participant had been able to infer each of the thoughts and feelings reported by both clients. David then correlated each perceiver's actual empathic accuracy scores for the various thought/feeling inferences with the same perceiver's accuracy ratings for the corresponding inferences to compute a "metaknowledge correlation" for each perceiver. When these metaknowledge correlations had been computed for all of the perceivers in his study, David discovered that the correlations were large enough to be statistically meaningful for only 8 of the 72 perceivers—about 11% of them.

In other words, only 11% of the perceivers in David's study displayed convincing evidence that they were sensitive to the actual variation in the accuracy of their empathic inferences across the entire set of inferences they made. The other 89% of the perceivers displayed no convincing evidence that they had this kind of metaknowledge. These results are consistent with my second assumption—that most perceivers will fail to display such metaknowledge when they infer the thoughts and feelings of a stranger or a recent acquaintance. On the other hand, additional research is still needed to evaluate my first assumption—that most perceivers will display such metaknowledge when they infer the thoughts and feelings of an intimate or a close friend.

In all this talk about different forms of metaknowledge, we are likely to lose sight of the Holy Grail—the fervently sought goal of a quick-and-easy way to measure individual differences in empathic ability within the "normal" range. It is discouraging to think that most people may lack the kind of metaknowledge they would need to provide valid self-estimates of their overall level of empathic ability on paper-and-pencil questionnaires. But should we be so discouraged as to give up our quest for the Holy Grail? If we cannot attain it by using self-report measures of empathy, perspective taking, or mind-reading ability, then can we attain it by following some other path?

According to Mark Davis and his colleague Linda Kraus, another path to this goal might exist. Mark Davis, of course, is the psychologist who developed the popular empathy scale that we used in our first empathic accuracy study. Like us, Mark was puzzled by the fact that people's scores on his empathy scale did not predict their scores on our performance measure of empathic accuracy. He and Linda Kraus decided to see if—by surveying a much broader research literature—they could figure out what was going on.

Using computerized databases to facilitate their search, Davis and Kraus sorted through hundreds of studies conducted from the mid-1950s to the mid-1990s, looking for ones that met three preestablished criteria. First, the study had to include at least one measure of interpersonal accuracy, whether it was accuracy in decoding nonverbal behavior, accuracy in trait inference, or accuracy on some other type of interpersonal judgment task. Second, the study had to include at least one measure of a personality trait or characteristic that the researchers had attempted to relate to their interpersonal accuracy measure. Third, the study's method and data analyses had to be relatively sophisticated in terms of the standards and guidelines that were available to researchers by the mid-1950s.

After much patient effort, Davis and Kraus identified thirty-six studies that met these criteria. Then, from the various findings reported in these studies, they examined a total of 251 correlations involving 32 different personality traits or characteristics and 30 different interpersonal accuracy measures. Their goal was to determine what personal characteristics, if any, might predict people's performance on interpersonal accuracy tasks.

Frequently represented in these studies were several self-report scales that had been designed to measure individual differences in empathy, social intelligence, and social sensitivity. These were the same kinds of empathy-relevant scales that had failed to predict perceivers' empathic accuracy scores in our own research. So we weren't surprised when Davis and Kraus reported that these kinds of scales also failed to predict perceivers' scores on the more extensive set of interpersonal accuracy tasks that they had examined. Whether the scale had been designed to measure self-reported empathy, social intelligence, or social sensitivity/thoughtfulness, the results were the same. There was essentially no relationship between the perceivers' scores on these empathy-relevant scales and their scores on the different interpersonal accuracy tasks.

These results led Davis and Kraus to conclude, like us, that most perceivers may lack the kind of metaknowledge they would need to make valid self-assessments of their own empathic ability. If this conclusion is correct, then what originally seemed like a direct path to the Holy Grail—simply asking people how empathic they are—is a path that might not get us there at all. Although Davis and Kraus acknowledged this possibility, they speculated that there still might be a more *indirect* path that researchers could take. Even if people can't give us valid reports of their own empathic ability, perhaps they can give us valid reports of other traits and characteristics (extraversion, for example) that might prove to be associated with their performance on interpersonal accuracy tasks.

Consistent with this reasoning, Davis and Kraus found that people's scores on certain other traits and characteristics did seem to predict their scores on interpersonal accuracy tasks. The predictive power of these traits and characteristics was admittedly rather weak, but their links to interpersonal accuracy were at least somewhat consistent from one study to the next. With appropriate caution, then, Davis and Kraus proposed the following tentative description of what socially accurate perceivers might be like:

> First, they are intelligent. . . . Second, [t]he accurate judge is more likely to see the world in a cognitively complex, sophisticated way [and] to score low on measures of rigid, dogmatic thinking. . . . Third, the successful judge has good psychological adjustment; that is, better judges tend to report being well socialized and responsible. . . . [They are] more mature and socialized individuals, but not necessarily less anxious ones . . .

Beyond these findings, Davis and Kraus also found that socially accurate perceivers tend to perceive themselves as being above-average in their awareness of the cues that help to define which behaviors are the most appropriate in a given situation. This finding makes sense in terms of the *accommodation hypothesis* that was first discussed in chapter 6. Highly accommodating people should be especially motivated to notice and correctly interpret the cues that signal other people's desires, beliefs, and expectations. Accordingly, it makes sense that the people who report the greatest awareness of such cues would also tend to perform well on interpersonal accuracy tasks.

Finally, Davis and Kraus found evidence that the social sensitivity of highly accurate perceivers is an attribute that is recognized, and is therefore validly judged, by others. This finding is particularly intriguing. It suggests that other people might be able to judge what we ourselves cannot—our own overall level of empathic ability. But why should this difference exist? One possible explanation is that other people are in a better position than we are to assess how our overall level of empathic ability compares to that of other perceivers. In other words, to the degree people can tell that we understand them better or worse than other perceivers do, they might be able to judge our overall level of empathic ability better than we can ourselves.

By the time Davis and Kraus published the results of their research survey in 1997, my colleagues and I had begun to despair of ever finding any personality traits or characteristics that would help us predict people's performance on our empathic accuracy tasks. For this reason, we were quick to recognize the importance of what Davis and Kraus had done.

First, Davis and Kraus had clearly established what we already suspected—that people's scores on empathy-relevant question-naires consistently fail to predict their scores on interpersonal accu-racy tasks. Second, Davis and Kraus had argued that we shouldn't be deterred by this failure. Instead, we should search the broader research literature for *other* personality traits and characteristics that might have predictive value, even if their relevance to empathic ability seemed more tenuous and indirect. Third, Davis and Kraus had actually "named names." They had identified *spe-cific* personality traits and characteristics that might offer at least a tentative portrait of the empathically accurate perceiver.

Would this tentative portrait be supported by the results of our empathic accuracy research? We hoped that it would, but we also had some doubt. A major source of my own doubt was that a finding described as reliable by Davis and Kraus had already proved to be unreliable in our empathic accuracy research. Whereas Davis and Kraus had found that interpersonal accuracy was consis-tently related to the degree to which perceivers reported being sen-sitive to the cues that help to specify which behaviors are socially appropriate, we had failed to find a consistent relationship of this type in a number of empathic accuracy studies.

But would some of the other traits and characteristics that pre-dicted interpersonal accuracy in Davis and Kraus's broader research survey also predict empathic accuracy scores in our own research? Two of my graduate student colleagues, Hao Pham and Kerri Rivers, decided to find out. After some discussion, they concluded that there wouldn't be enough time to assess all of the potential predictors identified by Davis and Krauss within a single experimental session. Still, they wanted to conduct a study in which they could assess at least some of these predictors, and then test to see if the participants' scores on these measures could be used to predict their overall accuracy in inferring the thoughts and feelings of the three female clients in our psychotherapy tapes.

The specific traits and characteristics that Hao and Kerri chose to measure in their study included verbal intelligence, interpersonal trust, and dogmatism (being open-minded as opposed to closed-minded). According to Davis and Kraus's findings, each of these attributes should positively affect performance on our empathic accuracy task. In other words, the perceivers should make more accurate inferences to the extent that they were verbally intelligent, trusting, and open-minded.

The actual results of the study weren't nearly so simple or straightforward, however. When the data analyses were complete, Hao and Kerri discovered that although verbal intelligence was indeed a statistically significant predictor of the men's empathic accuracy (the more intelligent men were the better mind readers), it was not a significant predictor of the women's empathic accuracy. Even more puzzling, although Davis and Kraus had found that higher interpersonal trust scores predicted higher levels of performance on the types of interpersonal accuracy tasks they examined, Hao and Kerri found just the opposite. They found that *lower* interpersonal trust scores predicted higher scores on our empathic task for both for the men and women in the study (in other words, it was the less-trusting, more-suspicious perceivers who proved to be the better mind readers). Finally, contrary to another of Davis and Kraus's findings, Hao and Kerri found that the perceivers' dogmatism scores were essentially unrelated to their empathic accuracy scores.

If you find this pattern of results confusing, you are not alone: my colleagues and I felt the same way. Why, we wondered, did the verbal intelligence measure predict the men's empathic accuracy scores but not the women's? Why did the dogmatism measure fail to predict the empathic accuracy scores of either gender? And why were *higher* trust scores associated with greater accuracy in the studies that Davis and Kraus examined, whereas *lower* trust scores were associated with greater accuracy in the study that Pham and Rivers conducted? The answers to these questions weren't obvious then, and they still aren't obvious today.

What *is* obvious is the lesson to be learned from such unexpected findings. They suggest that even Davis and Kraus's alternative path to the Holy Grail might not take us where we want to go. This alternative path is strewn with its own hazards and obstacles. It can, without warning, lead us off into mists of confusion, or bring us up short at an unexpected dead end.

When the paths you have taken have failed you, it is often best to return to the place where you started and look for renewed inspiration there. Early in the novel *The Magus*, Nicholas Urfe reads the following lines by T. S. Eliot:

> We shall not cease from exploration
> And the end of all our exploring
> Will be to arrive where we started
> And know the place for the first time.

If we follow this advice in the present case, what can we learn? When we go back to the start of this chapter, we find two facts about empathic ability that are worth re-considering. The first fact is that individuals really do differ in their overall level of empathic ability. Perceivers' empathic accuracy scores tend to be relatively consistent from one target person to the next, and the most straight-forward interpretation of this cross-target consistency is that it reflects stable individual differences in the perceivers' overall empathic ability. The second fact is that everyday mind reading is undeniably impaired in individuals who, by reason of their "biological abnormalities," "mental handicap," or "brain pathologies," have been categorized as autistic. This fact suggests that the study of autistic individuals might shed some light on the problem of assessing individual differences in empathic ability.

As the neurologist Oliver Sacks has noted, "No two people with autism are the same." Although all autistic individuals display impaired social development, the degree of their impairment ranges from severe to mild, depending on the type and severity of the underlying neurological disorder. In fact, a different term—Asperger Syndrome—is often applied to people whose autism is relatively mild. This term derived from the clinical observations of Hans Asperger, a contemporary of Leo Kanner's, who was one of the first to study these less-autistic individuals.

According to Oliver Sacks, the major advantage of studying people with Asperger's syndrome is that they "can tell us of their experiences, their inner feelings and states, whereas those with classical autism cannot." Sacks, for example, has recorded the insights of Dr. Temple Grandin, who earned her Ph.D. in agricultural science and who now teaches and conducts research at Colorado State University. At first glance, her impressive achievements suggest that she has managed to compensate fully for her "mind-blindness." This is not the case, however, as she has noted in her interviews with Dr. Sacks.

Temple Grandin reported that, as a child, she grew up without the awareness that she was different from others. However, by the time she went to high school, she had developed the sense that *they* were different from her. Sacks's description of her experience is compelling:

> Something was going on between the other kids, something
> swift, subtle, constantly changing—an exchange of meanings, a
> negotiation, a swiftness of understanding so remarkable that
> sometimes she wondered if they were all telepathic. She is now
> aware of the existence of these social signals. She can infer them,
> she says, but she herself cannot perceive them, cannot participate
> in this magical communication directly, or conceive of the many-
> leveled, kaleidoscopic states of mind behind it.

Donna Williams, a writer who was born in Australia and now
lives in England, is another autistic person whose intelligence and
self-insight have enabled her to describe her experience to others.
Many of her insights have been recorded by the British neurophys-
iologist Jonathan Cole, who devoted a lengthy chapter to them in
his book, *About Face*. In general, Donna Williams conveys the
impression of a person with a highly vulnerable sense of self—a
person who typically feels detached and disconnected from her
own feelings, her own actions, her own body. Her fragile sense of
self, already difficult to sustain, becomes even harder to control
when she is required to interact face-to-face with others.

At such times, she experiences an emotional and informational
overload that is so overwhelming that it threatens her precarious
sense of self. The other's voice is too noisy, too distracting, too difficult to track in its endless modulations. The other's face is too ani-
mated; the endless play of emotional expression is too complicated
to follow or interpret. Indeed, the other's face presents itself in a
fragmented, piecemeal way—as an eyebrow, then a nose and an
ear—rather than as a fully integrated configuration of features. The
other's gaze is too intense; she must actively avoid making eye contact because it threatens to overwhelm her fragile sense of self with
the unbearable "otherness" that confronts her.

According to Williams's autobiographical account, the autistic
individual tends to "shut down" in the face of this emotional and
perceptual onslaught, with the consequence that much of the
meaning of the social encounter is lost:

For me, when the directness of relating is too great, the walls go up. . . . Under overload conditions any of several meaning systems can shut down partially or completely, in combination or in isolation. Sensorially, this can mean that any one or any combination of the senses can become extremely acute. For me, this made some high-pitched sounds intolerable, and bright light became either intolerable or mesmerizing. Touch was as always intolerable. On a cognitive level, the meaning carried by intonation and gesture can be completely shut down, leaving the listener with no emotional cues. The meaning behind the significance of social rules can be completely lost (where it had previously been understood and cooperated with), and the comprehension of the meaning of words can drop away, leaving the listener lost as to both concept and significance.

These insights into Williams's experience suggest that autistic individuals are unable to deal with the emotions evoked in many social encounters and with the sheer amount of information that flows from their interaction partner's behavior. Rather than apprehending the other's behaviors in the form of integrated gestalts that are constantly updated with changes in the other's facial expressions, body movements, and vocal tones, they experience these behaviors as isolated "bits and pieces" that are often painfully stimulating. At times, they are able to organize some of these bits and pieces into a larger gestalt, but it requires a great effort for them to do so and, in general, they cannot. Even worse, to the extent that they *can* apprehend the other person in all of his or her "otherness," they find it harder to hold onto their own precarious sense of self.

Bernard Rimland, an expert in the field of autism, has offered the following insights about the condition in his foreword to Donna Williams' bestselling book, *Nobody Nowhere*:

Researchers in neuroanatomy are . . . discovering subtle *structural* anomalies in the brains of some autistic persons, especially in the cerebellar circuits that permit the normal brain to select, prioritize, and process information effectively. When these circuits malfunction, the automatic shifts of attention that make life flow smoothly for normal infants and children are grossly impaired in the autistic child, so that he or she becomes oblivious to many of the social cues and to the constant stream of cause-and-effect sequences that give coherence and meaning to normal experience.

The agonizing difficulties in the autistic person's ability to sort and process information, in my opinion, not only underlie many of the deficits in autism, but may also account for the islets of brilliance, or savant abilities, manifested by so many autistic persons, including Donna Williams.

Understanding the experience of autistic individuals may give us another path to follow in our attempts to measure individual differences in empathic ability. Before going down that path, however, we would first want to assure ourselves that there are varying degrees of mindblindness, and that autistic impairments in empathic ability are represented along a continuum that extends into the "normal" range. It would be useful to know, therefore, if more mildly autistic perceivers also differ from nonautistic perceivers in their average level of empathic accuracy. If they do, we might be able to use our insights into the autistic person's social experience to develop a self-report questionnaire that could predict perceivers' scores on empathic accuracy tasks.

In fact, a study comparing the empathic accuracy of mildly autistic and nonautistic perceivers has already been done. It was conducted in Belgium, at the University of Ghent, by Herbert Roeyers, Ann Buysse, Koen Ponnet, and Bert Pichal. With the help of the Flemish Parent Association and treatment facilities for adults with autism, they recruited 24 mildly autistic adolescents and adults to serve as participants. They also recruited the same number of nonautistic adolescents and adults, each of whom was carefully matched with one of the autistic participants so that both had the same gender, the same level of education, and similar occupations or interests.

Each of the participants was tested individually on three tasks that assessed different kinds of empathic inference. The first was an empathic accuracy task in which the participant was asked to infer the actual thoughts and feelings reported by two pairs of male and female strangers whose initial interactions had been captured on videotape. The second was a story task that required the participants to infer the beliefs of characters in situations that involved telling a lie, telling a white lie, mutual bluffing, sarcasm, persuasion, or mixed feelings. The third was a photograph task that required the participants to look at a set of photographs and use each target person's eye direction as a cue for inferring what the target person was currently thinking about.

Roeyers and his colleagues expected that the difference in performance between the autistic participants and their nonautistic counterparts would be most evident on the empathic accuracy task, because this task most closely approximated the challenges of trying to understand other people in everyday social interaction. And, in fact, this is what they found. In comparison to their nonautistic counterparts, the autistic participants were worse at inferring the thoughts and feelings of the freewheeling conversation partners in the empathic accuracy task. On the other hand, they proved to be just as good as their nonautistic counterparts at inferring the beliefs of the story characters, or in using eye direction as a cue to infer what the target persons in the photographs were currently thinking about.

This pattern of results suggests that mildly autistic individuals find it difficult to deal with the demands of everyday social interaction, in which rapidly changing information is simultaneously available in multiple "channels" (words, voice tone, facial expression, eye direction, and so on). However, when the information is restricted to a single, less dynamic channel (such as a well-paced verbal narrative in the story task or eye direction in the photograph task), mildly autistic individuals may perform about as well as their nonautistic counterparts.

Given this evidence that autistic impairments in everyday mind reading are not limited to the extreme end of the range, can we use our insights about the experience of mildly autistic individuals to develop items for a scale that could be used to predict empathic accuracy scores? Perhaps we can. If autistic impairments extend into the "normal range," then it should be possible to develop a self-report questionnaire that measures the extent to which people characterize their own social experience as being similar to that of high-functioning autistic individuals such as Temple Grandin and Donna Williams.

In fact, Simon Baron-Cohen and his colleagues Sally Wheelwright, Richard Skinner, Joanne Martin, and Emma Clubley have already developed such a questionnaire. Based on the premise that autistic-like behavior extends across a spectrum that connects diagnosed autistic individuals with normal individuals who display autistic-like behavior, their Autism-Spectrum questionnaire assesses five areas of such behavior. The first area, *limited social skill*, is measured by items such as "I find it hard to make new friends," and "I find it difficult to work out people's intentions." The second area, *problems in attention switching*, is measured by items such as "I prefer to do things the same way over and over again," and "I frequently get so strongly absorbed in one thing that I lose sight of other things." The third area, *attention to detail*, is measured by items such as "I often notice small sounds when others do not," and "I usually notice car number plates or similar strings of information." The fourth area, *problems in communication*, is measured by items such as "When I talk on the phone, I'm not sure when it's my turn to speak," and "People often tell me that I keep going on and on about the same thing." Finally, the fifth area, *limited imagination*, is measured by items such as "When I'm reading a story, I find it difficult to work out the characters' intentions," and "I find it difficult to imagine what it would be like to be someone else."

Baron-Cohen and his colleagues have reported that individuals with a diagnosis of Asperger syndrome or high-functioning autism score substantially higher on the Autism-Spectrum questionnaire than do randomly selected (presumably nonautistic) control individuals. Moreover, when the researchers compared the scores obtained by different groups within a university sample, they found higher scores for students majoring in math and math-intensive sciences than for students majoring in the humanities and social sciences, with male math majors reporting the highest level of "autistic-like" behavior. As you might have noticed, these people fit the classic nerd stereotype: they are good at math but are socially unskilled and report that they have difficulty "reading" other people.

Would university students' scores on the Autism-Spectrum questionnaire predict their scores on a standard performance-based measure of empathic accuracy? According to Baron-Cohen and his colleagues, they should. People who score high on the Autism-Spectrum questionnaire presumably have more autistic-like social experiences than people who score low. If such experiences are associated with impairment in everyday mind-reading ability, then people who score high on the questionnaire should perform poorly on standard empathic accuracy tasks, whereas people who score low on the questionnaire should perform well.

To the best of my knowledge, the research needed to test this hypothesis has not yet been conducted. However, the use of the Autism-Spectrum measure to predict individual differences in empathic accuracy would seem to offer a promising direction for future research. It might also be worthwhile to supplement the items on the Autism-Spectrum measure with ones based on the experiences reported by high-functioning autistic individuals such as Donna Williams and Temple Grandin. For example, "I tend to get overwhelmed by the emotions I experience when I interact with other people"; "The sheer physical presence of other people can be so intimidating that I lose track of what they are saying to me"; "I find it difficult to interact with other people because it is often such an intense, overwhelming experience."

In the absence of relevant data, we can only speculate about the relationship between autistic-like social experience and impaired empathic accuracy. However, the idea of a continuum linking autistic perceivers with more accomplished ones suggests another interesting possibility that we should consider. So far, we have talked about using a questionnaire with items focusing on how autistic people are different from nonautistic people. But suppose that we used a questionnaire with items focusing on how people who *aren't* mindblind are different from each other in their level of interest and motivation to understand others. Would people who score high on such a questionnaire prove to be better everyday mind readers than people who score low?

A potential answer to this question is suggested by the results of a study conducted by Geoff Thomas and Garth Fletcher at the University of Canterbury in Christchurch, New Zealand. In Thomas and Fletcher's ambitious study, 200 perceivers attempted to infer the thoughts and feelings of different target persons who appeared in 10-minute videotaped excerpts. The perceivers varied systematically in their relationship with the different target persons they viewed. In some cases, the target was a complete stranger whereas in other cases the target was either a friend or a dating partner.

Of greatest relevance to our present concerns, all of the perceivers in this study had previously completed a questionnaire that measured their *attributional complexity*—their interest and motivation in accurately inferring the underlying motives and intentions of other people. The perceivers who got high scores on the attributional complexity questionnaire should have been decidedly *non*autistic, taking a strong interest in other people's mental lives and actively attempting to infer their motives and intentions. In contrast, the perceivers who got low scores on the questionnaire should have been more like autistic individuals in their relative lack of interest in other people's thoughts and feelings.

When Thomas and Fletcher analyzed the data from their study, they found that the perceivers' attributional complexity scores predicted their level of empathic accuracy in some cases but not in others. Specifically, the perceivers' attributional complexity scores did not predict their accuracy in reading the thoughts and feelings of total strangers. However, these scores did predict the perceivers' accuracy in reading the thoughts and feelings of their dating partners. And, interestingly, the attributional complexity scores also predicted the perceivers' accuracy in the special case in which the perceivers were friends of the target persons (the dating partners) and had previously discussed with one or both partners the specific conflict issue that the dating partners were attempting to resolve in the videotaped excerpt.

Thomas and Fletcher interpreted these results by proposing that the perceivers' attributional complexity can play an important role in their empathy accuracy, but only when enough "background" information is available for this factor to make a difference. When perceivers have relatively little prior information on which to base their empathic inferences (as in the case of complete strangers), their degree of interest in understanding others may not matter much because the task is simply too difficult—not enough information is available for *any* perceivers to do very well. On the other hand, when the perceivers have sufficient background information on which to base their inferences (as in the case of well-informed friends or dating partners), their degree of interest in understanding others (as assessed by their attributional complexity scores) can play a more pronounced role in predicting the level of empathic accuracy that they are able to achieve.

❖ ❖ ❖

The reports of people like Temple Grandin and Donna Williams suggest that autistic individuals have impaired empathic ability because they are unable to structure and integrate the overwhelming streams of information that flow from their interaction partners' behavior. The impairment appears to operate at the level of their immediate perceptual experience, restricting the ability of autistic individuals to organize their perceptions into the kinds of gestalts that convey the underlying meanings of the other person's words and actions. Consequently, autistic individuals often fail to draw even the simplest and most basic empathic inferences from the relentless rush of cues flowing from their interaction with the other person.

In contrast, the more subtle impairment of "normal" individuals who score low rather than high in attributional complexity appears to be related less to problems in interpreting cues in the immediate context than in integrating such cues with previously acquired information about their interaction partners. Thomas and Fletcher's data suggest that individual differences in attributional complexity affect empathic accuracy only when the perceivers have sufficient background information on which to base their inferences (as in the case of well-informed friends or dating partners). On the other hand, attributional complexity differences don't seem to matter much when essentially no background information is available (as in the case of strangers). It appears, therefore, that low attributional complexity does not impair the ability of perceivers to interpret immediate contextual cues. Instead, it impairs their ability to identify and integrate relevant information derived from the entire cumulative context—past and present—of their interaction with the other person.

In summary, the more profound impairments in empathic ability may reflect problems in appropriately processing and integrating informational cues that are available in the *immediate con-*

text of one's interaction with the other, whereas the more subtle impairments in empathic ability may reflect problems in retrieving and integrating relevant cues that must be drawn from the temporally extended, *cumulative context* of one's interaction with the other. If this view of things is even approximately correct, it suggests that there might be two types of problems associated with impairments in everyday mind reading: failures to make appropriate perceptual integrations within the immediate social context and failures to make appropriate memory-based integrations across the cumulative social context.

The first of these failures is obviously the more profound, because if the appropriate perceptual gestalts fail to develop within the immediate social context, the perceiver would be unable to link them via memory to other relevant gestalts that were formed in the past. Perhaps the best the perceiver could hope to do in this case would be to piece such gestalts together later, some time after the immediate interaction has ended. And, indeed, this is a common theme of Donna Williams's reminiscences in her autobiographical account, *Nobody Nowhere*. Other persons' thoughts and feelings, which were so often completely opaque to her at the time she interacted with them, gradually yielded some of their meaning and their relation to the other persons' past behavior when she was able to reflect upon them later. However, as she notes at various points throughout her book, achieving these linkages and larger integrations could take a very long time—in some cases, months or even years.

So who are the highly empathic people? It is perhaps easier to begin by reminding ourselves who they aren't.

The highly empathic people aren't the ones who struggle every day with the various forms and degrees of autism, and with the corresponding forms and degrees of mindblindness that are associated with them. Autistic individuals must cope with what appears to be a basic perceptual impairment that limits their ability to read other people's minds. Although they vary along a substantial range of empathic ability, they are nonetheless limited to the lower range of this dimension.

Interestingly, autism is much more common in males than in females, a fact that Baron-Cohen speculated might be a source of the commonly held belief "that women are much better mind-readers than men." As we have seen in chapter 6, however, there appears to be no overall gender difference within the range of "normal" mind reading ability. The fact that there are more autistic men than autistic women should therefore not be used as a basis for claiming that, in general, women are better mind readers than men. Any such difference, if it exists, is instead relatively specific, applying primarily to males and females in the lower range of the empathic ability dimension.

Of course, within the "normal" range of empathic ability, stable and reliable *individual* differences do exist. Some individuals are consistently good mind readers; others are consistently average; and still others are consistently poor. Although it has proved difficult to find a quick and easy way to distinguish among these individuals, the available evidence suggests that the most empathically accurate people are those who have no signs of autism, who score high in attributional complexity, and who tend to be suspicious rather than trusting. And, for men at least, a high level of verbal intelligence is associated with better-than-average empathic ability.

Finally, some evidence suggests that the most accurate mind readers are those who are good at relating information from their partners' current behavior with information from their past behavior, and then integrating this accumulated information to make inferences about the specific content of their partners' thoughts and feelings. This evidence highlights an important distinction between the *immediate* social context and the *cumulative* social context—a distinction that we will examine more closely in the following chapter.

SOURCES FOR CHAPTER 7

Baron-Cohen, Simon. *Mindblindness: An Essay on Autism and Theory of Mind.* Cambridge, Mass.: MIT Press, 1995.

Baron-Cohen, Simon, Sally Wheelwright, Richard Skinner, Joanne Martin, and Emma Clubley, "The Autism-Spectrum Quotient (AQ): Evidence from Asperger Syndrome/High-Functioning Autism, Males and Females, Scientists and Mathematicians." *Journal of Autism and Communication Disorders* 31 (2001): 5–17.

Cole, Jonathan. *About Face.* Cambridge, Mass.: MIT Press, 1998.

Davis, Mark H. "Measuring Individual Differences in Empathy: Evidence for a Multidimensional Approach." *Journal of Personality and Social Psychology* 51 (1983): 167–84.

Davis, Mark H., and Linda Kraus. "Personality and Empathic Accuracy." In *Empathic Accuracy*, edited by William Ickes. New York: Guilford Press, 1997, pp. 144–68.

Fowles, John. *The Magus.* New York: Little, Brown, & Company, 1965.

Gesn, Paul R., and William Ickes. "The Development of Meaning Contexts for Empathic Accuracy: Channel and Sequence Effects." *Journal of Personality and Social Psychology* 77 (1999): 746–61.

Ickes, William. "Empathic Accuracy." *Journal of Personality* 61 (1993): 587–610.

Ickes, William, Ann Buysse, Hao Pham, Kerri Rivers, James R. Erickson, Melanie Hancock, Joli Kelleher, and Paul R. Gesn. "On the Difficulty of Distinguishing 'Good' and 'Poor' Perceivers: A Social Relations Analysis of Empathic Accuracy Data." *Personal Relationships* 7 (2000): 219–34.

Kagan, Nathan. *Interpersonal Process Recall.* East Lansing: Michigan State University Press, 1977.

Kanner, Leo. "Autistic Disturbance of Affective Contact." *Nervous Child* 2 (1943): 217–50.

Marangoni, Carol, Stella Garcia, William Ickes, and Gary Teng. "Empathic Accuracy in a Clinically Relevant Setting." *Journal of Personality and Social Psychology* 68 (1995): 854–69.

Mortimer, David C. "'Reading' Ourselves 'Reading' Others: Actual versus Self-Estimated Empathic Accuracy." Master's thesis, University of Texas at Arlington, 1996.

Roeyers, Herbert, Ann Buysse, Koen Ponnet, and Bert Pichal. "Advancing Advanced Mindreading Tests: Empathic Accuracy in Adults with a Pervasive Developmental Disorder." *Journal of Child Psychology and Psychiatry and Allied Disciplines* 42 (2001): 271–78.

Sacks, Oliver. *An Anthropologist on Mars.* New York: Knopf, 1995.

Thomas, Geoff, and Garth J. O. Fletcher. "Individual Differences in Mind-Reading Accuracy: The Profile of the Good Judge and Good Relationship." Unpublished manuscript, 2000.

Williams, Donna. *Nobody Nowhere.* New York: Avon Books, 1992.

Yirmiya, Nurit, Osnat Erel, Michal Shaked, and Daphna Solomonica-Levi. "Meta-analyses Comparing Theory of Mind Abilities of Individuals with Autism, Individuals with Mental Retardation, and Normally Developing Individuals." *Psychological Bulletin* 3 (1998): 283–307.

eight

FRAMING
YOUR
THOUGHTS

Consider the following little story, which two colleagues at a neighboring university sent me via e-mail:

A woman gets home, screeches her car into the driveway, runs into the house, slams the door, and shouts at the top of her lungs, "Honey, pack your bags. I won the lottery!"

The husband says, "Oh my god! No way! What should I pack, beach stuff or mountain stuff?"

And the wife yells back, "It doesn't matter. Just get the hell out!"

My colleagues thought this story was a nice illustration of how two people—even ones who are supposedly intimates—can apply very different interpretive "frames" to what is ostensibly the same situation. I agree that it is. What I find of even greater interest, however, is that male and female readers display essentially the same difference in the interpretive frames that they bring to this story. Male readers are generally slow to adopt the interpretive frame that female readers spontaneously apply—that the wife in the story has been waiting a long time for such an ideal opportunity to "throw the bum out."

Most women appear to see the punchline of this joke coming long before it arrives. On the other hand, most men (and I was certainly no exception) appear to be unsettled by both the punchline of the joke and the fact that we failed to anticipate it. Especially unsettling, I believe, is our realization that an interpretive frame that wouldn't automatically occur to us ("it's the perfect time to throw the bum out") *does* automatically occur to most women. It is not surprising, therefore, that men tend to find this joke less amusing than women do. Our masculine response is affected not only by the joke's implicit men-bad-women-good message but also by our failure to foresee, or even accept, the wife's dismissive interpretive frame.

As this example suggests, there are times when inferring another person's thoughts and feelings can be a very tricky business—one that can lead us to abrupt surprises and rude awakenings. Just when I think that I have you all figured out, you can suddenly say or do something that will cause my carefully built structure of understanding to collapse right in front of me like a house of cards. At such times, I am not only left to confront the blown-out remnants of that ruined structure; I am also forced to admit that the fault for its collapse was partially, if not entirely, mine. I now realize that I had mistakenly applied the wrong interpretive frame when I attempted to infer your thoughts and feelings.

❖   ❖   ❖

Yet it seems that there is also a frame of mind which can share
the frame of another at the same time. Frames multiply. The mind
is a frame which frames. But who, or what, frames this frame?
And from the "inside" or the "outside"?

—Nicholas Royle
Telepathy and Literature

This chapter is about how interpretative frames affect the success or failure of our attempts at everyday mind reading. My
thinking on this topic has been influenced most directly by the work
of Erving Goffman, one of history's greatest social psychological
theorists. I was first introduced to the concept of interpretive frames
in Goffman's book, *Frame Analysis*. Published in 1974, *Frame
Analysis* was the culmination of ideas that Goffman had developed
and explored in a series of previous books over the course of nearly
twenty years.

According to Goffman, frames are the "interpretative schemes"
that we apply to the different situations we encounter. Whenever we
are confronted with a new situation, we are required to deal, either
implicitly or explicitly, with the fundamental question, "What's
going on here?" It is how we answer that question—how we
"frame" or interpret the situation at hand—that not only defines
what is presumably occurring in the situation but also helps to
determine our subsequent actions, feelings, and beliefs.

What constitutes a new situation must be very loosely defined.
At one extreme, a "new situation" can suddenly emerge whenever
something new or unexpected happens in an otherwise familiar
context. The novel element can be extremely simple. Often, it is a
single action or utterance expressed by one person to which a
second person must respond. For example, when Angus asks
Angela if she wants to "fool around," she must "frame" or interpret
the meaning of this phrase before she can decide how to answer
him. If she interprets the phrase as referring to sex play, her answer
might be no; but if she interprets it as referring to horseplay, her

answer might be yes. Or, to take another example, when Don Vito instructs Frankie to "go whack your cousin," Frankie must interpret this new situation by deciding how he should frame the Don's command. Is Frankie being ordered to slap his silly cousin *on* the head or to shoot his silly cousin *in* the head?

At the other extreme, a "new situation" may be so slow to evolve that it might take months or even years before the participants become fully aware that things have changed. For example, a boy and a girl who were platonic friends throughout their childhood might not discover until their middle teenage years that they have gradually developed romantic feelings for each other—feelings that can no longer be denied. (Okay, I admit that I saw *The Blue Lagoon*). Or an elderly white woman might finally realize, after several years have passed, that her black chauffeur has also become her best friend. (I saw *Driving Miss Daisy*, too.)

The particular frame we adopt will typically depend upon how well the present situation matches previous situations in which one or another of our alternative frames has consistently proved useful and relevant. If we have successfully dealt with similar situations in the past, we are likely to have developed a frame that we recognize as being applicable to our current situation as well. On the other hand, if we have never encountered a similar situation before, or have encountered such a situation but have had no success in dealing with it, we are less likely to identify one of our available frames as being applicable in the present case. This means, of course, that our ability to apply an appropriate frame will be heavily influenced by our past experience as well as by our current knowledge of the situation at hand. It will also be influenced by the words and actions of any other people who are present, though there will be times when the information we get from them will be ambiguous or even misleading.

Erving Goffman was a master at revealing just how vulnerable we are when occasional gaps appear in the fabric of social reality. In *Frame Analysis*, he shows us how these gaps may occur when at least one person applies a different interpretive frame from that adopted by any other persons who are present. We often say in such cases that the parties involved "construe the situation differently"—sometimes with the awareness that they do so, but at other times with no such awareness at all. As a general rule, it is the cases in which one or both parties are unaware of their different construals that have the greatest potential for escalating tensions and dramatic resolutions. The mere fact that there are competing frames sets the stage for some initial misunderstanding and confusion. Later on, as the parties become more aware of their differences, they may be forced to confront the question of which view of social reality is the more correct.

It will often be the case that one person's frame is clearly wrong (that is, mistakenly applied) in comparison to the frame adopted by the other people are who present. Indeed, people can apply the wrong frame to a given situation for a variety of reasons. They may be mentally impaired, inexperienced, uninformed, misinformed, or self-deluded. They may the victims of their own fantasies or the victims of other people's fantasies, lies, or mistaken beliefs. They may be paying too much attention to cues that are irrelevant or anomalous. Conversely, they may have failed to give enough attention to the most relevant and diagnostic cues. Or they may be dealing with situational cues that are so ambiguous that the choice of what frame to adopt seems to be entirely "up for grabs."

The problem for a person who has adopted the wrong frame is that it immediately begins to define that person's "reality." The individual thinks, feels, and acts as if the situation actually *is* what it was just construed to be. This misapprehension of social reality can have consequences that range from the comic to the tragic, as illustrated in countless short stories, novels, plays, and movies. For example, its consequences are comic in the movie *Tootsie*, in which the Charles Durning character and the Dustin Hoffman character apply different frames regarding the nature of the latter's identity and sexual orientation. On the other hand, its consequences are tragic in

196 everyday MIND READING

Shakespeare's play *Romeo and Juliet*, in which the lovers' divergent frames are responsible for their deaths in the play's final scene.

The main point of *Frame Analysis* is that everyday social life is replete with such framing conflicts, a point that Goffman illustrated with dozens of examples taken from newspapers and other media reports. Some of the best examples come from his chapter on incidental "misframings," which can take the following forms:

- ❖ *Ambiguity*. "A driver wiggling his hand out the window can cause other drivers to be uncertain for a moment as to whether he means to signal a turn or to greet a friend."
- ❖ *Error*. "A student nurse attempting to straw-feed a patient whose face is bandaged can become upset when she learns that the reason for his apparent lack of thirst is that all along he has been dead . . ."
- ❖ *Frame disputes*. "It is reported that what is horseplay and larking for inner-city adolescents can be seen as vandalism and thievery by officials and victims."

Not all misframings occur so incidentally, however. Often they are induced quite deliberately, as when one party attempts to deceive another party about the true nature of the situation at hand. Such deceptions are, of course, all too common in everyday social life, and there are many existing terms in our language that refer to them. According to Goffman, "Those who engineer the deception can be called the operatives, fabricators, deceivers. Those . . . taken in can be said to be contained—contained in a construction or a fabrication. They can be called the dupes, marks, pigeons, suckers, butts, victims, gulls."

Although deceptive fabrications could be classified in many ways, Goffman found it useful to distinguish relatively benign fabrications from relatively exploitive ones. He discussed two types of *benign fabrications*, and provided examples for each:

✤ *Playful deceit.* "A contemporary example is the practice enjoyed by ghetto youths of teasing cruiser cops by acting as if a fight is in progress, thus twisting the man's tail."

✤ *Experimental hoaxing.* A subject in an experiment "may be led to think he is responding to a subject like himself in the next room, while all the time the response he receives to his own act has been randomly programmed beforehand, so that the interaction he ends up having is with a research design, not a person."

The topic of *exploitive fabrication*s is one that Goffman had already addressed at length in one of his earlier books, *Strategic Interaction.* Exploitive fabrications are ubiquitous in social life. They include activities ranging from con games to police interrogations, from shell games to stock swindles, and from sexual teases to long-term seductions. There are many different types of exploitive fabrications—so many, in fact, that Goffman did not attempt to review them all. Instead, he focused his attention on the elements that all of these activities have in common.

All exploitive fabrications involve the attempt by at least one individual (a fabricator) to contain at least one other individual (a victim). The fabricator's first goal is to fool the victim—to "pull the wool" over his or her eyes. In frame analysis terms, this amounts to persuading the victim to frame the situation in a naïve way that the fabricator can later exploit. If this first goal is achieved, then the fabricator's own frame—his or her more inclusive understanding of the situation at hand—will effectively "contain" or subsume the victim's less inclusive frame. Of course, the danger of such containment lies in its potential to be discovered by the victim. The fabricator must therefore endeavor to keep the victim contained until the fabricator's exploitive act (getting the victim's confession, taking the victim's money, having sex with the victim, etc.) is complete.

Events can take an interesting turn, however, if the victim becomes aware of the fabrication before the fabricator's goal has been achieved. Denouncing the fabricator immediately is one of the victim's options, and it will end the game very quickly. But the game can be continued—with an extra layer of containment and complexity—if the victim decides instead to turn the tables:

> [T]he discovering party [can] continue temporarily to act as if no discovery has been made, thus radically transforming the situation into one in which containment is itself contained. . . . Although often what has occurred is merely cognitive, something subjectively located within the mind of the one who makes the discovery he does not disclose having made, still a fundamental strategic event has taken place, one with objective import for the flow of events, as will be seen when the discoverer springs the trap that his inaction has baited. Indeed, here "acting as though nothing were wrong," concealing everything in one's head, becomes a very real strategic move, a juncture in the flow of events where a behavioristic, objective view quite misses the fundamental facts.

When I first read Goffman's *Frame Analysis* not long after it appeared, I was fascinated by its emphasis on the fragile nature of intersubjective reality. Goffman's central premise is clear: that any two people will understand each other on any given occasion is by no means guaranteed. Even if they share a common language and cultural background, they will presumably have to adopt the same (or a very similar) set of frames throughout the entire course of their conversation in order to effectively track each other's intended meaning. From this standpoint alone, everyday mind reading becomes a highly problematic enterprise.

As if all of that weren't bad enough, the difficulty of sustaining a succession of mutually held, intersubjective frames is subject to a number of additional complications in Goffman's analysis. First, it can be complicated by the *incidental misframings* that derive from ambiguity, error, or frame disputes. Second, it can be complicated by the *self-induced misframings* that derive from the illusions, delusions, or dissociations of the individual participants. Third, it can be complicated by the *other-induced misframings* that derive from the benign or exploitive deceptions perpetrated by one's interaction partners.

I wish I could tell you that when we began our studies of empathic accuracy in the fall of 1986, the relevance of *Frame Analysis* was so obvious to me that my colleagues and I immediately began to apply Goffman's ideas to our research. It didn't happen that way. Over a decade had passed since I had read Goffman's book, and although I retained a general sense of what frame analysis was all about, it simply didn't occur to me to go back and take another look.

The situation changed, however, after we had analyzed the data for our first four empathic accuracy studies and discovered just how difficult everyday mind reading really is. In general, most of the empathic accuracy scores in these studies were in the range of 10% to 40%. On average, same-sex strangers achieved about 20% of the possible "accuracy points" when they attempted to infer each other's thoughts and feelings, in comparison to an average of about 30% for same-sex friends. Occasionally, we would see an individual empathic accuracy score as high as 50%, but such cases tended to be rare in our experience as researchers.

Obviously, success in reading other people's minds really *is* difficult to achieve—even in a laboratory situation in which motivated perceivers can make these judgments carefully and deliberatively, as the passive observers of videotaped interactions that require no other response from them. But why should it be so difficult? After all, even the strangers in these studies were typically trying to find some common ground and "get to know" each other. And why didn't the friends do better? On a 0 to 100 scale, an average score of 30% seems like an objectively poor performance.

Goffman's frame analysis provided some plausible answers to these questions. Although the friends and the strangers that we tested in our studies probably spent little, if any, time trying to deceive each other, they probably did try to conceal some thoughts and feelings that they preferred to keep to themselves. And during the greater portion of their conversation, the portion in which they *did* want their interaction partners to understand they way they thought and felt, they generally had to assume that their partners shared the same successive frames of reference that they were using from the beginning of the conversation to its end.

As any linguistic theorist will tell you, this is a dubious assumption. Successive frames of reference can occur within the same conversation turn, and even within the same spoken sentence, so keeping track of these changing frames of reference should be difficult even for well-acquainted partners who are similar in their linguistic backgrounds and life experiences. For unacquainted partners, particularly those who are different in their linguistic backgrounds and life experiences, the task of keeping track of each other's changing frames of reference should be even more difficult, and—at times—impossible.

For well-acquainted partners, the task of keeping track of each other's changing frames of reference should generally be easier because of their greater familiarity with the frames that each partner has used in their previous conversations together. This interpretive advantage should be most evident when a particular word or phrase conjures up a memory in both partners of a mutually but exclusively known event that occurred at another place or time. For example, if Rayleen pokes her friend Shauna in the ribs and says, "Look at Hidy Girls," Shauna will look up expecting to see a grinning, jug-eared man. Why? Because Shauna was with Rayleen at Possum Kingdom Lake that day last July when another grinning, jug-eared man kept waving at them from a rowboat and shouting, "Hidy, Girls!" However, if Rayleen pokes her brand-new acquaintance Susan in the ribs and says the same thing, Susan will look up wondering what Rayleen can possibly have on her mind.

You might recall that Linda Stinson and I found evidence for this type of interpretive advantage in our study comparing the empathic accuracy of 24 pairs of male friends with that of 24 pairs of male strangers (see chapter 5). From the standpoint of frame analysis, we would expect that the male friends—who had developed common frames for discussing events in their shared past history—would be relatively successful in inferring each other's thoughts and feelings about events occurring at another place or time. On the other hand, we would expect that the male strangers—who had not developed such common frames and who lacked a shared past history—would be relatively unsuccessful in inferring such thoughts and feelings. And this, in fact, is what we found: The empathic accuracy of the male friends benefited to the extent that their interaction partners reported a high percentage of "other place, other time" thoughts and feelings, whereas the empathic accuracy of the male strangers suffered to the extent that their partners reported a high percentage of such thoughts and feelings.

Looking back on these results after I had reread Goffman's book, I realized that the friends' advantage over the strangers could be interpreted in terms of the greater availability to the friends of the appropriate common frames. And this realization quickly led to the next: that we could mine Goffman's theory for interesting hypotheses to test with our procedure for measuring empathy accuracy. But there were so many interesting hypotheses to be found in Goffman's book—where should we start?

When I discussed this question with one of my graduate students, Joli Kelleher, we decided that an interesting starting point would be to study the ability of fabricators to successfully enact a hidden agenda. In our opinion, the hidden agenda is one of the most fascinating but least studied phenomena in the field of social psychology. It is, by its very nature, an extremely subtle yet very demanding form of interpersonal deception. Unlike a secret that can remain unexpressed and can therefore be kept to oneself without much difficulty, successful effectance of a hidden agenda requires that the fabricator carry out the agenda publicly but in a disguised way that still influences others to think or act in a manner consistent with the fabricator's underlying motive.

To make it work, some subtle and complicated social engineering is required. Let's review the specific requirements. The fabricator of a hidden agenda must (a) carry it out publicly (b) but in a disguised way that (c) effectively influences others to think or act in a manner consistent with the fabricator's underlying motive, but (d) does not allow them to accurately infer the fabricator's agenda-relevant thoughts and feelings. The entire operation requires great finesse, because the fabricator routinely risks exposure on either of two fronts. First, there is the possibility that the fabricator's underlying motive will not be sufficiently disguised, so that the agenda-relevant behavior will be seen for the manipulative ploy that it really is. Second, there is the possibility that other people's public conformance to the agenda will eventually make the fabricator's motive apparent, even if the fabricator's own disguised behavior has not.

Could people in a laboratory study who are assigned the fabricator role successfully carry out a hidden agenda while simultaneously concealing their agenda-relevant thoughts and feelings? Joli Kelleher and I decided to find out. In collaboration with our colleague, Jeremy Dugosh, we conducted a study in which we unobtrusively videotaped the interactions of 33 mixed-sex dyads—pairs of opposite-sex strangers who had been left in our "waiting room" situation. Within each of these dyads, we randomly chose one dyad member to be the fabricator. The experimenter met privately with this person before the experimental session began and asked the person to carry out a specific hidden agenda—to keep the other dyad member laughing during the 6-minute period that the experimenter would leave them alone together in the waiting room.

Essentially, the procedure went like this. After meeting privately with the fabricator and giving him or her the hidden agenda to enact, the experimenter greeted the other dyad member (the naïve interactant) at a different location. Both participants were then brought together in our observation room, where they were seated side-by-side on the couch and asked to wait while the experimenter ran a quick errand. The participants were covertly videotaped during this 6-minute observation period—a period in which the fabricator attempted to get the naïve interactant to laugh as much as possible without revealing this "hidden agenda." The experimenter then returned, explained to the participants that their interaction had been videotaped, and asked them to consent to view the tape for the purpose of recording both their actual thoughts and feelings and their inferences about their partner's thoughts and feelings during the 6-minute observation period.

From the videotapes of the participants' interactions, our research assistants later recorded how frequently and how long each of the dyad members laughed. From the actual and inferred thought/feeling data, our research assistants also computed how accurately each of the dyad members was able to infer the other member's thoughts and feelings. By analyzing all of these data, we were able to establish a clear pattern of evidence indicating that the fabricators had been generally quite successful in enacting their assigned hidden agenda.

First, the data showed that the fabricators succeeded in getting their naïve interaction partners to laugh a lot during the observation period. The naïve interactants not only laughed more than the fabricators did themselves; they also laughed more than dyad members who were videotaped in interactions in which no hidden agenda was assigned. Second, the naïve interactants in the hidden-agenda dyads were particularly inaccurate when they attempted to infer the fabricators' agenda-relevant thoughts and feelings—much less accurate than they were when they attempted to infer the fabricators' agenda-*irrelevant* thoughts and feelings. Third, and even more convincing, there was no evidence in any of the naïve interactants' *own* thoughts and feelings that they realized that the fabricator had adopted the intentional goal of trying to get them to laugh. Only a few of the naïve interactants ever came close to achieving this insight, and these occurrences were limited to the rare instances in which the fabricators' own laughter provided a clue to their underlying motive that was a little too blatant and obvious.

The results of this study convinced us that fabricators can indeed carry out an assigned hidden agenda while keeping their agenda-relevant thoughts and feelings concealed from others (in this case, from the very people whose behavior the fabricators were successfully manipulating). But what if certain other people knew beforehand who the fabricators were and what their hidden agenda really was? Would the fabricators' agenda-relevant thoughts and feelings become more transparent to the well-informed perceivers who had acquired this special "inside knowledge"? In contrast, what would happen if certain other perceivers also knew beforehand that the fabricators had a hidden agenda but were deliberately *mis*informed about what that hidden agenda really was? Would the fabricator's agenda-relevant thoughts and feelings also become more transparent to these suspicious but somewhat misinformed perceivers? Or would the misinformation that these perceivers received about the fabricators' actual hidden agenda keep them from inferring the fabricators' agenda-relevant thoughts and feelings?

To answer these questions, we conducted a second study in which we varied the frames that perceivers would use to interpret the fabricators' behavior in our hidden-agenda videotapes. In this study, we asked 48 individual perceivers to view four of the hidden-agenda videotapes from our previous study and attempt to infer the fabricators' agenda-relevant and agenda-irrelevant thoughts and feelings. The individual perceivers were randomly assigned to one of three experimental conditions, with 16 perceivers in each condition.

The perceivers in the *accurate frame condition* were given

accurate information about the fabricator's motive in each of the four videotapes (that this person had a hidden agenda to keep the other person laughing while the experimenter was out of the room). In contrast, the perceivers in the *inaccurate frame condition* were given inaccurate but plausible information about the fabricator's motive (that this person had a hidden agenda to be charming and engaging because of a "secret crush" that he or she had on the other person). Finally, the control perceivers in the *no-frame condition* were given no information regarding the fabricator's motive, thereby obliging them to provide their own interpretive frame, if any came to mind.

All perceivers attempted to infer the fabricators' thoughts and feelings within each of the videotaped interactions, and we later computed their empathic accuracy for the fabricators' agenda-relevant and agenda-irrelevant thoughts and feelings. The results? We found that the perceivers in the accurate frame condition were significantly better at inferring the fabricator's agenda-relevant thoughts and feelings than were the perceivers in either the inaccurate frame or the no-frame conditions. On the other hand, the perceivers in all three conditions did equally well in inferring the fabricator's agenda-irrelevant thoughts and feelings.

A skeptic might be inclined toward a cynical interpretation of these results. Perhaps, the skeptic might argue, the perceivers in the accurate frame condition always inferred (or, at least, frequently and indiscriminately inferred) that the fabricator was thinking about trying the get the other person to laugh. If so, then these perceivers would *coincidentally* be more accurate in those specific instances when the fabricator actually did have this thought, but they could not be credited with having any genuine insight into the fabricators' agenda-relevant thoughts and feelings. Not a bad argument, huh? We wondered about that possibility ourselves, so we did a more fine-grained analysis of our data in order to examine it. And we found evidence to the contrary.

To be specific, we found that the perceivers in the accurate frame condition did not make such inferences ("s/he was trying to get the other person to laugh") consistently or indiscriminately. Instead, they made such inferences sparingly (only 14% of the time), and they tended to make them at the times when the fabricators really *had* been thinking such agenda-relevant thoughts. In contrast, the perceivers in the inaccurate frame and no-frame conditions almost never made such inferences (only 1 to 2% of the time), consistent with their ignorance about the fabricators' actual hidden agenda. It appeared, then, that by giving certain perceivers an accurate frame (one that matched the fabricators' actual hidden agenda), we enabled them to figure out which of the fabricators' thoughts and feelings really *were* agenda-relevant and to more accurately infer the specific content of these manipulative thoughts and feelings.

One final question was of interest: Did the perceivers in the inaccurate frame condition perform any better than those in the no-frame condition? The answer, in this case, was no. Although the inaccurate-frame perceivers had the advantage of knowing that the fabricators had a hidden agenda, they were burdened with the disadvantage of having been given a false but plausible belief about what that hidden agenda really was. If we assume that the effect of their advantage and the effect of their disadvantage canceled each other out, it is easy to see why they were no more accurate than the no-frame perceivers when they attempted to infer the fabricators' agenda-relevant and agenda-irrelevant thoughts and feelings.

In summary, the fabricators of hidden agendas can, with enough care and foresight, keep their agenda-relevant thoughts and feelings concealed from naïve perceivers. They can even keep such thoughts and feelings concealed from perceivers who know that they have a hidden agenda but who have incorrect knowledge about what that agenda really is. But their agenda-relevant thoughts and feelings are less easily concealed from accurately informed perceivers, who are able to catch glimpses of the fabricators' plans as they are actually being hatched.

❖   ❖   ❖

In most cases, we can size up a situation in a moment or two and apply the appropriate frame for interpreting what is going on. In some cases, however, the appropriate frame is not at all obvious at first glance. In cases such as these, we may temporarily have to suspend making a judgment about "What's going on here?" and wait until enough events have transpired to suggest how that question should be answered.

Imagine, for example, that you are eavesdropping on an initial therapy session between a male psychotherapist and his female client. If your eavesdropping begins at the very start of the therapy session and continues right through to its end, the odds are good that you will quickly develop a general view of the kind of person the client is and what kind of problem she is currently dealing with. In other words, you will quickly come up with an interpretive schema for understanding the client and her problem—a way of "framing" who she is and what she hopes to achieve.

Suppose, however, that you are eavesdropping on the same initial therapy session as it appears on a videotape that the therapist's 10-year-old son has previously snipped into pieces and then randomly respliced. The same events are depicted over the course of the videotape, but now they appear as a random jumble of flashbacks and flash forwards, with little or no temporal continuity. Eventually, you begin to get a sense of who the client is and why she is there, but developing this interpretive schema or frame takes considerably more time than it would have taken if you had witnessed the entire therapy session as it originally unfolded, from its beginning right through to its end.

How would your ability to infer the client's thoughts and feelings be affected under each of these two scenarios? In essence, this was the question that Randy Gesn and I posed in a study that closely mimicked these two hypothetical scenarios. Using the videotapes of the three client/therapist interactions that were originally developed by Carol Marangoni, Randy sliced and diced the tapes and then re-assembled the pieces to create versions of each tape that were appropriate for each of the two scenarios described above.

Randy began this process by using a video mixing board to extract from each tape the 15-second segments that immediately preceded each of the client's reported thoughts and feelings. In other words, the segments that he cut from each tape contained the fifteen seconds of client-therapist interaction that occurred right before (and included) the exact "tape stop" at which the client had reported that she had experienced a specific thought or feeling. Because each of the tapes had been edited by Carol Marangoni to include thirty of the client's reported thoughts and feelings, Randy's additional editing resulted in thirty 15-second segments being retained from tape (only seven and a half minutes' worth of each of the half-hour-long tapes that Carol had prepared).

Re-assembling the segments using the video mixing board, Randy created two versions of each psychotherapy tape: one in which the thirty segments were electronically spliced back together in their original sequence, and one in which the same thirty segments were spliced back together in a completely random sequence. He then recruited individual research participants to come to our laboratory and attempt to play amateur therapist. Half of the participants were shown the excerpts from each of the three therapy tapes in their original sequence, whereas the remaining participants were shown the excerpts from each of the tapes in the random sequence. But all of the participants had been given the same task to perform: to try to infer the specific content of the client's thought or feeling at the end of each of the 15-second excerpts.

We predicted that the perceivers in the original sequence condition would infer the clients' thoughts and feelings more accurately than would the perceivers in the random sequence condition. Surprisingly, however, when we analyzed the empathic accuracy data from our study, we found that this difference was much smaller than we had anticipated. It was small enough, in fact, not to qualify as a statistically reliable result. We found this outcome so puzzling that we spent a lot of time trying to figure out why it had occurred. And eventually we came up with a very interesting, but somewhat more complicated, hypothesis that we hoped might explain what was going on.

Suppose, we reasoned, that the process of constructing an appropriate frame or schema for understanding each client worked pretty much as we had expected. That is, the perceivers in the original sequence condition could construct such person-specific frames relatively easily, whereas the perceivers in the random sequence condition could not. But suppose further that such frames were only useful in helping the perceivers to accurately infer the clients' *frame-relevant* thoughts and feelings (for example, "I was thinking it wasn't fair that my husband plays golf most weekends while I stay home and do housework"). In contrast, such frames might actually impair the perceivers' ability to accurately infer the client's *frame-irrelevant* thoughts and feelings (for example, "I was thinking that the therapist is a really good listener"). If this more complicated process did in fact occur, it could conceivably account for what we had already found in our data: a weaker-than-expected difference in the overall empathic accuracy of the perceivers in the original sequence condition compared to those in the random sequence condition.

Fortunately, Randy and I were able to think of a way to test this new, more complicated hypothesis. In an earlier study, Tiffany Graham had already written single paragraphs that provided "capsule summary" descriptions of two of the clients in the psychotherapy tapes and the specific situation they each discussed with the therapist. Independent judges in Tiffany's study had already evaluated the content of these paragraphs and had helped her fine-tune them until everyone agreed that they provided concise, accurate summaries of the clients and their concerns. What Randy and I proposed to do was to use these paragraphs to represent the person-specific frames that perceivers were likely to construct during their viewing of the respective videotapes.

We recruited a group of new judges—several undergraduate research assistants who were working in our lab—and we asked them to view the original videotapes of these respective therapy sessions. Before they did so, however, we provided each judge with a copy of the capsule summary description for each client, a copy of the client's actual thoughts and feelings, and a copy of the specific times ("tape stops") at which these thoughts or feelings had actually occurred. Using all of this information, each of our judges paused the videotapes at each tape stop, read the thought or feeling that occurred at that point, and then compared the thought or feeling to the capsule summary description to determine whether the thought or feeling should be classified as frame-relevant (having content related to the capsule summary) or as frame-irrelevant (having content unrelated to the capsule summary).

Randy's next step was to compute separate empathic accuracy scores for the perceiver's frame-relevant and frame-irrelevant thoughts and feelings for each tape, and then test to see if our revised hypothesis would be supported. He found that it was. The results clearly showed that the perceivers in the original sequence condition were reliably more accurate than the perceivers in the random frame condition when they attempted to infer the content of the clients' frame-relevant thoughts and feelings. But, just as we had suspected, the perceivers in the original sequence condition were reliably *less* accurate than those in the random frame condition when they attempted to infer the content of the clients' frame-irrelevant thoughts and feelings.

So, you might ask, are person-specific frames helpful or harmful? According to our findings, it depends. Compared to their counterparts in the random sequence condition, the perceivers in the original sequence condition found it relatively easy to develop such person-specific frames. However, although these frames helped the original-sequence perceivers to infer the clients' frame-relevant thoughts and feelings, they made it more difficult for them to infer the clients' frame-irrelevant thoughts and feelings. The frames therefore had an effect similar to that of putting blinders on a horse: they made it easier for the perceivers to "see" some things while making it harder for them to "see" others.

What we have found in our laboratory is also evident in everyday life. The same frames that sharpen our perception of certain things can also blind us to others. This process is dramatically evident in cases in which our frame effectively blinds us to a target person's frame-*inconsistent* thoughts and feelings. For example, until the damage is already done, the devout viewer fails to see that the televangelist who appeared the most saintly was in the best position to fleece the flock. The idealistic voter fails to see that the candidate who had never been caught in a lie was in the best position to tell one. The complacent husband fails to see that the wife who had dinner on the table every evening had a lover in the bed most afternoons. And the aspiring bank vice-president fails to see that her most trusted clerk was also an accomplished embezzler. It is only in retrospect that the frame-inconsistent thoughts and feelings of these target persons become evident.

The sense of betrayal is acute in such cases because the perceivers discover that they cannot simply revise their original frames; they must reverse them completely. They must acknowledge that the apparently saintly televangelist is venal and materialistic, that the apparently truthful candidate is duplicitous, that the apparently faithful spouse is unfaithful, and that the apparently honest employee is a thief. Such radical reframings can have a traumatizing impact because they simultaneously call into question the perceivers' relationship with the other, their image of the other, and their image of their own competence as social perceivers. In a single stroke of belated insight, everything seems to have changed: You are not who I thought you were; I feel that I can't trust you anymore; and I'm not even sure that I can still trust my own judgment.

Such radical reframings, though dramatic, are not the rule in social life; they are the interesting exceptions. Most of the time, most of us act like "cognitive dogmatists" who apply our frames automatically, who fail to examine them critically, and who revise and update them reluctantly, if at all. We are creatures of our mental habits as well as our physical ones, and these mental habits are similarly resistant to change.

Our tendency to follow the cognitive path of least resistance is most evident in our routine, day-to-day interactions with others. These interactions are often carried out quite automatically, and they seldom present us with the kinds of novel interpretive problems that require the formation of new frames or the radical reformulation of existing ones. Our certainty about the accuracy of our interpretations may be unwarranted in such mundane encounters, but it is a certainty that has all the inertial guidance and momentum of longstanding habit. Over time, we each develop our own characteristic way of ascribing meaning to such familiar events, and it usually takes a decidedly unfamiliar event to jolt us out of the well-worn cognitive rut that we have settled into.

The best reason for believing that our interpretive frames are applied in such an automatic and economical manner is that even our most mundane interactions don't allow us the time to apply these frames more reflectively. According to psychologist Steven Pinker, speech perception occurs incredibly fast: "ten to fifteen phonemes per second for casual speech, twenty to thirty per second for the man in the late-night Veg-O-Matic ads, and as many as forty to fifty per second for artificially sped-up speech." According to psycholinguist Stephen Levinson, our inferences regarding the speaker's intended meaning occur with a speed that is equally astonishing: on-line testing reveals that such inferences are "already well underway" immediately after we hear the relevant word or expression. Moreover, our production of a reply based on these inferences is so rapid that our respective speaking turns "are, at least a third of the time, separated by less than 200 milliseconds." Indeed, the blazing speed with which we routinely carry out the sequence of speech perception, intentionality inference, and speech production has been labeled a "biological miracle" by Steven Pinker.

In order for us to respond to our conversation partners so quickly, the vast majority of our empathic inferences must be made automatically and effortlessly. And this, according to communication researcher Alan Sillars, accounts for why so many of our empathic inferences are experienced as "unmediated observations" rather than as consciously constructed attributions. As Sillars has said:

> The complexity of communication virtually requires an unques-
> tioning stance toward routine inference, since it is not possible to
> consciously attend to more than a tiny percentage of the inferences
> and decisions involved in interpersonal communication without
> constant disruptions and digressions in the flow of conversation.
> Thus, cognitive processing of communication is generally "geared
> to achieving the greatest possible cognitive effect for the smallest
> possible processing effort," as suggested by the "cognitive miser"
> metaphor for social cognition. In an occasional instance, people
> adopt a much more self-reflective and questioning stance toward
> communication; however, this primarily occurs during intervals
> between interactions, when the pace of activity has slowed. Further,
> there is generally little chance that meanings will be re-evaluated
> subsequent to interactions, once an interpretation has been supplied.

Most of the time, then, our interpretive frames are completely transparent to us; we look *through* them rather than at them. And because our interpretive frames are applied at so many different levels (to help us understand the meaning and intent of specific words, phrases, nonverbal behaviors, target persons, situations, and historical chains of events), and must be juggled so rapidly at each of these levels, we seldom have the luxury of looking *at* them with any degree of critical detachment.

It is only when our frame seems to differ from that of our inter-action partner, or of some third party who has our attention, that we begin to focus on how we are framing what is going on and to wonder if we should have framed it differently. In his essay titled "(Mis)Understanding," Alan Sillars has compared cases in which frame conflicts are relatively easy to identify and resolve with cases in which they aren't. According to Sillars, many misunderstandings are simple, obvious, and easy to resolve. If I tell an 8-year-old neighbor about a wonderful book called *Don Quixote,* and she tells me that she doesn't want to read a book about a donkey, it is easy for me to see that we have interpreted the meaning of the first two sylla-bles of the book's title quite differently. In cases such as this, it is evi-dent to at least one of the interactants that different interpretive frames have been applied, and corrective action can quickly be taken at that point to try to clear up the source of the misunderstanding.

Misunderstandings become murkier, more complicated, and harder to clear up, however, to the extent that our differing frames lead us to develop different views of what is going on, but both views are plausible, coherent, and not obviously inconsistent with the apparent facts of the situation. One of the best examples comes from one of Sillars's studies of marital conflict. In this study, each couple was videotaped during a conflict discussion. Afterwards, the husband and the wife were asked to independently view the video-tape and report the actual thoughts and feelings that each of them had at various "tape stops":

> [I]n one case in which the couple discusses the husband's drink-ing, the wife has a series of related thoughts: the husband knows he has a problem but he will not accept it; until he accepts it, they cannot work it out; he never wants to talk about it; he's always changing the topic and making it into a joke; he needs to wake up; he won't look at her because he knows she is right; she is sick of his tactics and may move out to make him understand. At the same time, the husband constructs a different scene: he drinks because he wants to, not as an escape; he loves her, even though

she is overly critical, insensitive, and needs to relax; he does not want to get into a deep argument and thinks that bickering is a waste of breath; she is getting offended for little reason and is trying to upset and intimidate him; she resorts to name-calling because she knows that he is right.

Who is right in this example? Each of them says that they are right, that the other person is wrong, and that the other person *knows* that he or she is wrong. Is it the case that one person is clearly right and that the other person is clearly wrong? Is it the case that the objective truth lies somewhere between their two alternative views of the situation? Or is it the case that there is no objective truth—only the competing subjective "truths" of two people who refuse to agree on a common construction of their social reality?

As a scientist, I am inclined to dismiss the last of these possibilities, which is based on the very unscientific premise that objective truths do not exist. On the other hand, I find the remaining possibilities intriguing because they resemble the kinds of theoretical conflicts and resolutions that scientists must deal with all the time. The husband and wife in this case have certainly framed the situation differently. But deciding between these competing frames is not easy to do, because each of these complex frames is not only internally coherent but also provides a relatively plausible and complete account of the "facts" of the situation.

These competing frames are, in effect, alternative *theories* that each partner has constructed to answer Goffman's basic question, "What's going on here?" And each partner has done a good job of constructing her or his theory, making sure that, despite its complexity, it is plausible, coherent, and reasonably consistent with certain facts about which all interested parties *are* able to agree. Everyone agrees that the issue is his drinking, that his wife considers it to be a problem, that he doesn't, that she repeatedly confronts him about it, and that he regards such confrontations as unnecessary and aversive.

So where do these two "theories" diverge? They diverge on two fundamental and interrelated issues: the issue of whether his drinking really is a problem, and the issue of which of them—her or him—is out of touch with reality. But these points of divergence might not be obvious at first glance, given the complexity, coherence, and plausibility of the two competing accounts. And a decision about who is right and who is wrong would require something analogous to a "crucial test" between the two competing theories—the collection of additional data that would ideally provide a definitive answer to the question of whether, and to what extent, his drinking really is a problem. However, a definitive answer is by no means guaranteed. The objective truth about these issues might be found to lie somewhere in the middle ground: his drinking is less of a problem than she thinks it is but more of a problem than he thinks it is, and both partners are therefore somewhat right and somewhat wrong.

As Alan Sillars has noted, relationship partners seldom operate like scientists, trying to pinpoint and resolve their differences in a dispassionate and objective way. Instead,

> . . . each partner falsely assumes that the partner shares the same bedrock perceptions of reality (e.g., "she knows I am right") and attributes the difficulty to the partner's motivated distortions (e.g., "he does not like to hear the truth"). There seems to be a sense that the "truth" is so obvious, it cannot be constructed otherwise. . . . [In addition], the wife's narrative provides a frame for assimilating and reacting to specific cues linked to the husband's withdrawal (e.g., the meaning of his jokes and topic shifts), whereas the husband's narrative likewise furnishes an interpretive frame for the wife's assertive behavior. The result is a mutually escalatory demand-withdraw sequence which further reinforces the original attributions of each person.

In other words, because each partner's interpretive frame can account not only for what the other person does when these differing frames are not discussed but also for what the other person does when they *are* discussed, the perceived validity of each partner's frame is doubly reinforced. Each partner feels justified in vigorously defending his or her respective frame during discussions of the conflict issue because, from the perspective of that partner, the other partner's "avoidant" or "distorting" behavior during these discussions offers direct, additional evidence for the validity of that frame. In consequence, both partners' positions increasingly harden. Each of them believes even more strongly that they are right, that their partner is wrong, and that their partner knows that he or she is wrong.

The hardening of one's frames, like the hardening of one's arteries, can have insidious long-term consequences. For example, husbands who begin to interpret some of their wives' helpful suggestions as "nagging" may eventually come to frame most of their wives' suggestions in this way. In consequence, their relationships with their wives may steadily deteriorate as they increasingly put a negative spin on comments that their wives intended to be both positive and constructive.

In a classic research investigation that is relevant to this process, Australian psychologist Patricia Noller studied how well husbands and wives were able to infer each other's intended meaning from paralinguistic (tone of voice) cues alone. Using a standard content method developed by Malcolm Kahn, a marriage and family researcher, Noller presented the members of each couple with a series of hypothetical situations—some in which the wife was required to speak and others in which the husband was required to speak. In each case, the speaker made a standard statement that was provided by the experimenter, but used his or her tone of voice to try to convey one of three alternative meanings that the experimenter had also prescribed.

For example, in one hypothetical situation, "You and your wife are both ready for bed at night. It is a night when sexual relations are a possibility," each husband was required to say, "Do you really want to have sex tonight?" However, depending on the experimenter's instruction, the husband attempted to use his voice tone to convey either a negative meaning ("You are not interested in having sex that night"), a neutral meaning ("You would like to make love only if she would like to, and are interested in her attitude"), or a positive meaning ("You are interested in having sex . . . and you hope that your eagerness will convince her to agree"). In another hypothetical situation, "You come home to find the washing you had left in the washing machine hanging on the line," each wife was required to say, "Did you do that?" However, depending on the experimenter's instruction, the wife attempted to use her voice tone to convey either a negative meaning ("You are angry because some of the clothes are hung in a way that will spoil their shape and you wish it had been left for you"), a neutral meaning ("You are curious about whether it was your husband or one of the children who hung it out"), or a positive meaning ("You are pleased that he has done such a thing to help you").

Patricia Noller asked the speaker's partner to try to identify the speaker's intended meaning in each situation and then analyzed the resulting data to determine if the partners' inferences were biased in any systematic way. She found evidence of such a bias for the husbands in her study, particularly those in relationships that both partners had previously described as unhappy. When these husbands were asked to identify the intended meaning of their wives' utterances, they tended to make errors in a negative direction—interpreting as negative many of the vocal cues that their wives had intended to be positive or neutral instead.

It appeared that the husbands in these unhappy relationships were using a negative "frame" to interpret the meaning of what their wives were attempting to say. To determine whether that was indeed the case, Noller had all of the participants in her study attempt to infer the intended meaning of the utterances expressed by *other people's* spouses as well. She found that the men in unhappy relationships were negatively biased in interpreting their own wives' voice cues, but were not similarly biased in interpreting the voice cues of other wives in the study. This finding suggested that the men in unhappy relationships had, over time, developed a negative frame that they applied uniquely to their own wives. Because the same negative frame was not evident in their reactions to other women, it appeared to be a partner-specific frame that had developed over the course of an unhappy marriage relationship rather than a more general and pre-existing frame that biased their interpretation of the voice cues expressed by women in general.

Some men, of course, *are* biased against women in general. Misogynists and abusive men come to mind in this regard, so it is reasonable to wonder what kind of interpretive frame such men might characteristically apply to the women they encounter.

The first person to raise this question in our lab was Will Schweinle. In August of 1997, I was sitting in my office one day when the area of my open doorway suddenly became dark. When I looked up to see what had happened, I found that an affable tall Texan named Will Schweinle was occupying nearly all of that space. Will, who introduced himself as a new graduate student from the Houston area, announced that he had come to UTA to work with me. His plan was to learn how to do empathic accuracy research so that he could study how abusive men differed from nonabusive men in their inferences about women's thoughts and feelings.

Frankly, this was a topic that I hadn't considered studying, but the more Will and I talked about it, the more intrigued I became. It seemed that there were two alternative hypotheses that one could apply in this case. Both hypotheses were plausible, but they were also incommensurable, so that evidence confirming one of them would tend to disconfirm the other. The first hypothesis was that abusive men are predisposed to infer that women are having critical and rejecting thoughts and feelings about men—even when women aren't actually having such thoughts and feelings. In other words, abusive men may inaccurately infer that women are harboring critical and rejecting thoughts and feelings about them, and then retaliate through some form of abuse. According to this hypothesis, the extent to which men abuse women should be predicted by the extent to which the men are biased to *overattribute* critical and rejecting thoughts and feelings either to their own female partners or to women in general.

The second hypothesis was that abusive men are unusually accurate, rather than inaccurate, when they attribute critical and rejecting thoughts and feelings to women. Because abusive men relate to women in a threatening, overbearing, and hostile way, they may actually evoke more critical and rejecting thoughts and feelings in women than nonabusive men do. If abusive men regard such thoughts and feelings as a threat to their potential control of the women's behavior, they may be hypersensitive to these actual feelings of criticism and rejection and respond to them with coercive acts that are intended to reassert their control. According to this hypothesis, then, the extent to which men abuse women should be predicted by the extent to which they can *accurately identify* women's critical and rejecting thoughts and feelings.

The difference between these two hypotheses is important. The first is based on the assumption that abusive men are exceptionally *in*accurate: they are quick to take offense when no offense is intended, inferring that women are being critical and rejecting even when they aren't. In contrast, the second is based on the assumption that abusive men are exceptionally accurate, at least with respect to women's actual critical and rejecting thoughts and feelings. That is, abusive men are assumed to be unusually good at detecting such thoughts and feelings when they actually occur, and in making accurate inferences about their content.

To determine which of these hypotheses was correct, Will and I conducted a laboratory study in collaboration with our colleague Ira Bernstein. Through ads placed in local newspapers, we recruited a sample of 86 married men of various ethnic backgrounds, who ranged in age from 19 to 72. These men were scheduled for individual testing sessions in our lab, where we asked them to view edited versions of the three psychotherapy tapes that Carol Marangoni had developed. In each of these three tapes, the female client discussed problems in her own marital relationship, sometimes expressing love and support for her husband or ex-husband, but at other times expressing criticism or rejection.

As in our previous studies, we stopped each tape at the points where the female client had reported having had a specific thought or feeling. The men's task was to write down the inferred content of the client's thought or feeling at each of these tape stops, and then circle one of two codes—CR or NCR—to indicate whether, in their judgment, the woman's thought or feeling expressed criticism or rejection (CR) or no criticism or rejection (NCR) of the woman's male partner. After they had inferred the thoughts and feelings of all three clients, we asked the men to respond confidentially to a series of questionnaire items that enabled us to determine the extent to which they reported abusing their own female partners. Most of the abuse they reported was verbal and emotional, but in some cases it involved physical abuse as well.

From the resulting data, my colleagues and I were able to answer the bias-versus-accuracy question that our study was designed to address. We found that the men who reported abusing their own female partners were biased, rather than accurate, when they inferred the thoughts and feelings of the female clients who appeared in our videotapes. Specifically, the most abusive men in our sample were the ones who overattributed critical and rejecting thoughts and feelings to the female clients, and were therefore relatively inaccurate when they tried to infer the actual content of the clients' thoughts and feelings.

These findings are important in their implication that abusive men have a general tendency to "frame" women's thoughts and feelings in a negative and inferentially biased way. Because the abusive men in our study overattributed criticism and rejection to three female clients they had never even met, our findings discourage the conclusion that abusive men are uniquely provoked by their own female partners. Abusive men seem to react negatively to women in general, not just to their own wives, so any impulse to "blame the victim" should be strongly resisted.

Although a history of distressed relationships with women may have contributed to the inferential bias displayed by abusive men, it seems likely that once this bias has been firmly established, it takes on a life of its own. Abusive men infer feelings of criticism and rejection that aren't really there, and then, through some act of abuse, retaliate against the women who supposedly harbor these feelings. Over time, the cycle of "biased attribution leading to abuse" becomes increasingly vicious. As the negative frame becomes more fixed and inflexible, it impairs the empathic accuracy of abusive men and provides them with a justification for actions that have devastating consequences for the women who become their victims.

Unfortunately, negative frames about other people—whether as individuals or as members of larger groups—are ubiquitous in social life. Suspicion, resentment, animosity, and outright hatred tend to thrive on such frames, which researchers often reduce for their convenience to the negative stereotypes that one person or group has developed about another.

Such a reduction is overly simplistic. As Goffman has noted, our frames about other people encompass much more than a catalogue of the others' positive or negative characteristics. By addressing the question, "What's going on here?" our frames implicate *the entire situation*: the respective parties who are involved, their relationship to each other, their current challenge or dilemma, and at least some sense of how this challenge or dilemma might have developed and how it might play out. In other words, the other person or group is never framed in isolation but is always seen within the context of an historically evolving situation that includes one's self and one's own reference group as well. Attempts to change negative stereotypes may therefore prove insufficient insofar as they address only one of the elements (the other person or group's attributes) within the larger situational frame.

Our negative frames about others are especially pernicious when they have become so fixed and inflexible that we are no longer willing to test them—either against the subjective reality of the other side's frames or against an objective reality that might serve as the final arbiter of our differences. In such cases, both sides become prisoners of their own respective frames, unwilling and eventually unable to see things from the other side's perspective. There is no longer any room for compromise, any room to explore the differences and attempt to find some common ground. There is, instead, the frame held by the Israeli and the frame held by the Palestinian, the frame of the Irish Protestant and the frame of the Irish Catholic—contrasting frames that have, over time, become inflexible, unyielding, and irreconcilable. The outcome is an empathic stalemate or, even worse, the death of any mutual understanding.

SOURCES FOR CHAPTER 8:

Gesn, Paul R., and William Ickes. "The Development of Meaning Contexts for Empathic Accuracy: Channel and Sequence Effects." *Journal of Personality and Social Psychology* 77 (1999): 746–61.

Goffman, Erving. *Frame Analysis*. New York: Harper & Row, 1974.

———. *Strategic Internation*. Philadelphia: University of Pennsylvania Press, 1969.

Kahn, Malcolm. "Nonverbal Communication and Marital Satisfaction." *Family Process* 9 (1970): 449–56.

Kelleher, Joli, William Ickes, and Jeremy W. Dugosh. "Hidden and Revealed Agendas: Effects of Frames on Empathic Accuracy." Manuscript under editorial review, 2003.

Levinson, Stephen C. "Interactional Biases in Human Thinking." In *Social Intelligence and Interaction*, edited by Esther N. Goody. Cambridge: Cambridge University Press, 1995, pp. 221–60.

Noller, Patricia. "Misunderstandings in Marital Communication: A Study of Couples' Nonverbal Communication." *Journal of Personality and Social Psychology* 39 (1980): 1135–48.

Noller, Patricia. "Gender and Marital Adjustment Level Differences in Decoding Messages from Spouses and Strangers." *Journal of Personality and Social Psychology* 41 (1981): 272–78.

Pinker, Steven. *The Language Instinct*. London: Penguin Books, 1994, p.161.

Schweinle, William E., William Ickes, and Ira H. Bernstein. "Empathic Inaccuracy in Husband to Wife Aggression: The Overattribution Bias." *Personal Relationships* 9 (2002): 141–58.

Sillars, Alan L. "(Mis)Understanding." In *The Dark Side of Close Relationships*, edited by Brian H. Spitzberg and William R. Cupach. Mahwah, N.J.: Erlbaum, 1998, pp. 73–102.

Stinson, Linda L., and William Ickes. "Empathic Accuracy in the Interactions of Male Friends Versus Male Strangers." *Journal of Personality and Social Psychology* 62 (1992): 787–97.

nine

MOTIVATED MISUNDER- STANDING

Based on what I have said so far, it might appear that greater understanding is always good for relationships—whether we are talking about the relationship between two people, two groups, or two nations. This idea has long been regarded as conventional wisdom, as illustrated by the old French aphorism: *Tout comprendre c'est tout pardonner*. The notion that "To understand all is to forgive all" is a charming and endearing one. However, as I will argue in this chapter, it is also naively optimistic. Indeed, the response to the French from some anonymous wag across the English Channel was both cynical and deflating: "To understand all is to forgive nothing."

Conventional wisdom holds that greater understanding is a general panacea for the various ills that afflict people's relationships. According to this view, if we just understood each other better, we would inevitably get along together better. And, perhaps, if we could somehow perfect the art of mutual understanding, we would eventually get along so well that we could all live together in perpetual bliss and harmony. Perfect understanding and accord in the Peaceable Kingdom.

I'm the first to agree that this is a wonderful ideal. But is it practical? Is it attainable? The answer to both questions is no. The sad fact is that greater understanding doesn't always make relationships better. Sometimes it makes them worse. Sometimes greater empathic accuracy can hurt or even destroy our relationships. And, for that reason, we may in such cases be motivated to avoid it. There are circumstances in which *not* knowing the other's thoughts and feelings, *not* being empathically accurate, is preferable to the alternative. Identifying these circumstances—what they are and when they occur—was the goal of the research that I describe next.

Jeff Simpson and I were walking along the beach at Nags Head, North Carolina the day I first told him my ideas about motivated inaccuracy. It was the summer of 1990, and we were attending a social psychology conference—one in a series of conferences that were held on the Outer Banks that summer. Later on, the Nags Head conferences were held in Boca Raton, Florida, but for the first several years they were held at Nags Head, in a rambling white clapboard conference center with large striped awnings that sat on a rise just above the beach. It was located less than a mile south of the sand dunes at Kill Devil Hills, where the Wright Brothers made their first successful powered flight in the winter of 1903.

At the time of that 1990 Nags Head conference, my graduate student colleagues and I had been doing research on empathic accuracy for about four years. I was looking for some new angles on the phenomenon, some interesting new problems to address, and the idea of *motivated inaccuracy* had recently come to the fore. Looking back, I can trace the origins of this idea to two distinct sources: a chapter that Alan Sillars had written for a book I had edited a few years earlier, and an incident a friend described that led me to think about the potential relevance of Sillars's insights to our empathic accuracy research.

In a chapter that he contributed to my 1985 edited book, *Compatible and Incompatible Relationships*, Alan Sillars offered many useful insights that he had gleaned from research on marriage partners' understanding of each other's perceptions about issues in their relationships. Toward the end of the chapter, he included the following paragraph. It must have made a strong impression on me when I first read it because I found myself searching for it a few years later:

> A fourth and final issue in the literature on understanding is whether understanding is always conducive to compatibility. In some situations greater understanding may increase conflict and dissatisfaction in a relationship—for example, when there are irreconcilable differences or when benevolent misconceptions previously existed. Some authors even suggest that unclear, tangential, or circumscribed communication is sometimes desirable to prevent understanding and preserve harmony in relationships.

I credit this paragraph with having planted the seed for the concept of motivated inaccuracy, the idea that, in relationship-threatening situations, partners will often be motivated to avoid accurately inferring each other's thoughts and feelings to spare themselves and their relationship the damage that might result if more accurate inferences were made. This idea seems to be implicit in certain idioms that people use when their conversations take a dangerous turn, leading them into topics that have the potential to generate conflict and instability within their relationship. For example, when people say things like "Let's not go there" or "Let's not get into that," they are implicitly acknowledging a danger zone in their relationship—an area in which the partners could discover things about each other's thoughts and feelings that they would prefer *not* to know.

A specific incident served as the catalyst for my thinking about motivated inaccuracy and led me to search Sillars's chapter for the paragraph cited above. It was a story that a friend related to me in the months that preceded the Nag's Head conference. He told me about a woman he knew who refused to see any of the all-too-obvious signs that her husband was having an affair. The man's schedule became more erratic; he was away from home many evenings and occasionally during the weekends. And there were unexplained phone hang-ups and other signs that, if investigated, would have suggested that he was involved with another woman.

But these signs weren't investigated—not at all. The man's wife rarely asked him about his absences, and she immediately accepted his explanation of them without any further questions. Nothing in her behavior indicated that she was motivated to know what was going on. In fact, her entire pattern of behavior indicated just the opposite: that she was motivated to *not* know what was going on, either in her husband's mind or in his activities away from home.

Obviously, this wasn't the first time that I had heard such a story. This woman's reactions were not unique; on the contrary, there were probably millions of other people—men and women alike—whose reactions under similar circumstances might resemble hers. But hearing this story had the same kind of impact on me that Archimedes's famous bath had upon him. I immediately recognized its relevance to the conceptual issues that I had been grappling with. I was struck with the certainty that the phenomenon of motivated inaccuracy really does exist, and that it should be possible to "capture" this phenomenon in an appropriately designed experiment.

Several weeks later, when Jeff Simpson and I discussed the possibility of collaborating on a research project during that walk on the beach at Nags Head, I told him my ideas about motivated inaccuracy and was pleased to see him become as excited about them as I was. During the next hour or so, we worked out the design and general procedure for a study that could be used to test these ideas—a study that Jeff agreed to conduct in his lab at Texas A&M

University with the assistance of one of his graduate students, Tami Blackstone.

The study we designed was an ambitious one, requiring nearly three years to complete. The first year was devoted to collecting the data, and the second and third years were spent coding the data, conducting the relevant statistical analyses, and writing and revising the research report to submit for publication.

We obviously had a lot riding on the outcome of this study, which we regarded as a major gamble from the outset. No previous research had ever documented the specific phenomenon that we were attempting to demonstrate, and it was almost too much to hope that we could find convincing evidence for it the very first time we tried. But the value of the prize seemed sufficient to justify the risk, so we decided to accept the risk and all of the costs that went with it. And, fortunately, there was a pay-off at the end.

In our wildest dreams, we hoped that the results of the study might demonstrate two things. First, we hoped to find evidence that couples display an exceptionally low level of empathic accuracy in a situation in which each partner's thoughts and feelings are potentially threatening to the other partner's view of the relationship. Second, we hoped to find evidence that, by *not* accurately inferring each other's thoughts and feelings in this type of situation, couples are able to minimize the damage to their relationship, keeping it intact by warding off the worst consequences of the potential threat.

Because the primary goal of our study was to demonstrate that the phenomenon of motivated inaccuracy really exists, our first task in designing the study was to specify some conditions in which this phenomenon might be likely to occur. After considerable discussion, we eventually agreed on three such conditions.

First, we agreed that the situation should be one in which the partners harbored thoughts and feelings that were, indeed, potentially threatening to their relationship. Establishing this condition within a controlled experiment meant that we needed to randomly assign half of the couples to a high-threat situation (one that was likely to evoke such relationship-threatening thoughts and feelings), and to assign the other half of the couples to a low-threat situation (one that was unlikely to evoke such relationship-threatening thoughts and feelings).

Second, we agreed that couples whose members were highly interdependent and who needed their relationship a lot should be more likely to display motivated inaccuracy than couples whose members were relatively independent and who needed their relationship less. We therefore decided to measure the strength of each couple's interdependence, expecting that more interdependent couples would be more likely than less interdependent couples to use motivated inaccuracy as a way of avoiding the worst consequences of the potential threat to their relationship.

Third, we agreed that couples who felt insecure about the long-term stability of their relationship should be more likely to display motivated inaccuracy than couples who felt secure about it. We therefore decided to measure the strength of each couple's insecurity as well.

Our next task was to develop a coherent procedure for the study. In its broadest outline, the procedure would require that we first measure each couple's level of interdependence and insecurity, and then place the couple in either a high- or a low-threat situation in which the partners' inferences about each other's thoughts and feelings could be assessed. We discussed a number of possible scenarios for this procedure, eventually settling on one that we regarded as optimal for the purposes we had in mind.

Here's how it worked. The participants were 82 heterosexual dating couples who were recruited from the college student population at Texas A&M. When the members of each couple reported to the lab, they were asked to fill out a set of questionnaires that included measures of how interdependent and insecure they perceived their relationship to be. The dating partners were then escorted to another room, where they were seated next to each other in chairs that faced a projection screen. The experimenter, Tami Blackstone, explained that we needed each of them to rate photographs of individuals who had agreed to take part in a dating study. She continued by saying that:

> We already have several personality measures from our volunteers, but we need ratings of their physical attractiveness and sexual appeal. We are asking dating couples to make these ratings because you, in effect, are experts on dating. Due to the delicate nature of arranging dates, we want to be as confident of our matches as possible. Later this semester, we may ask you to conduct interviews with our dating study volunteers. In the event you are asked, we would arrange for you to privately interview one of your two most highly rated individuals.

Tami explained that she would show each of the dating partners a series of slides that depicted six different members of the opposite sex. Their task would be rate each of these six target persons on two dimensions—physical attractiveness and sexual appeal. If a coin flip determined that the male dating partner would do his ratings first, he would rate six slides of different female targets, after which the female dating partner would rate six slides of different male targets. If the coin flip came out the other way, then the opposite order of rating would apply.

In either case, the person doing the attractiveness and sexual appeal ratings would convey them aloud to the experimenter in the form of a number from 0 to 10 (the so-called Bo Derek scale). This procedure guaranteed, of course, that each partner would hear all of the other partner's spoken ratings, because the two partners were sitting right next to each other throughout the entire rating session.

In the *high-threat condition* of the experiment, the opposite-sex target persons that both partners viewed were all highly attractive (in fact, the slides we used were of professional models whose age, style of dress, and location made them appear to be college students). In contrast, in the *low-threat condition* of the experiment, the target persons that both partners viewed were all below-average in their physical attractiveness. We expected that the target persons in the first condition would be rated as significantly more attractive and sexually appealing than those in the second condition (and this was, in fact, the case). We further expected that the dating partners in the first condition would feel more threatened by each other's perceptions than the partners in the second condition (and the self-report data we collected at the end of each session confirmed that this was the case as well).

After both dating partners had rated their respective series of slides, Tami surprised them by informing them that the entire rating session had been covertly videotaped. She explained that we needed the videotape for the next phase of the study, in which the dating partners would be asked about the specific thoughts and feelings they had experienced during the rating session. The partners were asked to give their written consent before they began this next phase of the procedure. They then viewed separate copies of the videotape, recording their own thoughts and feelings during a first viewing of the tape, and inferring their partner's thoughts and feelings during a second viewing.

We anticipated that many of the couples in our study, particularly those in the high-threat condition, would be experiencing feelings of jealousy and distress by the end of their experimental session. For this reason, Jeff and Tami conducted an unusually careful debriefing of each couple that was designed to reassure the partners that their reactions were completely normal given the nature of the situation we had put them in. The partners were informed that our rating task was *supposed* to evoke feelings of threat to their relationship, and that such feelings said more about the effectiveness of our procedure than about the actual state of their relationship. No couple was allowed to leave the lab until Jeff and Tami felt that this important point had been understood and appreciated.

But if the couples thought that we were through with them at that point, they were wrong. Four months after they had participated in the study, we contacted each of the dating partners by telephone and asked if they were still dating each other. One reason for doing this was to learn whether the couples who had been assigned to our high-threat condition were more likely to break up later than those who had been assigned to our low-threat condition. (We found that they weren't; in fact, the breakup rates were identical in both conditions.) Another reason for doing this, however, was to test our hypothesis that couples who had used motivated inaccuracy as a way of dealing with our relationship-threatening laboratory situation would actually be *less* likely to break up later than couples who had not. Support for this hypothesis would indicate that there are indeed situations in which too much empathic accuracy can hurt close relationships.

There is no instant gratification in such time- and labor-intensive research; months or even years can go by before you and your fellow researchers get to learn the results. But the three of us felt like 8-year-old kids on Christmas morning when, after two years of work, the results of the study finally emerged. Everything we had hoped to find was there.

To begin with, we found evidence for motivated inaccuracy exactly where we expected to find it: in the insecure but highly interdependent couples who had been in the high-threat condition of our experiment. This group of dating partners not only reported feeling the most threatened by each other's ratings of the highly attractive "target persons" but also were the most inaccurate when they attempted to infer each other's thoughts and feelings from the videotape.

Just how bad were they? They were so inaccurate that their average score was reliably lower than that of opposite-sex strangers whose empathic accuracy we had tested in a previous study. In fact, they were so inaccurate that their average score (about 5% of the available accuracy points) was essentially what we could expect them to score by chance alone. These two points of comparison offer strong evidence that the most threatened perceivers in our study were also extremely inaccurate—performing significantly worse than total strangers and at a level no greater than chance.

In contrast, the couples with the highest empathic accuracy scores were the ones that we had expected to be the least likely to display motivated inaccuracy: the secure, low-interdependent couples who had been in the low-threat condition of our experiment. This group of dating partners reported feeling the least threatened during the rating session, and their average level of empathic accuracy (about 18% of the available accuracy points) was substantially greater than chance. On the other hand, it did not differ from that of the opposite-sex strangers we had tested in our previous research, suggesting that even some of these less-threatened dating partners had used motivated inaccuracy as a defense.

The remaining couples in the study—those representing other combinations of interdependence/independence, security/insecurity, and high or low situational threat—had empathic accuracy scores that fell in between those of the two groups that I have just described. The pattern of data was just as we had predicted: the insecure, interdependent, and more situationally threatened dating partners displayed the most motivated inaccuracy; the secure, independent, and less situationally threatened dating partners displayed the least; and the remaining groups of dating partners fell somewhere in between.

But there was more. In addition to finding evidence for what we presumed was motivated inaccuracy, we found evidence that, by *not* accurately inferring each other's thoughts and feelings in our relationship-threatening laboratory situation, couples were able to protect their relationship from the long-term damage that might otherwise result. When we examined the breakups in these dating relationships four months later, we found no breakups at all within the group of couples for whom motivated inaccuracy had been most evident. In contrast, the overall breakup rate for the remaining couples was nearly 30%, a difference that was statistically reliable.

What does this finding mean? We think it provides the first direct evidence that perceivers can use motivated inaccuracy as a means of protecting their relationship when an accurate understanding of their partner's thoughts and feelings might destabilize and undermine it. More specifically, we think it points to a general tendency on the part of insecure but highly interdependent couples to "not go there" in an empathic sense whenever their interactions lead them into potential danger zones in their relationships. It appears that these couples have learned to steer clear of the danger zones by avoiding the knowledge of what their partners might be thinking and feeling at such times. The irony is that, by being extremely poor mind readers on these occasions, they do a better job of keeping their relationships together than do partners who are more empathically accurate.

Does this process occur consciously? Probably not. Motivated inaccuracy most closely resembles the psychological defense that Carl Rogers labeled *subception*—a "tuning out" of potentially threatening information before it is able to fully register in conscious awareness. And that is just how we described it in the journal article that reported the results of our experiment:

> Because perception is governed by cognitive processes that operate at different levels of awareness yet are under the same central regulative control, Erdelyi (1974) has suggested that many psychological processes associated with defense and vigilance should occur at subliminal levels of awareness. Using computer simulations, Hinton (1992) has recently modeled how perceptual selectivity could operate subconsciously at the level of neural networks within the brain. Evidence that motivated inaccuracy stems from subconscious processes would lend support to the proposition that motivated inaccuracy operates as a psycho-

logical mechanism serving a primary defensive function: to side-track or minimize conscious perceptions of threat to an existing relationship.

How do we know, however, that our results were based on motivated inaccuracy, as opposed to some other process? For example, perhaps the insecure but highly interdependent couples were exceptionally anxious in the high-threat condition of our study. If so, then their anxiety, rather than their feelings of threat, might have been responsible for the exceptionally low level of empathic accuracy that they displayed. Or perhaps these same couples had thoughts and feelings that were simply very difficult to infer. Could we rule out possibilities such as these?

Fortunately, by conducting some additional data analyses, we could. For although the insecure but highly interdependent couples were indeed highly anxious in the high-threat condition of our experiment, we found that their feelings of threat impaired their empathic accuracy to an extent that could not be accounted for by their anxiety alone. We also found that the thoughts and feelings of the insecure but independent couples in the high threat condition were *not* exceptionally difficult to infer, but were instead comparable in difficulty to those reported by the remaining couples in the study.

By the time we were done, the case for our motivated inaccuracy interpretation was consistent and reasonably strong. The major points of argument were as follows:

✤ As we hypothesized, the couples' level of insecurity and interdependence predicted how threatened they felt in our relationship-threatening laboratory situation. Their reported level of threat in turn predicted their level of empathic *inac-curacy*.

✤ The term *empathic inaccuracy* aptly describes the perform-ance of the insecure but interdependent couples who were in the high-threat condition of our experiment. These couples performed significantly worse than total strangers. In fact, their average level of performance was no better than chance.

❖ The overall pattern of findings could not be explained simply in terms of how anxious the perceivers were or how difficult their partners' thoughts and feelings were to infer. Instead, the partners' perceptions of threat were central to explaining our results.

❖ Four months later, the couples who had displayed the *least* empathic accuracy in our relationship-threatening laboratory situation were the *most* likely to still be together. At first glance, this outcome seems paradoxical because it flies in the face of the simple, commonsense view that greater understanding is always good for relationships. As we have seen, however, this outcome is not paradoxical at all. Instead, it is consistent with a more complex view which assumes that greater empathic accuracy about relationship-threatening issues can actually hurt people's relationships.

Given the encouraging results we had obtained, our next step was to try to develop a more general view of motivated inaccuracy and the conditions in which it does—and doesn't—occur. I won't risk boring you with the details of the work that went into this project, but I will risk boring you with the result.

What Jeff and I eventually came up with is one of those theoretical diagrams that look something like a flow chart. I have included this diagram as figure 9.1 on page 238. As you can see, its appearance is ungainly and its language is stilted. Because it reduces a complex aspect of human experience to a few lines and labels, it inevitably oversimplifies the phenomena that we are attempting to understand. Still, Jeff and I hoped that it would provide a useful starting point for our subsequent research.

Let me take you on a brief tour through this diagram, so that

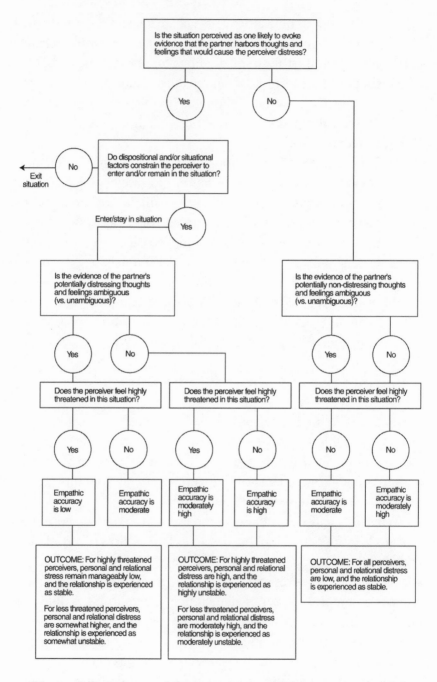

Figure 9.1. Ickes and Simpson's empathic accuracy model.

you can see what we had in mind. Starting at the top of figure 9.1, we assume that the perceiver makes a preliminary assessment of whether or not the current situation is likely to evoke a danger-zone issue in the relationship. The term *danger zone* is applicable whenever a perceiver has to confront an issue that could threaten the relationship by revealing a relationship partner's thoughts and feelings that the perceiver would find personally distressing.

If the situation appears to be nonthreatening in the sense that no danger-zone issue is likely to emerge (see the right-hand portion of figure 9.1), the perceiver should have at least some motivation to accurately infer the relationship partner's thoughts and feelings. Because experience teaches people that mutual understanding usually helps them to coordinate their actions in the pursuit of individual and common goals, perceivers should try to attain at least a moderate level of accuracy when they infer their partners' thoughts and feelings in nonthreatening situations. Acting mostly out of habit, perceivers will correctly infer their partners' intentions and desires, clear up misunderstandings about nonthreatening issues, keep minor conflicts from escalating into major ones, and gain a deeper understanding of their partners—all of which should enhance feelings of satisfaction and closeness in their relationships.

Inevitably, however, perceivers will at times encounter situations in which danger zones are anticipated—situations that have the potential to destabilize their relationships (see the left-hand portion of figure 9.1). When these situations arise, we predict that the first impulse of most perceivers should be to avoid or escape from them, if possible. In other words, the tactic of avoiding or escaping from danger-zone situations should be the first line of defense that perceivers can use to keep themselves from having to confront their partners' relationship-threatening thoughts and feelings.

The use of this tactic presumes, of course, that perceivers can recognize—and even anticipate—potential danger-zone areas in their relationships (for example, romantic feelings about former lovers or potential ones). Over time, the perceivers in most relationships should learn to identify and avoid such danger-zone areas in order to protect their cherished beliefs about themselves and their relationship. By doing so, perceivers can avoid dealing with danger-zone topics directly, acting as if it is better (and easier) to avoid confronting one's worst fears than it is to have one's worst fears confirmed and then be forced to deal with them.

Avoiding or escaping danger-zone issues is not always possible, however, and the part of our theoretical model that is relevant to these cases is depicted in the left and middle portions of figure 9.1. When perceivers feel obliged to remain in a relationship-threatening situation, the model predicts that their second line of defense should be *motivated inaccuracy*—a failure to accurately infer the specific content of their partner's potentially hurtful thoughts and feelings. The success of this strategy should vary, however, depending on the degree to which the inferred content of the partner's distressing thoughts/feelings is perceived as ambiguous versus unambiguous.

If the content of the partners' potentially threatening thoughts and feelings is perceived as ambiguous (see the left-hand portion of figure 9.1), perceivers should be able to use motivated inaccuracy as a defense. They can accomplish this by "tuning out" certain cues in the other person's behavior or by using psychological defense mechanisms such as denial, repression, or rationalization to avoid having to deal with the most threatening implications of their partners' potentially destructive thoughts and feelings. Obviously, the perceivers' empathic accuracy will be impaired by these defensive reactions—in some cases, quite dramatically. The same defensive reactions should provide an important payoff, however, by decreasing the perceivers' personal and relational distress and by helping to keep their relationship more stable.

Of course, there are circumstances in which motivated inaccuracy is simply not an option. What happens, for example, when perceivers feel obliged to remain in a relationship-threatening situation but cannot use motivated inaccuracy as a secondary strategy for dealing with relationship threat? The middle portion of figure 9.1 concerns this type of situation. In this case, the relationship-threatening content of the partner's thoughts and feelings is perceived to be clear and unambiguous (for example, the partner admits to being in love with someone else). The sheer clarity of this information should force the perceiver to achieve relatively high levels of empathic accuracy, resulting in increased dissatisfaction with the relationship and considerable instability.

All of this sounds pretty abstract, so let's look at the same set of processes using a concrete example. Darryl and Jackie Sue are former high school sweethearts who live together on a common-law basis in a trailer park on the outskirts of Lufkin, Texas. They get along together pretty good most of the time. For example, Jackie Sue has learned that whenever Darryl makes a joke about a "slippery piston," he is actually expressing his interest in having sexual relations with her. And, for his part, Darryl has learned that whenever Jackie Sue subsequently excuses herself to dab a little Floral Bouquet behind each of her ears, she is actually expressing her reciprocated interest in having sexual relations with him. Through such mundane acts of mutual attentiveness and accurate empathic inference, more exceptional and sublime acts of mutual lovemaking reliably occur. (Obviously, our story has begun in the right-hand portion of figure 9.1.)

One day, however, a potential danger zone appears in their relationship. It appears in the person of Jesse V. Holler, an earlier and more wildly amorous beau of Jackie Sue's who has recently been released from the state penitentiary at Huntsville. Jesse's name and newly freed status have just popped up in a conversation between Darryl and Jackie Sue, in response to which Darryl has just said, "I don't want to talk about him," and has exited the trailer home, driving off in his pickup truck to the Here We Are Bar down the road. (We are now in the upper left-hand portion of figure 9.1, a little to the left of the exit sign.)

Two days later, Darryl enters the trailer home after work to discover Jesse V. Holler sitting on the couch with Jackie Sue, engaged in conversation with her. Jesse V. gets up, shakes hands with Darryl, and says that he has just dropped by to pay his respects. Jackie Sue has the kind of ambiguous, vacant smile pasted on her face that Darryl can't easily interpret, so when Jesse leaves Darryl decides to put Jesse's visit out of his mind and to take at face value Jackie Sue's immediate profession of love and devotion. (Yes, this is the motivated inaccuracy part of figure 9.1, and Darryl—though he doesn't know it yet—is about to get his heart broke.)

Eleven days later, Darryl gets laid off from his job selling concrete gnomes and other lawn ornaments. He arrives home at 10:26 A.M. to find Jesse V. and Jackie Sue on the couch again. This time, however, Jesse V.'s tongue is inside Jackie Sue's ear and Jackie Sue's hand is inside Jesse V.'s pants. And this time Darryl does a much better job of reading Jackie Sue's mind, achieving an empathic inference that initiates a cascade of truly ugly events that become the lead story on Channel 9 the following day. (We have now arrived at the lower middle portion of figure 9.1, just as Jackie Sue has arrived at the lower middle portion of Jesse V.)

Are people in real-life relationships as likely to avoid confronting unpleasant realities as our view of motivated inaccuracy suggests? In the little story I just told, our protagonist, Darryl, steered clear of his personal danger zone on at least two occasions. The first time was when he said, "I don't want to talk about him" and took off for the bar. The second time was when he gave Jackie Sue the benefit of the doubt following her initial reunion with Jesse V. But Darryl, as far as I know, is a fictional character and not a real person. So it's appropriate to ask whether real people are as likely to steer clear of the danger zones in their real-life relationships as Darryl was in his fictional one.

Surprisingly, the answer seems to be yes. The available research findings suggest that, for the average relationship partner, the motive to avoid unpleasant realities is stronger than the motive to confront them (the guests on the Jerry Springer show are colorful exceptions to this rule). In general, the behavior of most relationship partners appears to be shaped by implicit mottos such as "Don't go looking for trouble," "Let's not make a big deal out of this," and "Everything's just fine; I don't see any problem here."

Consider, for example, Alan Sillars's study of how college roommates deal with areas of conflict in their relationships. Sillars found that passive-indirect responses were by far the most common, accounting for 52% of all reported incidents. A further breakdown of these passive-indirect responses revealed that 27% could be classified as avoidant, 14% as indirect, 8% as nonstrategies, and 3% as submissive. Moreover, the tendency to avoid dealing with the problem was especially pronounced when it was attributed to an aspect of the other roommate's personality that would be difficult, if not impossible, to change. Although active and cooperative problem solving did occur in many instances, it was limited primarily to the less volatile and contentious issues—the ones that did not pose obvious threats to the roommates' relationship.

You might think that the research on dating and marriage relationships would reveal a greater willingness to confront unpleasant realities head-on. In fact, however, essentially the opposite pattern has emerged. Across a large number of studies, the research findings suggest that dating and marriage partners prefer to look on the bright side of their relationship and to de-emphasize, redefine, or even ignore its darker aspects.

For example, psychologists John Holmes and Sandra Murray have found that individuals in both dating and marriage relationships tend to see their partners in overly idealized ways. Obviously, much of this idealization takes the form of exaggerating their partner's perceived virtues: evaluating the partner more favorably than they evaluate the average romantic partner, and viewing the partner more positively than the partner views himself or herself. Interestingly, however, some of this idealization also takes the form of putting the best possible spin on their partner's perceived faults: qualifying them with "yes, but" statements, deciding that they are harmless personality quirks, or even reinterpreting them as virtues.

Similarly, psychologist Caryl Rusbult and her colleagues have shown that individuals in dating or marriage relationships frequently ignore or shrug off their partner's "bad" behavior. In some cases, they tolerate the bad behavior without complaint, acting as if it had never occurred. In other cases, they make only a token protest before dropping the issue completely. And, in still other cases, they excuse the bad behavior by offering benign attributions about their partner's "actual" motive or intent.

These findings seem to fly in the face of a conventional wisdom that, according to Murray and Holmes, holds that "recognizing truths, even harsh truths, provides the foundation for satisfying close relationships by facilitating interpersonal adjustment and accommodation." Seeing the partner in an unrealistically positive light or putting the best possible spin on the partner's bad behavior suggests a willful distortion of the truth, not a clear-eyed appreciation of it. But, as Sandra Murray has argued, romantic partners have an excellent reason for wanting to "bend the truth" in just these ways:

> Few decisions are as important or life-altering as the decision to commit to an imperfect romantic partner. . . . In perhaps no other context do adults voluntarily tie the satisfaction of their hopes, goals, and wishes so completely to the good will of another. Given the vulnerability that such dependence implies, individuals need to possess a sense of conviction that the relationship is really a good one and that the partner can be counted on to be caring and responsive across time and situations . . .

... to resolve the tension posed by the practical necessity of insight and their hopes for happiness ... individuals with the strongest sense of conviction seem to dispel doubts [about their partners] by ascribing special significance to virtues, countering negative with positive beliefs about specific faults, and by organizing more general mental models in ways that link faults to greater virtues.

From this perspective, bending the truth is a small price to pay for a sense of security and stability that might otherwise be difficult to achieve within a close relationship. It should be noted, however, that Sandra Murray does not believe that we typically bend the truth in ways that are indiscriminate or unwise. On the contrary, she argues that by exaggerating our partners' virtues and putting a positive spin on their faults, we sustain a sense of commitment to our partners that would otherwise be difficult to achieve. This sense of commitment not only enables us to stick with our partners during stressful and trying times, but also encourages our partners to try to live up to the idealistic views that we hold of them. In essence, Murray argues that we are not so much blind as hopeful, and that there is a genuine, if unconventional, wisdom in that.

I believe that this same unconventional wisdom is brought to bear whenever we avoid relationship-threatening situations or use motivated inaccuracy as a way of trying to get through them unscathed. Unfortunately, we seldom lack for opportunities to get hurt by other people's unspoken thoughts and feelings. Fortunately, we don't have to accurately infer each and every one of them. By avoiding the danger zones as our first line of defense, and by using motivated inaccuracy as our second line of defense, we can spare ourselves a lot of unnecessary pain and distress. Even more important, we can keep potentially volatile situations under control, and can thereby buffer our relationships from genuine but short-term threats.

On the other hand, avoiding unpleasant realities is not always a good thing. If Jesse V. *had* just dropped by to pay his respects, Darryl's motivated inaccuracy would likely have been the most adaptive response, under the circumstances. However, because Jesse V. turned out to be a long-term, rather than a short-term, threat, Darryl's motivated inaccuracy only set himself up for a lot more trouble and heartache down the road. As this example suggests, motivated inaccuracy is best used as a strategy for avoiding knowledge about one's partner's more idle and fleeting thoughts and feelings that might temporarily threaten the relationship; it is not appropriate when the threat posed by one's partner's thoughts and feelings is more serious and persistent.

The key issue, according to John Holmes, is being able to decide "when . . . 'keeping the peace' and accommodating is healthy for a relationship, or when instead, avoiding real problems produces only a false sense of harmony and is ultimately destructive. . . ." In other words, the greatest wisdom may lie in knowing when you can afford to sustain the positive illusions you hold about your interaction partners and when you cannot afford to do so. Up to a certain point, you can use your illusions; but past that point, your illusions can start using you.

SOURCES FOR CHAPTER 9

Aldous, Joan. "Family Interaction Patterns." *Annual Review of Sociology* 3 (1977): 105–35.

Braiker, Harriet B., and Harold H. Kelley. "Conflict in the Development of Close Relationships." In *Social Exchange in Developing Relationships*, edited by Robert L. Burgess and Ted L. Huston. New York: Academic Press, 1979, pp. 135–68.

Drigotas, Stephen M., and Caryl E. Rusbult. "Should I Stay or Should I Go? A Dependence Model of Break-ups." *Journal of Personality and Social Psychology* 62 (1992): 62–87.

Erdelyi, Matthew H. "A New Look at the New Look: Perceptual Defense and Vigilance." *Psychological Review* 81 (1974): 1–25.

Hinton, Geoffrey E. "How Neural Networks Learn from Experience." *Scientific American* 267 (1992): 144–51.

Holmes, John G. "Social Relationships: The Nature and Function of Relational Schemas." *European Journal of Social Psychology* 30 (2000): 447–95.

Holmes, John G., and John K. Rempel. "Trust in Close Relationships." In *Review of Personality and Social Psychology: Close Relationships*, edited by Clyde Hendrick. Vol. 10. Newbury Park, Calif.: Sage, 1989, pp. 187–219.

Ickes, William, and Jeffry A. Simpson. "Managing Empathic Accuracy in Close Relationships." In *Empathic Accuracy*, edited by William Ickes. New York: Guilford Press, 1997, pp. 218–50.

———. "Motivational Aspects of Empathic Accuracy." In *Blackwell Handbook of Social Psychology: Interpersonal Processes*, edited by Garth J. O. Fletcher and Margaret S. Clark. Oxford, England: Blackwell, 2001, pp. 229–49.

Kursh, Charlotte O. "The Benefits of Poor Communication." *Psychoanalytic Review* 58 (1971): 189–209.

Levinger, George, and James Breedlove. "Interpersonal Attraction and Agreement." *Journal of Personality and Social Psychology* 3 (1966): 367–72.

Murray, Sandra L. "Seeking a Sense of Conviction: Motivated Cognition in Close Relationships." In *Blackwell Handbook of Social Psychology: Interpersonal Processes,* edited by Garth J. O. Fletcher and Margaret S. Clark. Oxford, England: Blackwell, 2001, pp. 107–26.

Murray, Sandra L., and John G. Holmes. (1996). "The Construction of Relationship Realities." In *Knowledge Structures in Close Relationships: A Social Psychological Approach*, edited by Garth J. O. Fletcher and Julie Fitness. Mahwah, N.J.: Erlbaum, 1996, pp. 91–120.

Rusbult, Caryl E., Dennis J. Johnson, and Gregory Morrow. "Impact of Couple Patterns of Problem Solving on Distress and Nondistress in Dating Relationships." *Journal of Personality and Social Psychology* 50 (1986): 744–53.

Rusbult, Caryl E., Julie Verette, Gregory Whitney, Linda F. Slovik, and Isaac Lipkus. "Accommodation Processes in Close Relationships: Theory and Preliminary Research Evidence." *Journal of Personality and Social Psychology* 60 (1991): 53–78.

Sillars, Alan L. "Attributions and Interpersonal Conflict Resolution." In *New Directions in Attribution Research*, edited by John H. Harvey, William Ickes, and Robert F. Kidd. Vol. 3. Hillsdale, N.J.: Erlbaum, 1981, pp. 279–305.

Sillars, Alan L. "Interpersonal Perception in Relationships." In *Compatible and Incompatible Relationships*, edited by William Ickes. New York: Springer-Verlag, 1985, pp. 277–305.

Simpson, Jeffry A., William Ickes, and Tami Blackstone. "When the Head Protects the Heart: Empathic Accuracy in Dating Relationships." *Journal of Personality and Social Psychology* 69 (1995): 629–41.

Watzlawick, Paul, John Weakland, and Richard Fisch. *Change: Principles of Problem Formation and Problem Resolution*. Oxford, England: W. W. Norton, 1974.

ten

WHO WANTS
TO KNOW?
WHO DOESN'T?

Aspiring theorists can get humbled pretty quickly. That happened to us.

About the same time that Jeff Simpson and I completed the first version of our theoretical statement, we decided to explore an entirely new angle in the data from our motivated inaccuracy study with Tami Blackstone. Jeff recruited another graduate student, Jami Grich, to help with this project, and the results they turned up convinced us that our just-completed theory was already in need of revision. The new results made it clear that we needed to pay more attention to the flip-sided questions, *Who wants to know?* and *Who doesn't?*

Recall that when the dating partners in our motivated inaccuracy study first arrived at the lab, they were asked to fill out a set of questionnaires before they were taken to another room to do the slide-rating task. Two of these questionnaires measured how interdependent and insecure the partners perceived their relationship to be, but there were other questionnaires that we had included as well. We thought that the additional questionnaire data might be worth examining at some point in the future. However, because we hadn't developed any hypotheses about them, we decided to put these data on hold and get back to them later.

What eventually led Jeff and Jami to get back to them was Jeff's interest in attachment theory as it applies to the study of adult romantic relationships. Jeff had recently developed his own line of research on adult attachment and was also co-editing a book on the topic with his colleague Steve Rholes. The more he learned about the work on attachment theory, the more convinced he became that we needed to re-examine the data from our motivated inaccuracy study from the unique vantage point that this theory provides.

As its name suggests, attachment theory concerns the type of *attachment*, or social bond, that develops between two people. Although the author of the theory, John Bowlby, believed that attachment processes were important throughout the entire lifespan, his first and most important goal was to explain how infants become attached to their primary caretakers (typically, their moms). He then went on to suggest how the course of the infants' subsequent development might be affected—for good or ill—by the type of attachment relationship that the infant and its mother establish.

Bowlby's key idea was that this very first relationship in the infant's life is also the most important in "setting the mold" for all of its future relationships. If the baby is securely attached to its mother, it comes to expect that other people—like mom—can be trusted and depended upon. The securely attached baby acquires both a positive view of self and a positive view of others, and these views make it easy for the child to form new relationships that are characterized by high levels of mutual trust and interdependence. In contrast, if the baby is *in*securely attached to its mother, it comes to question the extent to which people in general can be trusted and depended upon. At the same time, it acquires negative views of self and/or others that tend to precipitate problems in the child's subsequent relationships.

Believing that attachment was of fundamental importance throughout the entire lifespan, Bowlby encouraged researchers to study the role of attachment in adult relationships as well as the relationships between infants and their primary caretakers. However, because most of the early and influential research on attachment focused on mother-infant relationships, attachment theory during the 1970s and early 1980s was almost entirely the province of developmental psychologists. The situation changed dramatically after 1987, however, when psychologists Cindy Hazan and Philip Shaver proposed that attachment theory could also be applied to adult romantic relationships. They argued that although adult romantic relationships might appear on the surface to be quite different from infant-mother relationships, the underlying attachment processes might in fact be quite similar. They also argued, as Bowlby had before them, that the attachment styles people develop in infancy might carry over into their adult relationships.

These ideas were like a lit fuse that set off a decades-long explosion of research on adult attachment, most of which has been conducted by personality and social psychologists. One of these researchers' first goals was to identify the fundamental dimensions underlying different adult attachment styles. And, in journal articles published in 1992 and 1996, Jeff and his colleagues claimed to have done exactly that. Following up on an earlier article by psychologists Kim Bartholomew and Leonard Horowitz, Jeff and his colleagues reported data that led them similarly to conclude that there are two basic attachment dimensions: one representing people's varying levels of *anxiety* and the other representing people's varying levels of *avoidance* in their intimate relationships.

Drawing upon his knowledge of the research on infant and adult attachment, Jeff thought that the anxiety dimension might have a special relevance to the empathic accuracy of perceivers who felt that their relationships were being threatened. In the article that he, Jami, and I eventually wrote on the topic, he said:

> Because they have received inconsistent or unpredictable care and support from past attachment figures, highly anxious . . . individuals "have no confidence that [attachment figures] will ever be truly available and dependable." Consequently, such persons develop negative working models about themselves as relationship partners, viewing themselves as unworthy of love and affection. However, because they have not experienced consistently strong rejection from attachment figures, highly anxious-ambivalent people harbor positive (hopeful) yet guarded and apprehensive working models about whether significant others are likely to be available and emotionally supportive . . .
>
> According to Bowlby and Cassidy and Berlin, highly anxious-ambivalent individuals are likely to do three things in response to chronic uncertainty about the availability of their attachment figures. First, they should display . . . signs of greater distress . . . in situations that raise the possibility of losing their attachment figure. Second, they should closely monitor their attachment figure in these situations, especially if the knowledge gained could be used to keep the attachment figure more psychologically available in the future. Third, as a result of their heightened distress and closer monitoring, anxious-ambivalent individuals should find it more difficult to engage in and pursue other life tasks. [brackets in original]

What Jeff found particularly intriguing was the propensity of highly anxious individuals to closely monitor their "attachment figure" during times of apparent threat to the relationship. Researchers who study infant attachment had repeatedly shown that highly anxious babies and toddlers become "hypervigilant" as soon as it appears that their mothers might leave them. They keep their mothers under constant watch at that point, and they often run to their mothers, clinging and crying, if the threat of separation seems imminent.

Jeff speculated that highly anxious dating partners might also be hypervigilant in a relationship-threatening situation, but that in their case the hypervigilance would take the form of increased empathic accuracy. In other words, when anxious dating partners are faced with an imminent threat to their relationship, they might want to "get into the other person's head" to see how big a threat they are actually facing and what, if anything, might be done about it. Instead of being motivated to *inaccurately* infer their partner's potentially threatening thoughts and feelings, these highly anxious partners should be motivated to more *accurately* infer them.

This prediction was extremely interesting because it ran counter to the overall trend of the data in our motivated inaccuracy study. In general, the dating partners' empathic accuracy scores were relatively low in that study, and particularly so for the insecure but mutually dependent partners. So my colleagues and I were curious to learn whether highly anxious perceivers would prove to be exceptional by displaying *more* empathic accuracy in the same relationship-threatening situation that had motivated most perceivers to display *less*.

Fortunately, we had included a questionnaire that measured the anxiety and avoidance attachment dimensions in the set of questionnaires that the dating partners in our motivated inaccuracy study had completed before they participated in the slide-rating task. We were therefore able to correlate the perceivers' anxiety scores with their empathic accuracy scores to test Jeff's prediction. What we found was encouraging but also a little puzzling. Jeff's prediction was confirmed for the female dating partners: the higher their anxious attachment score, the greater was their empathic accuracy in our relationship-threatening slide-rating situation. However, the same prediction was not confirmed for the male dating partners, for reasons that weren't entirely clear.

Still, we now had some initial evidence that not everyone is motivated to *mis*infer their partner's thoughts and feelings in a relationship-threatening situation. Women with high anxious attachment scores seemed to behave in the opposite way. They acted as if they felt compelled to know what their male partners were thinking and feeling during the slide-rating task, even if that knowledge might threaten their relationships.

And, apparently, that's just what it did. Further data analyses revealed that the anxious but empathically accurate women reported a significant reduction in their feeling of closeness to their partner immediately after the slide-rating task. And because these same women also reported feeling highly threatened during the task, the results were consistent in suggesting that the anxious women paid an immediate emotional price for the greater accuracy of their empathic insights.

Why didn't the anxiously attached men display the same hypervigilant empathy as the anxiously attached women? Our data offered a couple of hints but no definitive answer. We found that the women were more visibly distressed than the men throughout the slide-rating task, and that the women rated themselves as being the more dependent partner within their dating relationships. These findings suggest that the anxious women might have felt more emotionally invested than the anxious men did, and were therefore more motivated to monitor their partners' potentially threatening thoughts and feelings.

The hypervigilant empathic accuracy of anxiously attached women clearly warranted some additional research attention. It got that attention from Jeremy Dugosh, who examined it in the studies he conducted for his master's and Ph.D. degrees. Jeremy wondered whether anxiously attached women would display the same motivated mind reading in a very different type of relationship-threatening situation. So he and I came up with an entirely new experimental scenario, one in which each woman saw a videotape of her male dating partner being interviewed by an attractive female interviewer.

In the *relationship-threatening condition* of the experiment, the female interviewer asked the male dating partner a scripted set of questions that made it easy for him to present himself as being popular, sexy, and desirable. Some of the questions were as follows: *If I asked you to give me just one reason why you are a desirable person to date, what would it be? If I asked you to name just one thing about yourself that is really sexy, what would it be? If you were at the beach, what part of you would attract the most attention?* We expected that, from the standpoint of the female dating partner who is watching the interview unfold, the man's answers to the questions in this condition would raise serious doubts about his esteem for her and for their relationship.

In contrast, in the *relationship-reassuring condition* of the experiment, the female interviewer asked the man essentially the same scripted questions, but in reference to the man's female dating partner instead of to himself: *If I asked you to give me just one reason why* [female dating partner's name] *is a desirable person to date, what would it be? If I asked you to name just one thing about her that is really sexy, what would it be? If she were at the beach, what part of her would attract the most attention?* We expected that, from the standpoint of the female dating partner who is watching the interview unfold, the man's answers to the questions in this condition would reassure her about his esteem for her and for their relationship.

The task of the female dating partners in each condition was to try to predict their male partner's answers to each of the interview questions. The men's answers during the interviews were spontaneous and unrehearsed, so the women's ability to predict the specific content of these answers could be used as a measure of their empathic accuracy. Moreover, because the women had completed an adult attachment questionnaire at the beginning of the experimental session, Jeremy was able to correlate their scores on the anxiety dimension with their accuracy in predicting the specific content of their male partners' answers during the interview.

Jeremy predicted that highly anxious women would display increased empathic accuracy in response to relationship threat, whereas less-anxious women would display decreased empathic accuracy instead. This prediction was confirmed: the highly anxious women were more accurate in predicting their dating partners' answers in the relationship-threatening condition than in the relationship-reassuring condition, whereas the opposite was true of the women with low anxiety scores. Moreover, when Jeremy tested the same prediction in a second study that he did for his doctoral thesis, he found the same pattern of results. He also found, however, that hypervigilant empathy was displayed only by highly anxious women; it was not evident when the perceivers were highly anxious men.

It appeared that we had our first definite answer to the question: *Who wants to know their partner's potentially threatening thoughts and feelings?* And the answer was: *Anxiously attached women do.* This answer makes sense in terms of the corresponding hypervigilance that anxious babies display when their mothers threaten to leave them, but it's an answer that only attachment theory could have provided. And even attachment theory would have failed to predict that the hypervigilant empathy of highly anxious women would not be found in highly anxious men.

On the one hand, the phenomenon of hypervigilant empathy is a fascinating one that researchers will want to explore in depth. On the other hand, it is a phenomenon that could not have been predicted from the theory that Jeff Simpson and I developed to account for motivated inaccuracy in close relationships. Given the accumulating evidence for the existence of this phenomenon, we were forced to recognize that there were gaps in our theory that needed to be addressed. So, in an updated version of the theory that Jeff and I wrote during the spring and summer of 1999, we modified it to take into account individual differences in the strength of people's motives to accurately read other people's thoughts and feelings.

The time we spent working on this project gave me the opportunity to think about whether it might be possible to assess people's mind-reading motives in a more direct manner. One possibility is to measure how strongly motivated they are to understand the thoughts and feelings of a particular relationship partner, as opposed to people in general. This type of measure has been advocated by Edgar Long, a family relations researcher who has developed scales for assessing perspective-taking in marriage and similar dyads. Long and his colleagues have used couples' scores on these scales to help predict the long-term stability of their relationships.

Another possibility is to measure the strength of people's motivation to infer a specific category of the thoughts and feelings that another person might have. For example, given the importance of relationship-threatening thoughts and feelings in the theory that Jeff Simpson and I have proposed, it might be useful to develop a measure of the extent to which people would or would not want to know the relationship-threatening information that their romantic partners possess. In fact, I have already developed such a measure, which my colleagues and I refer to as the MARTI scale. MARTI is a convenient acronym for the scale's full name: the Motive to Acquire Relationship-Threatening Information.

In the version of the scale designed for use with dating couples, the instructions begin by noting that:

> In dating relationships, there are things that partners might or might not want to know about each other. For each of the following hypothetical items of information, indicate whether you would prefer to *know* or *not know* the information by circling the appropriate alternative in each case. There are no right or wrong answers, but it is important that you be as honest and accurate as possible in responding to each item.

After reminding the participants that the items they will respond to are hypothetical and that no one but the researchers will see their responses, our instructions then ask: "If you could, which of the following hypothetical items of information about your dating partner would you prefer to *know* or *not know*? (Circle one of the two responses in each case.)" The participants then respond to a set of 21 items from which the following sample items have been drawn.

I would prefer to:

❖ The most unkind or unfair thing
   my partner has said about me to
   one of his/her current or former
   dating partners.   *know*   *not know*

❖ The most intimate detail of my
   past history that my partner has
   revealed to one of his/her
   current or former dating partners.   *know*   *not know*

❖ Which of *my* same-sex friends
   my partner is secretly the most
   strongly attracted to.   *know*   *not know*

❖ Whether my partner has ever dated
   one of my same-sex friends
   without telling me.   *know*   *not know*

❖ Whether my partner has, without
   telling me, ever had protected sex with
   any other members of the opposite
   sex while we have been dating.   *know*   *not know*

Even these few sample items should be sufficient to illustrate what people with high MARTI scores are like: they want to know all kinds of relationship-threatening infomation that other people might go out of their way to *avoid* knowing. They want to know about any critical, unfair, or unkind things that their partner has said about them behind their backs. They want to know about any information shared in confidence with their partner that their partner has subsequently shared with others. They want to know which of their own same-sex friends their partner is secretly the most attracted to. And they want to know about their partner's extracurricular sexual activities during the time that they have been together.

Do these people sound like they are asking for trouble? My colleagues and I thought so. It seemed to us that these people have the kind of "suspicious minds" that Elvis Presley referred to in his hit song by the same name. And if two of these people were to somehow get together, they—like the unhappy couple in Elvis's song—probably couldn't "go on together" for very long with their mutually suspicious minds operating in overdrive.

To see whether people with high MARTI scores really do have suspicious minds, Jeremy Dugosh collected data from 96 dating couples. Each of these couples came to our lab at the University of Texas at Arlington, where the partners were seated in separate cubicles and then asked to fill out a questionnaire. The questionnaire included both the MARTI scale and a trust scale developed by the Canadian psychologists John Rempel, John Holmes, and Mark Zanna. The trust scale was the appropriate one to use in our study because, like the MARTI scale, it focused on the specific relationship between the respondent and his or her dating partner.

The hypothesis we tested was so simple and straightforward that it was almost a no-brainer. We expected to find that people who scored high on the MARTI scale would tend to score low on the trust scale, and vice versa. In other words, the more relationship-threatening information the respondents wanted to know, the less they would report trusting their relationship partners. As predicted, we found that this inverse relationship was statistically reliable, confirming our hunch that high scorers on the MARTI scale were indeed people who had "suspicious minds."

In a follow-up study conducted at Texas A&M University, we found that people with suspicious minds engage in suspicious behaviors as well. Jeff Simpson and Carol Wilson asked 188 undergraduate students who had completed the MARTI scale to also complete a checklist measure of how often they had engaged in various behaviors designed to monitor or test for a romantic partner's possible disloyalty or infidelity. Among other behaviors, the participants reported how often they had eavesdropped on a partner's private phone conversation, called to see if the partner was where s/he was supposed to be, secretly followed or spied on a partner, set up test situations to see if the partner would lie, had someone else check to see who the partner was with, and closely monitored a partner's daily behavior for signs of infidelity. When we added up all of the suspicious behaviors reported by the participants in this study, we found—as expected—that the greatest number were reported by people who were motivated to acquire relationship-threatening information.

But what about Elvis's prediction—the prediction that romantic partners "can't go on together with suspicious minds"? Would dating partners who both scored high on the MARTI scale tend to break up sooner than partners who both scored low? To answer this question, Jeremy Dugosh and his undergraduate research assistants recruited a new sample of 81 dating couples. When these couples reported to our lab, the male and female partners each completed the MARTI scale and a measure of perceived relationship closeness. Jeremy and his assistants then waited five months before contacting the partners by phone and asking about the current status of their relationship.

The results were interesting. As we had expected, the dating partners who both scored high on the MARTI scale (the ones with "suspicious minds") were more likely to have broken up than the partners who both scored low. Nearly half of the mutually suspicious couples had broken up by the time we called them five months later, whereas less than a fourth of the unsuspicious couples had broken up by then.

Even more interesting, however, was the finding that having "*un*suspicious minds" seemed to buffer otherwise vulnerable couples from the risk of breaking up. Within the group of suspicious couples, those who had previously described their relationships as not very close broke up more often (53%) than those who had reported being closer (33%). On the other hand, within the group of unsuspicious couples, there was no such difference. In fact, the less-close couples were no more likely to break up than the more-close couples in this case (22% and 24%, respectively).

This pattern of results suggests that the avoidance of relationship-threatening information might buffer people against the influence of risk factors that could otherwise undermine their relationships. A low level of perceived closeness seems to be a risk factor for relationship dissolution, but only in combination with a strong motive to acquire relationship-threatening information. When this motive is weak (that is, when couples avoid such information), the relationships of less-close couples appear to be just as resistant to break-ups as those of close couples, at least within the time frame we examined in our study.

So far, my focus in this chapter has been on the question, *Who wants to know?* with a special emphasis on the personality traits and motives of people who want to know their partners' relationship-threatening thoughts and feelings. It is now time to turn the coin over and focus on the obverse question, *Who doesn't want to know?* giving a similar emphasis to potentially threatening thoughts and feelings.

In one sense, this question has already been answered—at least implicitly. The people who don't want to know their partners' thoughts and feelings are those who occupy the opposite end of the relevant dimensions from the people who do. In the most general case, they are the people who report having very little interest in what other people are thinking and feeling. In more specific cases, they are the people who score low on the anxious attachment dimension and on my measure of the Motive to Acquire Relationship-Threatening Information (MARTI). For one reason or another, the people who score low on these dimensions should be less interested in reading their partners' minds than the people who score high on them.

In addition to these cases, the available research evidence has identified some other categories of people who don't want to know what another person is thinking or feeling. The first category includes the women in our motivated inaccuracy study who scored high on the *avoidant*, rather than the anxious, attachment dimension. These women report that they feel uncomfortable with "too much" intimacy in their close relationships; they also tend to avoid dealing with problems in the relationship whenever they can. A second category includes anxious-abusive men—highly anxious men who report a pattern of abusive behavior directed toward women. Let's take a look at the people in these two categories and see how they operate.

Although Jeff and Jami's reexamination of the data from the motivated inaccuracy study focused primarily on the women who scored high on the anxious attachment dimension, the women who scored high on the avoidant attachment dimension turned out to be of interest as well. These high-avoidant women did not differ from low-avoidant women in their empathic accuracy scores, because both groups tended to display the motivated inaccuracy that was characteristic of the data as a whole. However, the high-avoidant women *did* differ from the low-avoidant women in the number of times that they failed to make an empathic inference, either by leaving blank the relevant slot on the inference form or by writing "I don't know" instead.

This pattern of behavior provides direct evidence that the avoidant women did not want to infer, or perhaps even to think about, their dating partners' potentially threatening thoughts and feelings. After we had explicitly instructed them to try to accurately infer all of their dating partners' thoughts and feelings, leaving no slots on the inference form blank, the high-avoidant women still chose to ignore our instruction in many more instances than the low-avoidant women did. It was as if the high-avoidant women were telling us that they simply "didn't want to go there" at times when their motivation to avoid confronting their partners' potentially threatening thoughts and feelings was stronger than their desire to comply with the task instructions we had given them.

As you might expect, the women who scored high on the *anxious* attachment dimension responded very differently. The high-anxious women attempted to infer more of their partners' thoughts and feelings than the low-anxious women did, and their inferences were generally more accurate as well, consistent with our hypervigilant empathy interpretation. Whereas the highly avoidant women acted as if they wanted to stay out of their partner's heads when the results could be distressing, the highly anxious women acted as if they felt compelled to get in their partners' heads, despite the distressing results.

Once again, however, we are left to ask why these contrasting motives were so strongly evident in the female, but not the male, dating partners. And, once again, we can speculate that the answer to this question might lie in the greater emotional investment of the women in these relationships. If the women felt that they had more to lose than the men, they should have been more strongly motivated to preserve the relationship in the face of an apparent threat. For the highly avoidant women, preserving the relationship meant doing their best to stay out of their partners' heads, whereas for the highly anxious women it meant doing their best to get inside of them.

We have come to the dark side of "everyday mind reading," but things are about to become darker still. For if the desire to keep the partner motivates the hypervigilant empathy displayed by highly anxious women, the desire to control the partner appears to motivate the biased perceptions of a certain category of highly anxious men—those who report abusing women. Whereas anxious women try to understand their partners to keep them close, anxious-abusive men try *not* to understand their partners to keep them oppressed. By not attending to their partners' actual thoughts and feelings and imposing a biased view of them instead, anxious-abusive men create a distorted reality in which women deserve to be abused and treated in a very unempathic way.

Recall that in our first attempt to study the psychology of abusive men, Will Schweinle, Ira Bernstein, and I found that men who reported abusing their own female partners were systematically biased when they inferred the thoughts and feelings of the female clients who appeared in our stimulus videotapes (see chapter 8). Specifically, the abusive men overattributed critical and rejecting thoughts and feelings to these women, and were therefore relatively inaccurate when they attempted to infer the actual content of the women's thoughts and feelings.

To gain further insights into the behavior of abusive men, Will Schweinle designed a follow-up study that he conducted for his dissertation research. In this study, the participants—80 married men —were again recruited through newspaper ads and tested in individual sessions. At the start of each session, the participant filled out a set of questionnaires. One of the questionnaires was used to obtain the man's scores on the anxious and avoidant attachment dimensions; another was used to measure his sensitivity to being rejected by women.

After completing the questionnaires, each participant viewed the videotape of Client A from the set of tapes that Carol Marangoni originally recorded (see chapter 5). Client A was a very articulate woman in her mid-twenties who recounted for the therapist the circumstances leading up to her divorce. During the course of the tape, she relates how she and her ex-husband met, fell in love, were married after a very brief courtship, and then soon began to experience escalating tension over the issue of control in the relationship. She expresses the opinion that her former husband had been much too controlling, and she cites that perception as a major reason for her eventual desire to end the relationship.

In previous studies in which Client A's tape was used, we found that our male participants reported widely varying emotional reactions to it. Men who presumably identified with Client A's point of view generally felt sympathetic and concerned, whereas men who presumably identified with the point of view ascribed to Client A's ex-husband seemed to feel somewhat irritated with, or even contemptuous of, her. For this reason, Will and I decided that Client A's tape would be the ideal one to use in his study, which was designed to capture the specific emotions the participants were feeling whenever they attempted to infer one of Client A's reported thoughts or feelings.

While each of Will's participants was sitting in his cubicle and viewing Client A's videotape, a tiny camera concealed next to the television screen was used to tape his facial expressions throughout the empathic inference task. Client A's conversation with the therapist was simultaneously recorded as the "soundtrack" of this covert videotape, which Will showed to each participant immediately after he had completed all of his empathic inferences. When the participant viewed this new tape, Will stopped it for him at each of the same "tape stops" used before. However, the participant's task on this occasion was to check any of a set of emotion words that described the specific emotions he remembered experiencing when he first heard Client A's conversation with her therapist at that point.

By means of this procedure, Will was able to get each participant to characterize the specific emotions he was feeling at each of the times when he inferred one of Client A's thoughts or feelings. The participant could see his own facial expressions and behavior at each tape stop, and by hearing the client-therapist interaction in the background, he could ideally remember the specific emotions that he had experienced at that time. The participant could then report these emotions by checking all relevant ones from a list that included *irritated, annoyed, sympathetic, concerned, indifferent, unaffected, insulted, contempt, uncaring,* and *sad.*

Better still, Will was later able to use these covert videotapes to determine how much time each participant spent looking away from Client A, whose image had appeared in the center of the participant's television screen throughout the entire session. Will and I recruited two of our undergraduate research assistants—Wayland Scott and Brea Yell—to do the necessary data coding. By tracking the men's head and gaze displacements, Wayland and Brea were able to measure very reliably how long each man spent looking away from Client A. Will then analyzed the resulting data to test his hypothesis that abusive men are more likely than nonabusive men to disattend or "tune out" when a woman attempts to express her actual thoughts and feelings about her relationship.

This disattention hypothesis was strongly confirmed. In fact, the amount of time the men spent looking away from Client A was correlated with virtually every attribute of abusive men that was measured in the study. In particular, it was correlated with:

- ❖ the degree to which the men reported abusing their own female partners;
- ❖ the degree to which they reported having sexually harassed other women during the previous year;
- ❖ their scores on the anxious attachment dimension;
- ❖ their scores on a questionnaire that measured their sensitivity to rejection by women; and
- ❖ the strength of their bias to overattribute criticism and rejection when they tried to infer the content of Client A's thoughts and feelings.

This pattern of correlations offers strong and consistent evidence that abusive men are the ones most likely to deal with a woman's "complaints" by disattending them. Rather than listening patiently to a woman's legitimate concerns, the abusive man may "tune out" these concerns and stereotype the woman as being critical and rejecting. By stereotyping her in this way, the abusive man can not only free himself from the obligation to take the woman's "complaints" seriously; he can also feel justified in getting angry at her for her habitual criticism and rejection.

Further insights about the psychology of abusive men were revealed by other findings from Will's study. For example, consistent with the results of our first study, Will found that the strength of the men's overattribution bias was correlated with the extent to which they reported abusing their own female partners. In addition, the kinds of emotions the men reported feeling at the time they inferred Client A's thoughts and feelings were related to the men's overall empathic accuracy scores. Specifically, the men who reported feeling sympathetic and concerned tended to be the best at reading Client A's mind, whereas the men who reported feeling uncaring tended to be the worst.

Taken together, these results suggest that anxious-abusive men are likely to *mis*infer women's thoughts and feelings as a means of exerting control. Having already made up their minds that women are critical and rejecting, abusive men act as if they don't want any challenges to that point of view. Accordingly, they tend to "tune out" the woman's attempts to express her actual thoughts and feelings. And the less they attend to her actual thoughts and feelings, the less accurately they infer them. Through the vicious cycle created by this process, their inferential bias becomes increasingly entrenched and self-sustaining, leading them to consistently "find" evidence of criticism and rejection in women's thoughts and feelings even when these sentiments aren't actually there.

All of this behavior seems to serve the purpose of *negating* women's actual thoughts and feelings so that anxious-abusive men are not obliged to deal with them. If women's actual thoughts and feelings do not have to be taken into account, abusive men are freer to act without any regard to them. Moreover, any sign of protest on the women's part can be taken as evidence that the men were right all along—the women really *are* critical and rejecting.

Do anxious-abusive women generally act the same way as anxious-abusive men—"tuning out" what their partners are thinking and feeling instead of displaying the hypervigilant empathy that anxious but nonabusive women display? Or do anxious-abusive women, like the character of Martha in Edward Albee's play *Who's Afraid of Virginia Woolf*, torture their partners with the cruel and unusual accuracy of their empathic inferences? I don't know the answers to these questions, but I'll be very interested to see what future research findings will have to say in this regard.

In the meantime, the behavior of anxious-abusive men makes the important point that sometimes power isn't sought through *greater* knowledge, but through *less*. By refusing to acknowledge and understand another person's thoughts and feelings, one is freer to assert the preeminence of one's own. But is the power that one achieves in this way the true power of the rational person or the false power of the self-deluded tyrant? I don't think we need to do research to answer that question.

SOURCES FOR CHAPTER 10

Bartholomew, Kim, and Leonard M. Horowitz. "Attachment Styles among Young Adults: A Test of a Four-Category Model." *Journal of Personality and Social Psychology* 61 (1991): 226–44.

Bowlby, John. *Attachment*. Vol. 1 of *Attachment and Loss*. New York: Basic Books, 1969.

Bowlby, John. *Separation: Anxiety and Anger*. Vol. 2 of *Attachment and Loss*. New York: Basic Books, 1973.

Cassidy, Jude, and Lisa J. Berlin. "The Insecure/Ambivalent Pattern of Attachment: Theory and Research." *Child Development* 65 (1994): 971–91.

Dugosh, Jeremy W. "Adult Attachment Style Influences on the Empathic Accuracy of Female Dating Partners." Master's thesis, University of Texas at Arlington, 1998.

————. "Effects of Relationship Threat and Ambiguity on Empathic Accuracy in Dating Couples." Ph.D. diss., University of Texas at Arlington, 2001.

Goleman, Daniel. *Emotional Intelligence: Why It Can Matter More than IQ.* New York: Bantam Books, 1995.

Hazan, Cindy, and Phillip R. Shaver. "Romantic Love Conceptualized as an Attachment Process." *Journal of Personality and Social Psychology* 52 (1987): 511–24.

Ickes, William, Jeremy W. Dugosh, Jeffry A. Simpson, and Carol L. Wilson. "Suspicious Minds: The Motive to Acquire Relationship-Threatening Information." *Personal Relationships* 10 (2003): 131–48.

Ickes, William, and Jeffry A. Simpson. "Managing Empathic Accuracy in Close Relationships." In *Empathic Accuracy*, edited by William Ickes. New York: Guilford Press, 1997, pp. 218–50.

————. "Motivational Aspects of Empathic Accuracy." In *Blackwell Handbook of Social Psychology: Interpersonal Processes*, edited by Garth J. O. Fletcher and Margaret S. Clark. Oxford, England: Blackwell, 2001, pp. 229–49.

Long, Edgar C. "Measuring Dyadic Perspective Taking: Two Scales for Assessing Perspective Taking in Marriage and Similar Dyads." *Educational and Psychological Measurement* 50 (1990): 91–103.

————. "Maintaining a Stable Marriage: Perspective Taking as a Predictor of Propensity to Divorce." *Journal of Divorce and Remarriage* 21 (1993): 121–38.

Long, Edgar C., and David W. Andrews. "Perspective Taking as a Predictor of Marital Adjustment." *Journal of Personality and Social Psychology* 59 (1990): 126–31.

Rempel, John K., John G. Holmes, and Mark P. Zanna. "Trust in Close Relationships." *Journal of Personality and Social Psychology* 49 (1985): 95–112.

Schweinle, William E. "The Role of Men's Attribution Biases and Affect in Wife Abuse and Sexual Harassment." Ph.D. diss., University of Texas at Arlington, 2001.

Schweinle, William E., William Ickes, and Ira H. Bernstein. "Empathic Inaccuracy in Husband to Wife Aggression: The Overattribution Bias." *Personal Relationships* 9 (1986): 141–58.

Simpson, Jeffry A., William Ickes, and Tami Blackstone. "When the Head Protects the Heart: Empathic Accuracy in Dating Relationships." *Journal of Personality and Social Psychology* 69 (1995): 629–41.

Simpson, Jeffry A., William Ickes, and Jami Grich. "When Accuracy Hurts: Reactions of Anxious-Ambivalent Dating Partners to a Relationship-Threatening Situation." *Journal of Personality and Social Psychology* 76 (1999): 754–69.

Simpson, Jeffry A., William S. Rholes, and Julia S. Nelligan. "Support Seeking and Support Giving within Couples in an Anxiety-Provoking Situation: The Role of Attachment Styles." *Journal of Personality and Social Psychology* 62 (1992): 434–46.

Simpson, Jeffry A., William S. Rholes, and Dede Phillips. "Conflict in Close Relationships: An Attachment Perspective." *Journal of Personality and Social Psychology* 71 (1996): 899–914.

eleven
PERCEPTIVE
PROFESSIONALS

Does the research on empathic accuracy have any practical value? Can the findings from this research help us live better, more successful lives as parents, relationship partners, and working professionals? These are not just rhetorical questions, as the following cautionary tale suggests.

In 1995, Daniel Goleman's new book, *Emotional Intelligence*, was greeted with enormous critical and popular acclaim. *Time* magazine devoted a cover story to the book in which it was claimed that emotional intelligence (or EQ, as *Time* called it) was more important than "academic" intelligence (IQ) in determining people's success in life. Within a very short time, the book became an international best-seller that spawned many imitators. It also created a surge of interest and activity in various researchers, educators, policymakers, and business consultants, all of whom scrambled to get aboard the EQ bandwagon. But were the extraordinary claims made for emotional intelligence supported by the available research? According to psychologist John Mayer, they weren't:

> Claims for emotional intelligence escalated markedly in popularizations of the concept. Emotional intelligence was said to be as or more important than IQ in predicting success in life. . . . The claim was astonishing, as intelligence . . . regularly predicts academic grade point average at $r = .50$ level; moreover, the prestige of an occupation (as rated by independent observers) correlates about $r = .80$ with the average IQ of the people in the occupation.
>
> To claim that emotional intelligence outpredicts intelligence means that it should have correlations above those $r = .50$ and $r = .80$—a stiff hurdle. Those searching for documented evidence for the 1995 claim in the popular book were disappointed. For example, a widely reported Bell Labs study of engineers was said to indicate that emotionally intelligent engineers outperformed others at work. The study in question, however, involved no psychological measurements at all, and emotion was barely mentioned . . .
>
> Rather than retreat from such claims, however, the popular claims escalated—doubled, in fact. For example, emotional intelligence became "twice as important as IQ and other technical skills," in Goleman's [1998] book, and this claim was repeated by him in a much-read article in the *Harvard Business Review*. This time, documentation was produced: The figure was based on a survey of job descriptions that indicated that "emotionally intelligence-related criteria appeared twice as often as technical requirements." . . . Job performance is, of course, not best measured by the study of job descriptions. What *is* measured is merely the words used in job advertisements. . . . Understanding what actually predicts success requires employing actual measures . . . of on-the-job performance.

Writing this commentary in 2001, Mayer concluded that "there is little or no evidence thus far that emotional intelligence is the best predictor of success in life, let alone twice as important as IQ." Although the concept might have genuine value, the early claims for it were, in retrospect, both exaggerated and over-hyped.

Mayer's cautionary tale is pertinent to the present case because empathy is a characteristic that many writers have argued is an important—and even central—aspect of emotional intelligence. Writers ranging from E. B. Titchener in the early 1900s through Howard Gardner in the 1980s to Peter Salovey and John Mayer in the 1990s have all regarded the ability to understand others' feelings as a quintessential social skill. On the other hand, empathy is not the only aspect of emotional intelligence. As Mayer has noted, contemporary writers use emotional intelligence as a broad, umbrella-like term that stretches to include not just empathy but emotional self-awareness, emotional self-regulation, self-motivation, and certain social skills. So if strong claims are not warranted for a concept as broad as emotional intelligence, we should think twice before making such claims for the more focused concept of empathic accuracy.

Keeping Mayer's cautionary tale in mind, what can we say about the practical implications of the research on empathic accuracy? As much as I would like to encourage an unstoppable buzz for the book you are reading, I am not inclined to make any extraordinary claims. Accordingly, my goal in this chapter is a relatively modest one. In the sections to follow, I discuss only those empathic accuracy findings that appear to have direct implications for people who aspire to be "professionals" in four types of social roles. The specific roles I consider are those of *parents*, of *partners* in close relationships, of practicing *psychotherapists,* and of other *professionals* whose livelihood depends on their everyday mind reading skills.

Are empathically accurate parents better parents? Are they more successful than less-empathic parents in the art of raising healthy, happy children?

These questions were the starting point for the dissertation research of Laura Crosby, a psychologist who completed her Ph.D. at the Fielding Institute in Santa Barbara. Realizing that the questions she was asking were too broad and inclusive to investigate in a single study, she decided to ask a more focused and specific question instead: *Do the children of empathically accurate mothers have more positive self-concepts than the children of less-accurate mothers?*

To answer this question, Crosby placed notices and newspaper ads in the mid-state area of Santa Fe and Albuquerque, New Mexico, inviting children aged nine to eleven and their mothers "to participate in a research study by completing two questionnaires and watching and recording videotaped conversations." Complimentary movie tickets were given as an incentive, and 40 mother-child pairs agreed to participate in the study, which required them to provide data on two separate occasions.

In their first testing session, the mother and child were given different questionnaires to complete—a background information questionnaire for the mother and a self-concept scale for the child. In their second testing session, they began by watching a training tape of another mother and child interacting and having a conversation, and then practiced inferring the thoughts and feelings of these target persons at various tape stops. After this practice period, the mother and child participants were themselves videotaped during a 10-minute conversation about some decisions they were in the process of making, such as planning a trip, making a purchase, or choosing a pet.

When the videotaping was finished, the mother was asked to sit in the waiting room while the child viewed the tape and reported all of the thoughts and feelings that he or she remembered having experienced during the videotaped conversation. This procedure had to be modified because, as Laura Crosby said, "It became evident during the pilot study that the children were mesmerized while watching themselves on tape and were able to make only a very few [tape] stops." Crosby's solution to this problem was to stop the tape several times for the child at points when the videotape revealed "changes in the child's facial expression, speech volume, and eye and body movements." With this procedural change in place, Crosby was able to get all of the children to report approximately 20 thoughts and feelings.

Once this step had been completed, the child went to sit in another room with a research assistant while the mother was asked to view the videotape of the conversation she had had with her child and attempt to infer the child's specific thoughts and feelings at each of the stop points. After completing this task, she was then asked to infer the thoughts and feelings of another mother's child in a second videotape—a standard tape that was viewed by all of the mothers who participated in the study.

When Crosby analyzed the data from her study, she was pleased to find that the mothers who were the most accurate in inferring their own child's thoughts and feelings had the children with the most positive self-concepts. In particular, their children scored high on two different measures of how good they felt about themselves in their relationships with family members. And, interestingly, it was the mothers' ability to infer their *own* child's thoughts and feelings that was important in this regard: their ability to infer the thoughts and feelings of the other mother's child in the standard tape was unrelated to their own child's self-esteem. Even more intriguing was Crosby's additional discovery that the empathic accuracy of mothers who had experienced separations from their child through joint custody arrangements was significantly lower than that of mothers who had not.

Interpreting these findings proved to be difficult, however, because of the chicken-or-egg ambiguity that is often inherent in correlational results. With regard to Crosby's first finding, do moms who understand their kids better do a better job of making their kids feel understood and appreciated, thereby raising the kids' self-esteem? Or do kids who already have high self-esteem also express their thoughts and feelings more clearly in what they say and do, so that it is easier for their moms to understand them? Or do both of these processes occur in a positive feedback loop, such that empathic moms contribute to their children's self-esteem in a way that encourages the children to express themselves more openly, which in turn promotes the moms' empathic accuracy?

With regard to Crosby's second finding, do the separations that some moms have from their kids disrupt the mother-child relationship enough to impair the moms' empathic accuracy? Or do divorced moms already have low empathic ability, and could that "empathy deficit" be responsible—at least in part—for both their divorced status and the resulting separations? Or do both of these processes occur in a vicious cycle wherein empathically challenged moms are more likely to divorce and thereby precipitate the kinds of separations that increasingly limit their ability to understand their children's thoughts and feelings?

Unfortunately, we can't decide between these alternative interpretations on the basis of the single study that Crosby has reported. The mothers' empathy may come first and contribute to their children's self-esteem; or the children's self-esteem may come first and contribute to the open expression of feelings that promotes the mothers' empathy. One thing is clear, however: Crosby's study breaks new ground in suggesting that empathic accuracy plays an important role in the mother-child relationship. Although it is still too early to claim that empathically accurate parents contribute more to their children's self-esteem than less accurate parents do, the results of Crosby's study suggest that they might. Her pioneering work should encourage other researchers to try to replicate and clarify the meaning of her findings.

❖　❖　❖

Are empathically accurate people better friends? Better dating partners? Better marriage partners? According to the results of the relevant research, the answers to these questions are not simple and straightforward, but more subtle and complex. The reason for this complexity is that greater empathic accuracy, though usually beneficial over the long-term period in which relationships develop, can be either helpful or harmful at any particular point in the relationship. And, as we have seen in chapters 8, 9, and 10, whether increased empathic accuracy helps or hurts relationships "in the moment" depends both on how it is used and on the context in which it is applied.

Obviously, for a relationship to even begin, the participants must achieve at least a modicum of empathic accuracy. If empathic accuracy were totally lacking in both partners, the most they could do is to emit noises and generate additional behaviors in each other's presence. They could not, in this case, achieve *intersubjectivity*—a shared, common ground understanding—and they would therefore fail to have a human relationship in any usual sense of the term. They might as well be department store mannequins for all the "transpersonal meaning" that would get exchanged.

And if it is true that a modicum of empathic accuracy is needed for a relationship to begin at all, it is also true that increased empathic accuracy is necessary for the relationship to develop and progress over time. As the research findings in chapter 5 suggest, people make the transition from being strangers to being intimates by getting to know each other "from the inside." This process requires the partners to spend time together; to establish common ground; to share their more intimate thoughts, feelings, and perceptions with each other; and to recall this information in order to more effectively "read" each other's unexpressed thoughts and feelings. Through this process, greater empathic accuracy helps to change and redefine the partners' relationship in a way that typically makes it better over an extended period of time—turning strangers into friends and acquaintances into intimates.

Things are not nearly so simple or straightforward, however, at any particular moment in the partners' relationship. For as Jeff Simpson and I have proposed in our theoretical model on page 238 (fig. 9.1), greater empathic accuracy does not always make the relationship better—it sometimes makes it worse. More specifically, the model predicts that when our partner's thoughts and feelings are benign and carry little or no threat to our relationship, greater empathic accuracy should make the relationship better. However, when our partner's thoughts and feelings are distressing and relationship-threatening, greater empathic accuracy should make the relationship worse.

Perhaps the clearest support for these contrasting predictions is found in a study of nearly 100 married couples that Jeff Simpson, Minda Oriña, and I conducted in the Bryan-College Station area of south central Texas. In this study, the members of each couple came to our lab, where they were separated and asked to fill out some self-report questionnaires that included a measure of how close they felt to their partner. The two spouses were then brought back together and were videotaped for 7 to 10 minutes as they attempted to resolve an existing problem in their marriage. Following this discussion, the spouses were separated again and asked to independently view a videotape of their interaction—first to record the specific thoughts and feelings they remembered having experienced, and then to infer their partner's thoughts and feelings. As soon as the empathic inference task had been completed, both partners were again asked to rate how close they felt to their partner on the same type of measure they had completed at the beginning of the session.

Consistent with the predictions of the empathic accuracy model, when the partner's actual thoughts and feelings were relationship-threatening (as rated by both the partners themselves and by outside observers), greater empathic accuracy on the part of the perceiver was associated with the extent to which the perceiver *felt less close* to the partner at the end of the session than they had at the beginning. However, when the partner's actual thoughts and feelings were nonthreatening, greater empathic accuracy on the part of the perceiver was associated with the extent to which the perceiver *felt closer* to the partner at the end of the session than at the beginning. This pattern of results showed, just as we had predicted, that greater empathic accuracy does not always benefit people's relationships. Temporarily at least, it hurt the spouses' relationships in the first case, though it helped them in the second.

Remember, however, that not all perceivers are equally likely to be affected by their partners' relationship-threatening thoughts and feelings. According to the results of the study by Simpson, Ickes, and Grich (described in chapter 10), women who score high on the anxious attachment dimension are particularly likely to make accurate inferences about their partners' relationship-threatening thoughts and feelings. They are also particularly likely to feel threatened, upset, jealous, and less close to their partners as a result. On the other hand, women who score high on the avoidant attachment dimension seem to go out of their way to *avoid* inferring their partners' relationship-threatening thoughts and feelings, presumably to spare themselves some of the personal and relational distress that might otherwise occur.

So far, we have considered how the perceiver's empathic accuracy can result in injury to the perceiver herself. But we should also consider how the perceiver's empathic accuracy can be used to injure the perceiver's interaction partner. Although the theoretical model presented in chapter 9 does not address this latter possibility, it represents another important way that the perceiver's empathic accuracy can hurt the relationship. When partners discuss and debate their differences, as they did in the married couples study described above, they often use their empathic accuracy to gain new insights about "which buttons they can push" if they ever feel the need to hurt or upset each other. With the aid of these insights, perceivers can determine where their partners are most vulnerable and then attack these vulnerabilities if they choose to do so.

Some perceivers will choose to do so a lot—others, very little. As I noted at the end of chapter 10, some people, like the character of Martha in Edward Albee's play *Who's Afraid of Virginia Woolf*, will miss few opportunities to push their partners' buttons in just this way, torturing their partners with the cruel and unusual accuracy of their empathic inferences. What motivates these people will vary greatly from one person to the next: a sadistic personality, low impulse control, dislike for the partner, the desire for revenge, an appetite for conflict—the list can go on and on. By the same token, there is a similar diversity in the factors that motivate people who consistently *refrain* from injuring their partners in this way: an altruistic personality, high impulse control, the desire for harmony, an aversion to conflict, and so on.

There is little doubt, however, that such individual differences do exist. Although I don't know of any hard data to support this assertion, I suspect that some compelling evidence for "serial spousal button-pushing" could be gleaned from police reports of the events that precipitate a certain category of domestic violence calls. At the other end of this dimension, there are cases like the man who informed me in an e-mail message that "my wife and I are somewhat unique in that we have been married some 24 years and have never had an argument. That is not to say that she and I always agree but we simply choose not to argue when we have a difference of opinion." I suggest that, after 24 years of marriage, it is not that these partners don't know where each other's buttons are. It is just that they choose not to push them.

To summarize, the results of a number of studies have revealed that empathic accuracy can sometimes help, but at other times hurt, close relationships. And on those occasions when it hurts, the injury can be suffered not only by the *perceiver* who infers the partner's hurtful thoughts and feelings, but also by the *partner* who winds up getting punished by the perceiver's blunt empathic insights. Empathic accuracy can therefore affect our relationships in complicated ways. Given these complications, I propose that that the available research findings suggest five implications for improving the quality of our close relationships.

First, we must acknowledge the importance of empathic accuracy in defining the very nature of our relationships with others. Friends and intimates understand each other better than strangers do, and if relationships are to progress beyond their starting point, the partners' ability to "read" each other must inevitably increase. If people don't take the time to talk face-to-face, to share their respective thoughts and feelings, and to construct an intersubjective reality that provides a framework for integrating their individual realities, their relationship will always remain undeveloped and superficial.

Second, the complexity of the research findings suggests that we need to get beyond simplistic aphorisms such as "If we only understood each other better, we would all get along together better." When interpersonal differences are correctly perceived as irreconcilable, greater understanding may not help things at all; it may simply increase the level of tension and frustration for everyone concerned. Although it is important to understand what the relevant differences are and why they exist, increased understanding by itself is often insufficient to make the relationship better. In some cases, it actually makes things worse. In the absence of a genuine mutual desire to improve the quality of the relationship, understanding can be hollow and ineffective. So we shouldn't make a fetish out of increased understanding; it is probably not as important as love and commitment to the success of our intimate relationships.

Third, we should also acknowledge that even (and perhaps especially) in our most intimate relationships, there are some things we are probably better off *not* knowing. With the benefit of hindsight, I think most people now agree that the 1960s humanist-hippie ideal of expressing all of one's thoughts and feelings openly and completely ("letting it all hang out") was a naïve and unrealistic one that left a lot of broken relationships in its wake. There are some things that your relationship partners think and feel that you would be hurt and upset to discover, just as there are other things that *you* think and feel that *they* would be hurt and upset to discover. Certain of these things are important enough that they have to be confronted anyway, but many of them are not. In love, as in war, discretion may be the better part of valor; and there is no shame, and some credit, in going out of your way to avoid causing yourself and others unnecessary pain.

Fourth, it is important to know when to be empathically accurate and when not to be. As Jeff Simpson, Minda Oriña, and I have noted elsewhere, accurately "reading" your partner in order to anticipate a need, avert a conflict, or keep a small problem from escalating into a large one is a healthy and adaptive way to use your everyday mind reading skill. On the other hand, accurately "reading" your partner in order to feed your jealousy, extort an unpleasant truth, or pick at the scab of an emotional wound that would be better left alone is an unhealthy and maladaptive way to use this ability. Often, what separates the wise and experienced couples from the foolish and inexperienced ones is this higher-level sense of *discretion*: of knowing when to get in your partner's head and when to stay out of it. Once again, empathic accuracy by itself is not sufficient to guarantee that a relationship will work well—the sense of discretion is also vitally important.

Fifth, there are, of course, many cases in which the problem really *is* a lack of understanding on the part of one or both partners. As we saw in chapter 8, partners' misunderstandings are often innocent and unmotivated, resulting from the different cognitive frames that they are applying to what is ostensibly the "same" situation. But while these innocent misunderstandings are often easily corrected by supplying one's partner with the intended cognitive frame, more pernicious misunderstandings—those resulting from hidden agendas and the "empathic stalemates" of irreconcilable cognitive frames—are not. In fact, applying one's empathic accuracy to uncover a partner's hidden agenda or unwillingness to compromise will usually make the relationship worse in the short run, though confronting these hard truths is often a necessary part of deciding what direction the relationship should take in the future.

To this list of practical implications, I would like to add a final speculation. It appears that four ingredients may provide the basic recipe for success in one's close relationships: (1) enough *empathic accuracy* for the relationship to progress to the stage of friendship or intimacy; (2) enough *love and commitment* to sustain the relationship in the face of various challenges and threats; (3) enough *discretion* to allow the partners to share some things and keep other things to themselves; (4) and enough *courage* to confront the ugly truths in the relationship that the partners cannot afford to avoid, overlook, or ignore. As with most recipes, people will differ in the proportions of these ingredients that they consider ideal. On the other hand, the entire recipe is likely to fail if any one of these ingredients is missing.

What practical implications does the research on empathic accuracy have for improving the performance of psychotherapists? Clearly, the most general implications involve ways to improve the selection and training of psychotherapists. More specific implications concern the kinds of cues that therapists should attend to most closely during their therapy sessions, and the kinds of pitfalls they should avoid in working with particular patient types—for example, distressed marriage partners, people who have "suspicious minds," aggressive-abusive men, and women who display a high level of anxious attachment.

The most important practical implication of our empathic accuracy research is that it provides a reliable method for measuring people's performance as everyday mind readers. Some of the most compelling evidence for this claim is found in the results of the 1995 study by Carol Marangoni and her colleagues. In that study, 80 undergraduate men and women attempted to infer the actual thoughts and feelings reported by each of three female clients who had been videotaped during their respective sessions with a male, client-centered therapist. The results of the study showed that there were reliable individual differences in the perceivers' empathic accuracy—with some perceivers being consistently good, other perceivers being consistently average, and still other perceivers being consistently poor at inferring the specific thoughts and feelings of the female clients.

This performance-based measure of empathic accuracy has three important advantages. First, it does not rely on people's self-reported (and often erroneous) beliefs about how empathically accurate they are; it assesses this ability directly with standard stimulus videotapes. Second, because people's performance on this measure has proved to be consistent across the different target persons who appear on the videotapes (particularly when the number of empathic inferences is large), we can use the data to compute an overall, cross-target empathic accuracy score for each of the perceivers we test. Third, because this overall measure has proved to be statistically reliable, we can use it to meaningfully rank and compare the perceivers in terms of their general proficiency as everyday mind readers.

In practical terms, this means that we can distinguish the people who are empathically skilled from those who are empathically challenged, and then use this information as a selection criterion. So instead of selecting aspiring psychotherapists (students who have applied for advanced training as clinical psychologists, counseling psychologists, or psychiatrists) solely on the basis of their undergraduate grade-point averages and their scores on the Graduate Record Exam, we could also require them to complete a standard empathic accuracy performance test. The results of this test could then be used, along with the GPA and GRE data, to help selection committees decide which students to admit to graduate schools and other professional programs that train aspiring counselors and psychotherapists.

This type of alternative selection procedure would inevitably raise some important but as-yet-unanswered questions. One might ask, for example, "What kinds of applicants make the best psychotherapists—those with exceptionally high grades and GRE scores but below-average empathic accuracy, or those with only moderately high grades and GRE scores but above-average empathic accuracy?" I won't pretend that I know the answer to this question, or to a related one such as "Other things (like GPA and GRE scores) being equal, are we better off selecting the more empathically accurate candidate over the less-accurate one?" Still, I think there are two good reasons for believing that the candidates' empathic accuracy might prove to be a uniquely valid predictor of their future on-the-job performance as practicing psychotherapists.

First, empathic accuracy has long been regarded as one of the most important criteria for success as a psychotherapist. Writing nearly 50 years ago, Carl Rogers identified *accurate empathy* as one of the three "necessary and sufficient facilitative core conditions" for therapeutic change—the other two conditions being the therapist's genuineness and nonjudgmental caring for the client. Many subsequent writers—including Robert Elliot, Arthur Bohart, Leslie Greenberg, Godfrey Barrett-Lennard, Dan Buie, Arnold Goldstein, and Gerald Michaels—have shared Rogers's view that the therapist's empathic accuracy is one of the most important elements in the psychotherapy process. And additional evidence for the perceived importance of empathic accuracy can be found in the repeated attempts of clinical researchers such as Charles Truax, Robert Carkhuff, and Nathan Kagan to measure this elusive capacity.

Second, the available research findings support the belief of clinical researchers and practitioners by showing that the therapist's empathy really does play an important role in successful psychotherapy outcomes. In 2001, clinical psychologists Leslie Greenberg, Jeanne Watson, Robert Elliot, and Arthur Bohart published their summary of the results of 47 studies that examined "the empathy-outcome association" during the 39-year period from 1961 to 2000. They reported that, across this set of studies involving more than 3,000 clients, the therapist's empathy emerged as one of the strongest single predictors of good treatment outcomes. The empathy-outcome association was the strongest when the clients rated their therapists' empathy by reporting the extent to which they *felt understood*, but it was also significant when therapist empathy was rated by outside observers or by the therapists themselves.

Clearly, a major advantage of our empathic accuracy research is that it offers another, more objective way to measure the therapist's empathy—by assessing how accurately the therapist can infer the actual, reported thoughts and feelings of clients who appear in a set of standard videotapes. And note that we can use such tapes not only to assess people's empathic accuracy but also to train them to become more empathically accurate. Recall that in the study of "amateur psychotherapists" conducted by Carol Marangoni and her colleagues (see chapter 5), the perceivers who received feedback about the client's actual thoughts and feelings during the middle portion of each tape displayed greater empathic accuracy by the end of the tape than did the perceivers in the no-feedback condition. Moreover, this form of empathy training appeared to be highly efficient, in that relatively few feedback trials were required to produce this significant increase (an estimated 10 percent overall improvement) in the perceivers' empathic accuracy scores.

The obvious practical implication of this finding is that similar feedback training could be used to improve the empathic skills of students who are enrolled in graduate or professional programs in psychiatry, social work, or clinical and counseling psychology. Once the students have been admitted to these programs, based in part on an assessment of their empathic accuracy by means of standard stimulus tapes, their empathic skills could be further enhanced by subsequent training with additional tapes in which feedback about the clients' actual thoughts and feelings is provided. I believe that this two-step selection and training process could be effective in producing counselors and psychotherapists who are already highly empathic by the time they are ready to leave graduate school and begin their own clinical practices. More research is needed, however, to see if this belief is justified.

In addition to the general benefits I have just discussed, the research on empathic accuracy may offer psychotherapists the benefits of more specific insights as well. For example, the findings from one study suggest that therapists should pay more attention to what their clients say than to the clients' nonverbal behavior. This was the study, first described in chapter 8, in which Randy Gesn and I asked the participants to infer the thoughts and feelings of highly edited versions of the psychotherapy session stimulus tapes that Carol Marangoni had recorded for her dissertation research. There is an aspect of this study that I haven't told you about yet; and it concerns the different versions of the stimulus tapes that Randy created in order to vary systematically the "information channels" that different participants received.

To see which information channel might contribute the most to the perceivers' empathic accuracy, Randy created different versions of the stimulus tapes for each of three different channel conditions. First, there was a *video and audio condition*, in which the clients on the tapes could be both clearly seen and clearly heard. Second, there was a *video and filtered audio condition*, in which the clients could be seen but their words could not be understood because their speech had been electronically filtered so that only the paralinguistic cues (inflection, tone of voice, loudness, etc.) remained. Third, there was an *audio only condition* in which the clients' video images did not appear on the blank TV monitor but their conversation with the therapist was clearly audible.

In which of these conditions would you expect the perceivers' average empathic accuracy scores to be the highest? If you chose the video-and-audio condition, congratulate yourself on being right: the average empathic accuracy score was indeed the highest in this condition, at 34.1%. But continue making your predictions: How much would the lack of visual information impair the empathic accuracy of the participants in the audio-only condition, in comparison to those in the video-and-audio condition? And how much would the unintelligible words impair the empathic accuracy of the participants in the video-and-filtered-audio condition, in comparison to those in the video-and-audio condition?

Here is where the results may surprise you. There was only a small drop in empathic accuracy in the audio-only condition, where the participants' average score of 32.7% was only negligibly less than the 34.1% that we found in the video-and-audio condition. So taking away the visual stuff—all of the nonverbal information that includes the clients' facial expressions, hand gestures, body postures, and so on—did little if anything to impair the perceivers' empathic accuracy, *as long as they could clearly hear everything that the client and therapist said to each other*. On the other hand, when the clients' words were rendered unintelligible in the video-and-filtered-audio condition, the perceivers' average empathic score of 13.9% was less than half of those found in the other two channel conditions, *despite the fact that virtually all of the relevant visual and paralinguistic information was readily available*.

The lesson here is simple: When it comes to our everyday mind reading ability, words matter. In the Gesn and Ickes study, the clients' words mattered so much that eliminating the intelligibility of these words reduced empathic accuracy by more than half, whereas eliminating the video image but leaving the words intact reduced empathic accuracy scarcely at all.

But this lesson is not *just* simple; in some quarters, it is actually heretical. During the 1970s, many writers clamored to get aboard an earlier bandwagon than the one launched by Daniel Goleman in the 1990s. This was the bandwagon of nonverbal behavior, from which it was trumpeted that the nonverbal information provided by facial expressions and other body movements was generally more important than verbal information in helping us to infer a person's

underlying thoughts and feelings. The psychologists Ray Birdwhistell and Albert Mehrabian were among the first to make this
claim—a claim that was later presented as fact by writers such as
Dale Leathers (". . . *nonverbal, not verbal, factors are the major
determinants of meaning in the interpersonal context*") and Mary
Ritchie Key (*"In some way that we don't understand completely
yet, the Nonverbal Act seems to be more important in interpersonal
relationships than language itself"*). Even respected clinical
researchers such as Albert Scheflen were eager to climb aboard the
nonverbal behavior bandwagon, encouraging psychotherapists to
pay more attention to what their clients were doing and to be less
preoccupied with what their clients were saying. In retrospect, it is
striking how the hyping of nonverbal behavior over verbal behavior
in the 1970s foreshadows the hyping of EQ over IQ in the 1990s.

Was this emphasis on nonverbal behavior misplaced? Yes and
no. Given the results of the Gesn and Ickes study, I think that—as
a general rule—empathic accuracy really does depend more on
what clients say during therapy sessions than on their nonverbal
behavior. And I suggest that what applies inside the consulting
room applies outside of it as well: our everyday mind reading at
home, at work, and in most other contexts is based more on what
other people say than on what they do. Certainly, there are some
contexts (making love, for example, or dealing with a person who
can't or won't speak) in which actions count much more heavily
than words. However, in most of our everyday life situations, I
would argue that just the opposite is true.

But let's see what you think. To help you decide whether you
find this argument plausible or not, I would like you to indulge me
by considering the results of the following thought experiment.
Let's suppose that, back in 1876, a prescient inventor named
Alexander Graham Pixel developed the telemime (a device for
transmitting the images of others without the accompanying
sounds) to compete with Alexander Graham Bell's telephone (a
device for transmitting the sounds of others without the accompa-

nying images). In terms of the sheer number of subscribers, whose technology—Pixel's or Bell's—do you think would have won the battle in the marketplace?

We'll never know for sure, of course, but I would place my bets with Bell. Why? Because, generally speaking, we really *do* seem to get more useful information about other people's thoughts and feelings from what they say than from what they do nonverbally. (For example, imagine trying to mime your instructions to the house sitter when you leave on vacation. Or to mime your way through two weeks' worth of office gossip when you return.) So, in that sense and in light of the findings from the Gesn and Ickes study, I think the 1970s emphasis on nonverbal behavior was, in retrospect, somewhat misplaced.

In another sense, however, the nonverbal behavior craze was both necessary and appropriate. In the 1970s there was a sudden and ubiquitous awareness—a kind of zeitgeist recognition—that there was more to human social behavior than the exchange of conversation (polite or otherwise): *There was all of this nonverbal behavior going on too!* As social scientists recognized that the study of nonverbal behavior was a new and largely unexplored research frontier in which exciting, career-building discoveries might be made, they jumped aboard the nonverbal behavior bandwagon and drove it at breakneck speed on their "land rush" into the new frontier. And to a large extent, their expectations were fulfilled: many aspects of nonverbal behavior such as eye contact, facial expressions, interpersonal distance, and hand and body movements were shown to play an important role in communicating the thoughts and feelings of the people who displayed them. So, in this sense, the 1970s emphasis on nonverbal behavior was not misplaced at all.

What was wrong with this scenario was not the belief that nonverbal behavior is important; it was the rush to claim that nonverbal behavior is generally *more* important than verbal behavior in conveying a target person's thoughts and feelings. To see if you really believe this claim, assume that—at this very moment—you can irrevocably trade in all of your telephones for telemimes at no additional charge. Would you do it? Okay, not counting the folks who make most of their calls to 1-900 numbers, would you do it? Probably not. Although nonverbal information is undeniably important, to claim that it is generally more important than verbal information in conveying a person's thoughts and feelings is like claiming that we could replace all the words in library books with captionless moving pictures without losing much essential information in the process. Can you imagine what would happen to *Das Kapital? The Brothers Karamazov? Finnegans Wake? Being and Nothingness?*

The conclusion I draw from the Gesn and Ickes study is that words are important because they are generally, though not always, the best and most reliable indicators of the larger and murkier complex of thoughts and feelings to which they direct our attention. Words are important because they suggest as well as state, imply as well as proclaim. When people string their words together into phrases and sentences, the words they use often reveal or betray their underlying thoughts and feelings. Our empathic accuracy therefore depends not only on the words themselves, but also on our ability to "read between the lines." As Leslie Greenberg and her colleagues have expressed it in the context of psychotherapy: "Truly empathic therapists do not parrot clients' words back or reflect only the content of those words; instead, they understand overall goals as well as moment-to-moment experiences, both explicit and implicit. Empathy in part entails capturing the nuances and implications of what people say, and reflecting this back to them for their consideration."

Apart from documenting the importance of the words clients use, what other implications do the research findings on empathic accuracy have for psychotherapists? For one thing, they suggest some pitfalls that psychotherapists should avoid in their attempts to treat the partners in distressed relationships. These pitfalls include: (1) the hazards of forcing partners to more accurately infer each other's relationship-threatening thoughts and feelings when they are not prepared to do so; (2) the instability of relationships involving partners who have an anxious attachment orientation, a pervasive bias to "see" criticism and rejection where none is intended, or a strong motive to acquire relationship-threatening information; and (3) the reluctance of partners who have an avoidant attachment orientation to confront the danger-zone issues in their relationship.

To avoid the first pitfall, the therapist must accept the fact that many relationships are predicated on the partners' routine *avoidance* of each other's relationship-threatening thoughts and feelings. For many couples, the implicit agreement to follow the policy of "don't ask, don't tell" may be the primary reason why their relationship has worked as well as it has. If the therapist fails to appreciate this fact, more harm than good can be accomplished when the partners are pressed to confront their most relationship-threatening issues before they feel capable of doing so. And the risk of this harm (the therapist's intervention evoking the kinds of volatile feelings that could precipitate greater conflict or even divorce) may further increase when the therapist feels obliged to treat the couple within the accelerated timeframe of a few brief sessions that have been authorized by the bureaucracy of a managed care organization. To help minimize this risk, the therapist who wants to foster greater empathy in one or both partners should begin by having them discuss relatively benign, non-threatening issues, and then gradually introduce more relationship-threatening issues only when the partners themselves feel ready to confront them.

To avoid the second pitfall, the therapist must realize that some people are predisposed to "look for trouble" in their intimate relationships, and that their readiness to confront relationship-threatening issues may be part of the problem rather than part of the solution. People in this category can include suspicious partners who have a strong motive to acquire relationship-threatening information; aggressive-abusive men who have a pervasive bias to "see" criticism and rejection in their wives' thoughts and feelings; and women with an anxious attachment orientation, who act as if they are compelled to know their husbands' relationship-threatening thoughts and feelings (see chapter 10). Although different interventions may be required in each case, the therapist should learn to recognize these predispositions to "look for trouble" and make them a focus of the therapy.

To avoid the third pitfall, the therapist must realize that some people are so motivated to *avoid* confronting the danger-zone issues in their relationships that they will appear not to care about a relationship which they actually value greatly. Perceiving such clients as stubborn, uncooperative, or uncaring can blind the therapist to the reality of a fearful, threatened person who needs continued reassurance rather than blunt confrontation.

What other professionals might benefit from the research on empathic accuracy? The answer is any of them whose livelihoods depend on their everyday mind reading skills. They can include teachers, trial attorneys, politicians and diplomats, health care professionals, managers, negotiators, and salespeople. On the other hand, they can also include professional pimps, prostitutes, grifters, and con artists. Because empathic accuracy can be used to harm as well as to help, it can be as essential to the sadism of a professional torturer as it is to the altruism of a professional nurse. Used for good, however, empathic accuracy can help to enlighten minds, enact progressive legislation, alleviate suffering, increase productivity, and bring buyers and sellers together.

As in the case of psychotherapy, there are many other professions in which our procedure for assessing empathic accuracy could be used to select promising trainees. In each of these cases, the kinds of videotapes used as standard stimulus materials would be specific to the profession. Apprentice teachers, for example, might be required to infer the thoughts and feelings of grade school children whose interactions were videotaped. Fledgling trial lawyers might infer the thoughts and feelings of potential and actual jury members. Aspiring politicians might infer the thoughts and feelings of the members of different constituent groups. Medical students might infer the thoughts and feelings of patients who are being interviewed about their symptoms. Aspiring managers might infer the thoughts and feelings of rank-and-file employees; aspiring negotiators, the thoughts and feelings of business rivals; and aspiring salespersons, the thoughts and feelings of customers who were videotaped on the sales floor while they considered making a major purchase.

The advantage of using such targeted assessment procedures should be obvious. Other things being equal, the education majors who have good insight into children's thoughts and feelings should make better grade school teachers than the ones who don't. Similarly, the interns who can accurately infer patients' thoughts and feelings should make better attending physicians than the ones who can't. The MBA students who can accurately "read" employees' thoughts and feelings should make better managers than their less-accurate counterparts. And so on. Because training people for professional positions is both costly and time-consuming, it makes good economic sense to want to select those applicants who already demonstrate an above-average ability to understand the kinds of people they will be working with every day.

By the same token, it also makes good economic sense to want to further develop the empathic skills of the professionals in each of these domains. And, as in the case of the psychotherapy example cited above, it should be possible to create feedback training videotapes for other professions in which immediate, veridical feedback is provided about the target persons' actual thoughts and feelings. With the aid of these tapes, teachers might learn to better understand their students; politicians to better understand their constituents; doctors to better understand their patients; managers to better understand their employees; salespersons to better understand their customers; and so on. Although it is not yet known how much improvement could be expected through the use of this technique, or how general and enduring its effects would be, I think the available research findings are promising enough to warrant at least a cautious optimism about the effectiveness of applying this form of empathy training in the workplace.

We must remember, however, that empathic accuracy has a dark side as well. The same procedures that could help us select and train more empathically accurate teachers, physicians, managers, and diplomats could also be used to help select and train more empathically accurate criminals and con artists at all levels of society—from the exploitive politician to the opportunistic beggar. These procedures might be used to accomplish great good, but they might also be used to accomplish great harm. When applied by saints, empathic accuracy can increase harmony, relieve suffering, and promote the general welfare. When applied by sinners, empathic accuracy can produce just the opposite effects. It must therefore be used wisely, with that higher-order sense of discretion that I have emphasized throughout this chapter.

SOURCES FOR CHAPTER 11

Barrett-Lennard, Godfrey T. "The Empathy Cycle: Refinement of a Nuclear Concept." *Journal of Counseling Psychology* 28 (1981): 91–100.
———. "The Phases and Focus of Empathy." *British Journal of Medical Psychology* 66 (1993): 3–14.
Birdwhistell, Ray. *Kinesics and Context.* Philadelphia: University of Pennsylvania Press, 1970, p. 158.
Bohart, Arthur C., and Leslie S. Greenberg, eds. *Empathy Reconsidered: New Directions in Psychotherapy.* Washington, D.C.: American Psychological Association, 1997.

Bohart, Arthur C., Robert Elliot, Leslie S. Greenberg, and Jeanne C. Watson. "Empathy." In *Psychotherapy Relationships That Work: Therapist Contributions and Responsiveness to Patients*, edited by John C. Norcross. New York: Oxford University Press, 2002.

Buie, Dan H. "Empathy: Its Nature and Limitations." *Journal of the American Psychoanalytic Association* 29 (1981): 281–307.

Crosby, Laura. "The Relation of Maternal Empathic Accuracy to the Development of Self Concept." Ph.D. diss., The Fielding Institute, Santa Barbara, California, 2002.

Elliot, Robert. "Research on the Effectiveness of Humanistic Therapies: A Meta-Analysis." In *Handbook of Research and Practice in Humanistic Psychotherapy*, edited by David J. Cain and Julius Seeman. Washington, D.C.: American Psychological Association, 2001, pp. 57–82.

Fast, Julius. *Body Language*. New York: Pocket Books, 1971.

Gardner, Howard. *Frames of Mind: The Theory of Multiple Intelligences*. New York: Basic Books, 1983.

Gesn, Paul R., and William Ickes. "The Development of Meaning Contexts for Empathic Accuracy: Channel and Sequence Effects." *Journal of Personality and Social Psychology* 77 (1999): 746–61.

Goldstein, Arnold P., and Gerald Y. Michaels. *Empathy: Development, Training and Consequences*. Hillsdale, N.J.: Erlbaum, 1985.

Goleman, Daniel. *Emotional Intelligence: Why It Can Matter More than IQ*. New York: Bantam Books, 1995.

———. *Working with Emotional Intelligence*. New York: Bantam Books, 1998.

———. "What Makes a Leader?" *Harvard Business Review* 76 (1998): 93–102.

Greenberg, Leslie S., Jeanne C. Watson, Robert Elliot, and Arthur C. Bohart. "Empathy." *Psychotherapy: Theory, Research, Practice, Training* 38 (2001): 380–84.

Ickes, William, Carol Marangoni, and Stella Garcia. "Studying Empathic Accuracy in a Clinically Relevant Context." In *Empathic Accuracy*, edited by William Ickes. New York: Guilford Press, 1997, pp. 282–310.

Kagan, Nathan. *Interpersonal Process Recall*. East Lansing: Michigan State University Press, 1977.

Key, Mary Ritchie. *Paralanguage and Kinesics (Nonverbal Communication)*. The Scarecrow Press, 1975, p. 20.

Leathers, Dale G. *Nonverbal Communication Systems*. Boston: Allyn and Bacon, 1978, p. 4.

Marangoni, Carol, Stella Garcia, William Ickes, and Gary Teng. "Empathic Accuracy in a Clinically Relevant Setting." *Journal of Personality and Social Psychology* 68 (1995): 854–69.

Mayer, John D. "A Field Guide to Emotional Intelligence." In *Emotional Intelligence in Everyday Life: A Scientific Inquiry*, edited by Joseph Ciarrochi, Joseph P. Forgas, and John D. Mayer. Philadelphia: Psychology Press, 2001, pp. 3–24.

Mayer, John D., and Peter Salovey. "What Is Emotional Intelligence?" In *Emotional Development and Emotional Intelligence*, edited by Peter Salovey and David J. Sluyter. New York: Basic Books, 1997, pp. 3–31.

Mehrabian, Albert. "Communication without Words." *Psychology Today* 2 (1968): 51–52.

Mehrabian, Albert, and Susan R. Ferris. "Inference of Attitudes from Nonverbal Communication in Two Channels." *Journal of Consulting Psychology* 31 (1967): 248–52.

Salovey, Peter, and John D. Mayer. "Emotional Intelligence." *Imagination, Cognition, and Personality* 9 (1990): 185–211.

Scheflen, Albert E. *How Behavior Means*. New York: Doubleday, 1974.

Simpson, Jeffry A., William Ickes, and Tami Blackstone. "When the Head Protects the Heart: Empathic Accuracy in Dating Relationships." *Journal of Personality and Social Psychology* 69 (1995): 629–41.

Simpson, Jeffry A., William Ickes, and Minda Oriña. "Empathic Accuracy and Preemptive Relationship Maintenance." In *Close Romantic Relationships: Maintenance and Enhancement,* edited by John H. Harvey and Amy Wenzel. Mahwah, N.J.: Erlbaum, 2001, pp. 27–46.

Simpson, Jeffry A., Minda Oriña, and William Ickes. "When Accuracy Hurts, and When It Helps: A Test of the Empathic Accuracy Model in Marital Interactions." *Journal of Personality and Social Psychology*. Forthcoming.

Titchener, Edward B. *Lectures on the Experimental Psychology of the Thought-Processes*. © 1909. Reprint, New York: Arno Press, 1973, p. 21.

Truax, Charles B., Robert R. Carkhuff. *Toward Effective Counseling and Psychotherapy: Training and Practice*. Chicago: Aldine, 1967.

twelve
THE SIXTH
SENSE

Richard Francis Burton, that master of intrusiveness, was the originator of the term that we now call ESP. This, at least, is the view of his biographer, Edward Rice, who claimed that the ESP acronym has it origin in Burton's phase "extra-sensuous perception."

Richard Burton did not believe in an afterlife, but he clearly did believe in a "sixth sense." Whether he consistently regarded it as supernatural, however, is a matter to be debated. As a young man, Burton developed an interest in psychic phenomena that began during his earliest travels in India. This interest was further nurtured following his return to England in 1849 by the spiritualist movement that was then in vogue. According to Fawn Brodie:

> Like almost everyone in the British upper classes, the Burtons toyed with spiritualism, then fashionable, and took part in numerous séances. Burton was fascinated by the table rappings and

related phenomena, but suspected fakery. . . . But he had seen too much evidence of clairvoyance, somnambulism, hypnosis, and occult phenomena associated with what he called the "Jogis" in India, to dismiss the whole movement as based entirely on fraud.

In a speech before the British National Association of Spiritualists . . . he said that he believed perception to be possible without the ordinary channels of the senses, but went on bluntly: "The supernatural is the natural misunderstood or improperly understood . . ."

A similar description of Burton was offered by Byron Farwell, another of his biographers. Like Brodie, Farwell noted that Burton "believed in extrasensory perception and a sixth sense." Evidence of Burton's equivocation is again suggested, however, by a reference in one of his unpublished books to "that 'sixth sense' developed by the life-long habit of observation." In this context, the term 'sixth sense' seems to refer to a natural ability, not a supernatural one.

But if Richard Burton found it difficult to decide whether the sixth sense should be regarded as a natural or as a supernatural phenomenon, he was in excellent company. According to psychologists Leonard Zusne and Warren Jones, many of the best minds of Burton's time struggled with a similar conflict "between advancing science, abetted by the newly promulgated theory of evolution, and traditional religion . . ."

They felt the conflict between the monistic view of humans as organisms and the dualistic view of humans as persons in a particularly acute manner because these two views were nearly equally balanced in them. . . . To those who played the most significant roles in the work of the SPR [Society for Psychical Research], psychical research was not just an avocation. . . . It was something they had to do as part of their quest for answers to the paradoxes posed by the two views of humanity, and the motivating force came from the near-equal strength of these two views in them. They could have accepted either the scientific or the religious view, but as soon as they began to lean toward one, the other made itself felt. . . .

Frederic Myers, one of the founders of the Society for Psychical Research, was the first person to introduce the term "telepathy" at the Society's meeting in London in December 1882. Telepathy, he said, was intended "to cover all cases of impression received at a distance without the normal operation of the recognized sense organs." It is interesting that Myers's definition did not specify that the impressions in question had to emanate from another mind or consciousness. In subsequent usage, however, the word telepathy was commonly assumed to imply a supernatural or paranormal connection with some other mind —either that of a living person or that of a disembodied spirit.

According to the literary scholar Nicholas Royle, the concept of telepathy "did not just appear from nowhere." It is obviously rooted in the spiritualist movement and the first wave of research on psychic phenomena that took place during the second half of the nineteenth century. But, as Royle has argued, it had a less obvious, though no less important, connection to other emerging "tele-phenomena." Indeed, "it is part of the establishment of tele-culture in general."

> It is necessarily related to other nineteenth-century forms of communication from a distance through new and often invisible channels, including . . . telegraphy, photography, the telephone and gramophone. It is thus part of a culture which is still in the process of being articulated, and in this respect perhaps the question 'Do you believe in telepathy?' need not be regarded as categorically essentially distinguishable from questions such as, 'Do you believe in the telephone?' or 'Do you believe in television?'

From this perspective, it is not surprising that the concept of telepathy had such widespread and immediate appeal. If disembodied words could be transmitted in an instant across vast distances, why couldn't thoughts and other "psychic impressions" be transmitted in an analogous manner? Indeed, Sigmund Freud referred explicitly to this analogy when, a few decades later, he speculated that thought-transference might be regarded as "a psychical counterpart to wireless telegraphy."

What made the notion of telepathy particularly appealing was that it offered the promise of connecting the technological future with the spiritual past. To the millions of people whose religious beliefs were intensely challenged by the scientific theories of Charles Darwin and his contemporaries, telepathy appeared to be a fundamental bridging concept. Ideally, it could be used to integrate the new magic of science with the old magic of religion, thereby reconciling the natural with the supernatural and the physical with the metaphysical.

This integration was not readily achieved, of course, as Burton and many others of his generation eventually acknowledged. And even now, over 120 years after the founding of the Society for Psychical Research, the question of whether telepathic communication really exists is still in dispute.

On the one hand are the inveterate skeptics—people such as Charles Hansel and James Randi. They have repeatedly challenged the validity of studies purporting to have found evidence for ESP, and they have documented many instances in which the results could be attributed to other factors, including cheating, fraud, collusion, and insufficient experimental controls. On the other hand are the credulous enthusiasts. They take it for granted that ESP exists; they believe the apparently supportive research findings; and they vigorously resist any skeptics' attempts to "explain it all away."

Occupying the middle ground between these two positions are people whose own skeptical need to be convinced is balanced by a genuine open-mindedness. Their position is represented by a current generation of scientists who seek to investigate ESP and other anomalous experiences without bias or prejudice, using the most valid and defensible methods available. Surveying the studies conducted by these scientists, respected scholars such as Daryl Bem, Charles Honorton, Ray Hyman, and Robert Rosenthal have carefully reviewed the results. And the general consensus of these reviewers is that it is difficult to explain away all of the evidence for extrasensory perception. Although the existence of ESP has not been definitively proved, it has not been definitively discredited either.

If we allow, then, for the possibility that extrasensory perception might actually exist, is it reasonable to believe that an element of telepathy underlies our own everyday mind reading? The answer to that question depends, of course, on what one accepts as reasonable grounds for subscribing to such a belief. My own opinion, based on the current scientific data, is that there is no compelling evidence for the role of telepathy in empathic accuracy. Like Burton, I believe in a "sixth sense." But, also like Burton, I believe that this sixth sense is a natural, rather than a supernatural, phenomenon. In the rest of this chapter, I will explain why I have come to subscribe to these beliefs.

If telepathy *were* to play a role in our everyday mind reading, where should its influence be most evident? According to folklore, anecdotal reports, and speculation extending back at least 150 years, its influence should be most evident in twins. There is a long tradition of belief that twins have a special psychic and empathic affinity with each other, and that instances of telepathic communication are especially likely to occur in twins.

Guy Lyon Playfair, in his review of the research on this topic, has identified Alexandre Dumas's novel *The Corsican Brothers* (1844) as containing what is "possibly the earliest reference in modern times to the idea that twins can communicate across space." Scientific interest in this idea began to emerge about half a century later. In 1883, Francis Galton, one of the most eminent scientists of his day and a cousin of Charles Darwin, estimated that about one-third of twin pairs experienced some form of telepathy. This estimate was based on a number of anecdotal cases that Galton had compiled. Similar anecdotal cases were subsequently reported, first by Edmund Gurney, Frederic Myers, and Frank Podmore in 1886, and later by Horatio Newman in 1942.

A couple of decades later, Robert Sommer, Humphry Osmond, and Lucille Pancyr, three Toronto-based psychologists, conducted structured interviews with fourteen pairs of identical twins and seven pairs of same-sex fraternal twins. Consistent with Galton's much earlier estimate, they found that about a third of the twins reported having had telepathy-like experiences. Some of the examples they cited (statements made by one of the twins) suggest extrasensory perception:

> "Yes, I felt that I could communicate thoughts, perhaps through telepathy. For example, when my twin was about to do something he shouldn't, I could communicate by thoughts rather than tell him directly."
>
> "Yes, sometimes if she's thinking of me, I can communicate with her."
>
> "I always know her mood without talking to her or even seeing her."
>
> "Once when Carol was in Saskatoon and I was in Vancouver, I had the vague feeling that something was wrong. I didn't know who it was at first, then I realized it was Carol, and I almost phoned home. She was ill, although not seriously."

The majority of the examples, however, seem to have less to do with telepathy than with an empathic affinity that derives from applying an interpretive frame that is very similar to one that the other twin would use in a particular situation:

> "Her decisions are so similar to my own. Questions asked by my twin are often identical to those asked by me."
>
> "I can communicate ideas with a minimum of explanation. I can also tell how my twin was feeling even when my father couldn't. We often managed to pick up identical gifts for the

same person even though one of us lives in Ontario, the other in Saskatchewan."

"We both say the same thing at once. In the store if I don't feel like waiting on a customer and I want my brother to, he usually does."

"I have the feeling of riding horseback when watching my twin . . . the feeling is more vivid when she is active."

"Yes, I frequently know when there's something wrong, not specifically though. I feel on edge and unhappy for no reason. I know what she's doing and all the events up to that time, and this is probably why I know how she feels."

For this larger set of examples, telepathy provides neither the most plausible nor the most parsimonious interpretation. A simpler and more straightforward interpretation is that twins are able to understand and even replicate each other's experiences because their interpretive frames are unusually similar. Both kinds of twins—fraternal ("two egg") twins and identical ("one egg") twins—are born at the same time and experience many of the same life events at the same points in their development. This similarity in their age and stage of development should give them a similar vantage point on many commonly experienced life events. It should also help to ensure that twins discuss and share their interpretations of such life events more often than nontwin siblings do. For these reasons, twins might develop interpretive frames that are more similar than those of nontwin siblings whose ages, friendship networks, and current life interests can differ greatly.

Similar interpretive frames might be especially evident in identical twins, who are not only the same age and gender but also have exceptionally similar brains and central nervous systems. Indeed, an unusual similarity in their interpretive frames could account for the finding that identical twins respond more similarly to the items on psychological tests than either fraternal twins or nontwin siblings do. The usual interpretation of this often replicated finding is that identical twins are more similar in their personalities and cognitive abilities than are fraternal or nontwin siblings. But the alternative interpretation should also be considered: that identical twins apply more similar frames when they respond to the items on psychological tests and therefore achieve more similar scores on the tests for that reason.

Of course, both interpretations could be correct; they are not necessarily incommensurable. In fact, the psychologist George Kelly proposed that the crucial element in personality similarity *is* the extent to which two people "frame" or construe the world in similar ways. If Kelly was right about this, then the similarity in people's interpretive frames is potentially confounded with the similarity in their genes, their personalities, and their cognitive abilities.

But before we worry too much about these confounded influences, let's begin by asking whether there is any compelling scientific evidence for extrasensory perception in twins. In my opinion, the answer is no.

This opinion is based primarily on the results of two relevant studies—the first conducted in America by Gary France and Robert Hogan and the second conducted in England by Susan Blackmore and Frances Chamberlain. Although these studies cannot be regarded as definitive (they both used relatively small samples and methods that were good but not perfect), their experimental designs and results are similar enough to suggest two tentative conclusions. The first conclusion is that, on average, neither twins nor nontwin siblings exhibit any compelling evidence of a telepathic form of ESP. The second conclusion is that twins may express more similar or "concordant" thoughts than nontwin siblings; and, when they do, it is because of a natural, rather than a supernatural, cause.

To see how these conclusions were derived, consider the procedure used in the Blackmore and Chamberlain study. The two siblings in each session—twins or nontwins—were randomly assigned to be either the sender or the receiver, swapping these roles halfway through the session. Each sender-receiver pair was given three tasks to perform, and they did each of these tasks twice: once under a condition designed to test for evidence of thought concordance and once under a condition designed to test for evidence of extra-sensory perception. For example, in the first task (Numbers Test):

> The numbers 1–10 were used as targets. In Condition 1 (thought concordance) the sender was asked to write down and concentrate on the first number between 1 and 10 that came to mind. The receiver at the same time tried to pick up what number was being thought about and write it down. This was repeated five times. In Condition 2 (ESP) the procedure was exactly the same except that the experimenter selected the number using random-numbers tables and told the sender which number to concentrate on.

The logic of this procedure was that the siblings could generate a significant proportion of identical responses by means of thought concordance in Condition 1. (Given the freedom to choose their own number, both might tend to think of the same number at a rate exceeding chance). In contrast, the siblings would have to use ESP in order to generate a significant proportion of identical responses in Condition 2. (Given no freedom to choose their own number, the receivers would have to "read" the senders' minds in order to report the same numbers at a rate exceeding chance.)

Blackmore and Chamberlain's findings, when aggregated across the three tasks, revealed no evidence of telepathy in either the twins or the nontwin siblings. On the other hand, their findings did reveal that the level of thought concordance displayed by the twins (the identicals and the fraternals combined) was reliably greater than that displayed by the nontwin siblings. These results led Blackmore and Chamberlain to conclude that most, if not all, cases of coincident thoughts and feelings in twins represent nothing more than thought concordance. To the extent that twins are likely to "frame" their experiences similarly, they will have concordant thoughts and feelings at a rate that noticeably exceeds chance. "This in turn may encourage them to think they have experienced the paranormal or have psychic ability whether they do or not."

❖ ❖ ❖

It is debatable whether or not great minds think alike, but the preliminary scientific evidence suggests that twins do. "Thinking alike" is not, however, the same thing as telepathy. Instead, it is a similarity in cognitive processes that is based on the similarity of interpretive frames, a similarity that is natural rather than supernatural. It does not require the presumption of a Psychic Twins Hotline—a magical connection based on ESP.

But if thought concordance in twins is not necessarily based on ESP, what is? Perhaps the best available candidate is the phenomenon that Guy Playfair has termed crisis telepathy. Guy Playfair cited Sir Hubert Wilkins, an early ESP researcher, as having expressed the opinion "that it is the highly emotional or exciting thoughts that are most apt to get through [telepathically], and to make an impression on another mind." If Wilkins's speculation is correct, it is possible that the emotional empathy of twins is based in part on ESP, even if their thought concordance is not.

To illustrate the phenomenon of crisis telepathy, Playfair has offered the following dramatic examples:

> One day in 1948, 20-year-old Alice Lambe of Springfield, Illinois, felt a massive blow on the left side of her body and a sharp pain. She fell off her chair, cried out to her father "Something's happening to Diane," and passed out. Something was indeed happening to her sister, 70 miles away at the time. She was in a train crash which left her with two fractured ribs and concussion. Alice's aches and pains continued throughout her sister's period of convalescence.
>
> In another crash coincidence, reported in 1975, a hospital worker not only felt severe pain in her left leg but also came out in bruises all over her left side. At the same time, her sister was involved in a car crash 400 miles away. The most tragic of all such cases was that of a pair of twins whose fate was reported by their non-twin sister Mrs Joyce Crominski. According to her, one twin had woken up one night suffering unbearable chest pains.

An ambulance was called, but she died on the way to the hospital—as did her twin sister whose chest had been crushed in a road accident. Mrs Crominski reckoned that the crash and the rude awakening had been simultaneous.

... An articulate young man named Marcus Lewis described, on the BBC2 program hosted by Esther Rantzen (12 February 1997), how he had telephoned his mother in the middle of the night to ask her if his brother Alex was all right. She sleepily assured him that he was, as far as she knew, but twenty minutes later she received another call—from the hospital to which Alex had been taken after a motorcycle accident. (He may well have been "lying in the gutter" at the exact time of Marcus's call). Both twins gave a more detailed account of this incident in the BBC2 programme *Mysteries with Carol Vorderman* (2 December 1997).

Anecdotes like this, though admittedly intriguing, do not establish the phenomenon of crisis telepathy as a scientific fact. Obviously, the first thing a professional statistician would ask is *"How many times do people feel sympathetic pains or have visions of their loved ones suffering when their loved ones aren't really suffering at all?"* If these false alarms are relatively frequent and the apparent "hits" are relatively rare, then chance alone (that is, random coincidence) may provide a perfectly satisfactory explanation for both types of outcome.

Another problem with establishing the validity of crisis telepathy is that ethical constraints would make it difficult to "capture" this phenomenon in a laboratory study using human participants. Obviously, it would be blatantly unethical to conduct an experiment in which the members of twin pairs were physically separated, one twin was randomly assigned to suffer an intensely painful stimulus, and the reactions of the other twin were monitored for evidence of similar and simultaneous pain. Researchers who want to study emotional telepathy must therefore rely on less extreme emotional inductions—ones that do not involve inflicting intense pain on any of the participants.

A few studies of this type have, in fact, been conducted. In general, they have used only a small number of twin pairs and have relied on relatively subtle ways of manipulating one twin's emotional state to see if it has a corresponding effect on the other twin's state. It is not surprising, therefore, that the results of these studies are mixed. They do not, in my view, provide convincing scientific evidence of emotional telepathy. On the other hand, they do not entirely discredit the possibility of emotional telepathy either.

If we assume, for the purposes of the present argument, that the emotional empathy of most twin pairs is not based on some form of extrasensory perception, the most reasonable alternative explanation is that it is based on emotional concordance.

Emotional concordance, analogous to thought concordance, occurs when individuals have the same feelings in response to the same stimulus event. Subjectively, of course, the event is not exactly the same for each individual. However, to the extent that they "frame" or interpret the event similarly, it will tend to evoke a similar emotional experience in each. Although emotional concordance alone cannot account for the few anecdotal cases of crisis telepathy (emotional empathy at a distance), it may account very well for the vast majority of cases in which twins experience similar emotions at the same place and time.

Perhaps the strongest evidence for emotional concordance in twin pairs comes from an ambitious study conducted in Germany by Franz Neyer and his colleagues Rainer Banse and Jens Asendorpf. The data were collected at the Max Planck Institute for Psychological Research in Munich (a place that I was thrown out of once in my younger days, but that's another story). The participants in the study were 108 pairs of elderly German twins—75 identical and 33 fraternal. All of the twins were retired (their average age was 71), and the majority of them were women.

The members of each twin pair were videotaped while they discussed positive and negative events that had occurred in their relationship during the past few years. They were then seated in separate rooms, where they were each shown a tape of their just-completed interaction. Their task during the first viewing of the tape was to move a lever back and forth within a horizontal plane to create a continuous record of the intensity of their positive and negative feelings throughout the entire videotaped discussion. Their task during the second viewing of the tape was to use the same lever to rate the intensity of their twin's positive and negative feelings throughout the same discussion period.

From the resulting data, Neyer and his colleagues were able to assess how accurate the twins were in inferring each other's positive and negative emotional states. Even more important, they were able to use sophisticated statistical analyses to estimate the extent to which the twins' accuracy reflected two potentially important influences. The first influence was the *actual similarity* in the twins' positive and negative feelings. The second influence was the *assumed similarity* in their positive and negative feelings (the degree to which the twins based their ratings of their cotwin's feelings on what they themselves had been feeling at the same point in time).

Neyer and his colleagues found strong evidence that both of these influences were important. The twins' accuracy in inferring each other's feelings depended, to a large extent, on their having had similar feelings themselves at each point and then assuming that their cotwin's feelings were similar to their own. Roughly half of the time, when the twins assumed that their cotwins had been feeling essentially the same way that they had been feeling, they were correct in making such projection-based inferences. Moreover, Neyer and his colleagues concluded that the twins' projection-based accuracy was "much stronger" than that observed in other close relationships, such as those of marriage partners.

What about the other half of the time? Here the findings were mixed. In some cases, the twins made errors of *over*projection: they inappropriately assumed that their cotwins were experiencing similar feelings when their cotwins' feelings were actually different from their own. In other cases, however, the twins were able to recognize the difference between their own feelings and those of their cotwins and make accurate inferences that obviously required a greater sensitivity than projection alone could provide.

Neyer and his colleagues were surprised, however, to find that the emotional empathy of the identical twins was not reliably greater than that of the fraternal twins. They had expected to find an empathic advantage for the identical twins, reasoning that the greater genetic similarity of the identical twins would cause them to have more similar emotional reactions and interpretive frames than the fraternal twins would. But their statistical test revealed this difference to be unexpectedly slight, for reasons that aren't yet apparent.

One possibility is that the effect of the twins' genetic similarity depends upon their level of psychological closeness. Identical twins vary in their closeness just as fraternal twins do, and the twins in close relationships should develop a better sense than those in more distant relationships of the instances in which their cotwin either does or does not share their own current feelings. Perhaps identical twins who aren't close are the most likely to overproject their own feelings onto their cotwins, thereby canceling out any advantage that their greater genetic similarity might confer.

In summary, the emotional inferences of these elderly twins revealed a mix of accuracy and error. Although much of their accuracy depended on their appropriately projecting their own highly similar feelings onto each other, they also overprojected at times and thereby misinferred what their cotwins were actually feeling at those times. To their credit, however, they could also recognize at least some of the instances in which their own feelings and their cotwins' feelings diverged.

❖   ❖   ❖

If you are thinking that the results of this study tell us nothing about whether telepathy is a basis for emotional empathy in twins, you're right—they don't. Neyer and his colleagues did not set out to do a telepathy experiment. If they had, they would have included another condition in their study—one in which the twins attempted to infer each other's feelings while being physically isolated from each other. Without the benefit of such a condition, the results of Neyer, Banse, and Aserdorpf's study cannot be used to rule out the possibility that telepathy plays a role in the emotional empathy of at least some pairs of twins.

On the other hand, their results do suggest that telepathy isn't *necessary* in order for twins to achieve a relatively high level of emotional empathy. To infer what their cotwins are (or would be) feeling in a particular situation, twins can simply assume that their cotwins' feelings are (or would be) similar to their own. By making such inferences routinely, they will be accurate much of the time.

From a scientific standpoint, this type of explanation is preferable to one that involves telepathy because it does not require the invocation of any quasi-magical or paranormal process. It also promises greater theoretical parsimony in its implication that people's ability to understand each other depends largely on the degree to which their own respective thoughts and feelings are already similar or concordant. Although the possibility of emotional telepathy cannot be ruled out, there is no compelling scientific reason to rule it in either.

There are, of course, other reasons why people might believe in telepathy as a basis of empathic understanding. Just as in Burton's time, some people today believe in telepathy because it promises to help them reconcile their spiritual beliefs with their scientific ones. Other people believe in telepathy because it promises to give them unusual insights, a magical connection to others, or a sense of being special, unique, or chosen.

For most of us, however, the temptation to believe in telepathy probably derives from the difficulty of pinpointing the source of our empathic intuitions, which we often experience as elusive, diffuse, and ineffable. Tobin Hart has described his experience as a practicing psychotherapist in this way:

> ... there are sometimes moments when understanding of the other deepens beyond what I can easily explain. I seem to experience the other's feelings directly in my own body or recognize patterns, histories, or meanings that do not appear to come from interpreting the words and gestures that we exchange. . . . Phenomenologically, information is often encountered as if it were coming from another source, perceived as outside or deep inside. . . .

In my opinion, it is this aspect of empathic intuition—the ineffable sense that it comes from unspecified sources both outside and inside of us—that is primarily responsible for the belief that empathy involves something mystical or magical, a telepathic "sixth sense."

Empathic intuition often is experienced as the nebulous awareness of "patterns, histories, or meanings" that seem to be larger and more informative than the target person's words and actions would imply. And empathic intuition often does seem to derive from sources both outside and inside of us. But does this mean that empathic understanding must be magical or paranormal—even in the slightest degree? Or are there nonmagical, scientific explanations for these widely acknowledged qualities of the empathic experience?

According to research findings that have accumulated during the past three or four decades, there are. With respect to the belief that our empathic experience often derives from sources of information of which we are at best only minimally aware, the research evidence clearly confirms our reliance on such cues. As psychologist Elaine Hatfield and her colleagues John Cacioppo and Richard Rapson have noted:

> Despite the subjective experience that information is processed sequentially, the human brain is clearly capable of parallel processing. . . . For example, while we are carrying on a rational conversation, we may also be continuously monitoring our partner's emotional reactions to what we have to say. We may unconsciously and automatically scan her face for second-by-second information as to her emotions. Is she feeling happiness, love, anger, sadness, or fear? We can use a variety of subtle indicators (e.g., facial muscle movements, "micro-expressions," crooked expressions, or the timing of reactions) to decide whether the other person is telling the truth or lying. We may even be able to judge her mood by observing facial muscle movements so minute that they *seem* detectable only in electromyographic (EMG) recordings.
>
> Other types of . . . information are also available. People can listen to the speech of others—to the volume, rhythm, speed, pitch, disfluencies, and word choice, as well as to the length of their pauses. They can observe the way others stand, gesture, or move their hands, legs, and feet. They can also observe instrumental behaviors. *Such observations are made so frequently that they tend to become automated; that is, the information is processed quickly, with minimal demand on cognitive resources and minimal impact on conversant awareness.* [italics mine]

In their response to the observations of therapists such as Tobin Hart, Elaine Hatfield and her colleagues have concluded that: ". . . there is really not much mystery to the observations of therapists and others that, though not *consciously* aware that their clients (say) are experiencing joy, sadness, fear, or anger, they 'somehow' do sense and react to these feelings. Today, emotion researchers assume conscious awareness of only a small portion of the information we possess about ourselves and others."

What about the sense we share with Tobin Hart that our empathic intuitions often seem to derive from sources both outside and deep inside of us? Is there a scientific explanation for this aspect of our empathic experience as well?

Sure is. In fact, there are at least three of them, all of which might eventually prove to fit together as neatly as the pieces of a puzzle. At the most general level, Elaine Hatfield and her colleagues have documented the evidence for *emotional contagion*—a phenomenon that occurs when one person "catches" and experiences the same type of emotion that another person is currently feeling. At a more specific level, psychologists Robert Levenson and Anna Ruef have reviewed the evidence for *physiological synchrony*—a phenomenon that occurs when one person's physiological responses seem to "track" or vary in tandem with those of another person. Finally, at an even more specific level, neurophysiologists Vittorio Gallese, Giacomo Rizzolatti, and their colleagues at the University of Parma have found evidence for the existence of *mirror neurons*—recently identified nerve cells that fire not only when their owner performs a certain action but also when he or she observes someone else performing the same action.

In their book *Emotional Contagion*, Elaine Hatfield, John Cacioppo, and Richard Rapson review the research evidence for the phenomenon they call *primitive emotional contagion*. They define this phenomenon as "the tendency to automatically mimic and synchronize facial expressions, vocalizations, postures, and movements with those of another person and, consequently, to converge emotionally" with the other.

According to Hatfield and her colleagues, primitive emotional contagion occurs whenever we "catch" or "are infected by" another person's current emotional state. Just as we catch other people's germs in an automatic, unintentional way, we similarly catch other people's emotions in a manner that is "relatively automatic, unintentional, uncontrollable, and largely inaccessible to conversant awareness." The existence of this phenomenon, if confirmed, could plausibly account for our sense that our empathic intuition derives from sources both outside and inside of us.

In fact, Hatfield and her colleagues found considerable evidence in the research literature that people really do mimic, mirror, and in other ways match the verbal and nonverbal behavior of other people. Normally developing infants, for example, spontaneously imitate the facial gestures of adult models—opening their mouths, pursing their lips, and sticking out their tongues in response to the same gestures made by the adult. (Infants are also "infected" by other people's yawns and respond with yawns of their own.) After just a few weeks of life, infants mimic in a rudimentary way their mothers' facial expressions of happiness and anger; a few months later, they reflect more nuanced expressions of joy, anger, and sadness. Babies also find other people's laughter and other babies' cries highly contagious, and during the first year of life they spontaneously mimic the sounds and cadence of their mother's speech.

As babies develop into children, adolescents, and then adults, they display more varied and subtle ways of matching and synchronizing their behavior to the behavior of others. They continue to mirror other people's facial expressions, even those of total strangers. They match or mirror other people's movements, interaction rhythms, and body postures. They "mimic and synchronize their speech productions with others to within one-twentieth of a second." They converge with their conversation partners in the rate and cadence of their speech, the pitch and amplitude of their voices, the peculiarities of their accents and inflections, and the length of their pauses, utterances, and speaking turns.

All of this unconscious coordination is more than an end in itself; it is an important means by which people achieve emotional rapport and mutual understanding. As Hatfield and her colleagues discovered in the results of many laboratory studies, when we mimic other people's behavior—their speech, rhythms, gestures, expressions, and physical attitudes—we gain a better, more direct sense of their feelings and psychological attitudes as well.

The specifics of the research findings need not concern us here, since a few mundane examples might be sufficient to make the point. Consider how adopting a Marine recruit's rigid, unblinking posture makes you feel tense and alert, whereas adopting your roommate's slouchy, glassy-eyed posture infuses you with the vegetative sense of the couch potato. Then consider, after watching the film *Midnight Cowboy*, how imitating Ratso Rizzo's insistent whine makes you feel anxious and needy, whereas imitating Joe Buck's soft-edged drawl makes you feel relaxed and unhurried. Next, consider how matching the leaden movements, lifeless expression, and slowed speech of a clinically depressed person undermines your previously upbeat mood. Finally, consider how you feel holding a pen lengthwise between your teeth (slightly happy?) as opposed to holding the end of the same pen between your pursed lips (slightly concerned?).

There are, of course, important qualifications to the phenomenon of emotional contagion—qualifications that Hatfield and her colleagues have been careful to note. Some people are more susceptible to the phenomenon than others, catching other people's moods more easily, more intensely, and more often. On the other side of the equation, some people are more likely than others to "infect" people with their emotions, reflecting both the intensity of the feelings and the expressiveness of the person transmitting them. Finally, emotional contagion is stronger in some types of situations, and in some types of relationships, than in others. Still, despite these qualifications, the evidence is compelling that emotional contagion is a universal experience that occurs in most, if not all, of our day-to-day interactions with others.

❖   ❖   ❖

But what connects the behavioral synchrony that occurs outside of our bodies with the emotional rapport that we feel inside of them? The answer, according to psychologists Robert Levenson and Anna Ruef, is the phenomenon that they call *physiological synchrony*. As they discovered, evidence of physiological synchrony is well documented in the psychological literature:

> A striking number of physiological systems have shown evidence of synchrony across individuals, without any intentional attempt by those individuals to achieve this state.... One of the more fascinating manifestations of physiological synchrony in humans was first reported by McClintock, who described the tendency of women who were college roommates and close friends to have menstrual cycles that became increasingly synchronized over time (i.e., their days of onset became closer). Many studies of this phenomenon have been conducted over the ensuing years ... [and] the evidence from these studies provides strong support for the existence of menstrual synchrony, especially under conditions in which women live in close proximity or otherwise have a great deal of exposure to each other.

Menstrual synchrony might not seem to have any obvious or direct connection with emotional rapport, but for other forms of physiological synchrony this connection is more obvious and direct. Levenson and Ruef cited the following examples:

❖ One team of researchers found high levels of synchrony in the heart rates of mothers and their infants when they played together. "Assuming that emotional rapport is quite high during mother-infant play, this study could be viewed as evidence for a connection between emotional rapport and heart rate synchrony."

❖ Another team of researchers found significant covariations in skin conductance between discussion-group members who reported disliking each other. This result was evident in both all-male and all-female discussion groups.

❖ Other researchers have found evidence of synchrony in the heart rates of therapists and their patients during psychotherapy sessions. One team of researchers "found that the therapist's and patient's heart rates moved in similar directions as the levels of 'tension' in the interview varied, but moved in opposite directions when the patient expressed 'antagonism' toward the therapist."

To date, however, the best and most convincing evidence that physiological synchrony provides a basis for emotional empathy comes from a classic study that Levenson and Ruef themselves conducted. The overall goal of the study was to demonstrate that when perceivers are asked to infer the emotional states that were actually experienced by husbands and wives during laboratory discussions, the perceivers' inferences will be accurate to the extent that their own physiological responses vary in sync with those of the husband or wife whose emotional states they are currently trying to infer. In other words, the greater the physiological linkage between the perceiver and the target person on the videotape, the more accurate the perceivers' emotional inferences should be.

Testing this prediction required a lot of advance preparation. The first thing the researchers had to do was to videotape the laboratory interactions of actual married couples. At the time each couple's discussion was videotaped, both the husband and the wife were hooked up to separate physiological recording devices that made continuous records of their heart rates, skin conductance levels, and other physiological responses. Several days later, the spouses came back to the laboratory and individually viewed the videotape of their earlier interaction while using a joystick control to create a continuous record of how positive or negative their feelings had been throughout the interaction. When all of the physiological and emotion-rating data had been collected from the couples, the researchers were then ready to proceed with the main part of their study.

To conduct the main part of the study, the researchers recruited 31 adults to participate as perceivers. Each perceiver was asked to infer the changing emotional states of a husband and a wife who appeared in two different videotaped discussions. Before viewing these discussions, each perceiver was hooked up to the same physiological recording devices that the marriage partners themselves had been hooked up to. (The output from these devices enabled the researchers to track the changes in the perceiver's own physiology that occurred while he or she was attempting to infer the successive emotional states of the designated spouse in each of two videotaped discussions.) Just as the spouses themselves had done, the perceiver used the joystick control throughout each discussion to make a continuous record of the inferred positivity or negativity of the target spouse's emotional states.

Using sophisticated statistical analyses, Levenson and Ruef were able to correlate the degree of physiological synchrony between the perceiver and the target spouse with the perceiver's level of accuracy in inferring the target spouse's changing emotional states. The results were encouraging, but not entirely as expected. The researchers found that the degree of physiological linkage was strongly related to the perceivers' accuracy in inferring the target persons' negative emotions, but was only weakly related to the perceivers' accuracy in inferring the target person's positive emotions. Their interpretation of these findings:

> . . . was based on the notion of emotional contagion and on the patterns of autonomic nervous system activation associated with certain negative emotions. We reasoned that subjects who are empathically accurate are those who are most sensitive to emotional contagion and thus are most likely to experience the same emotions as the target at approximately the same time. These emotions would produce similar patterns of autonomic activation in both subject and target, thus creating physiological linkage.

> To explain the [relatively weak] association between empathic accuracy and physiological linkage for positive emotions, we . . . drew on findings that negative emotions are more likely than positive emotions to produce patterned autonomic nervous system activity. In our view, emotions produce autonomic activation so that the necessary physiological support is available for patterns of behavior that are prototypical for those emotions. Because negative emotions are more closely associated with behavioral patterns that make higher metabolic demands (e.g., fleeing in fear, fighting in anger) than positive emotions, the negative emotions are more likely to produce the kind of strong autonomic nervous activation necessary for physiological linkage to occur between the subject and the target.

In making this argument, Levenson and Ruef were careful to note that emotional contagion undoubtedly occurs for both positive and negative emotions. Smiles and laughter, for example, have been found to be highly contagious behaviors. However, to the extent that positive feelings are less likely to produce the strong and distinct patterns of autonomic activation that negative feelings do, the degree of physiological linkage is likely to be less evident.

Emotional contagion and physiological synchrony appear to be crucial to our understanding of emotional empathy. Together, they take us a long way toward explaining how we are able to apprehend other people's emotional states in such a spontaneous and seemingly ineffable way. But even more fundamental than these processes are the activities of a special class of neurons called *mirror neurons*—nerve cells that fire not only when their owner performs a certain action but also when he or she observes someone else performing the same action. By equating the meaning of similar actions by self and other at the most basic neurological level, mirror neurons seem to account for both the ineffability of our empathic experience and our sense that it derives from sources both outside and deep inside of us.

In a *New Scientist* article called "Read My Mind," writer Alison Motluk described how mirror neurons were discovered in the early 1990s:

> Vittorio Gallese, Giacomo Rizzolatti, and their colleagues at the University of Parma have identified an entirely new class of neurons. These neurons are active when their owners perform a certain task, and in this respect are wholly unremarkable. But, more interestingly, the same neurons fire when their owner watches someone else perform that same task. The team has dubbed the novel nerve cells "mirror" neurons, because they seem to be firing in sympathy, reflecting or perhaps simulating the actions of others . . .
>
> Gallese and his colleagues didn't set out to find anything so radical when, in the early 1990s, they started recording the activity of neurons in a macaque's brain. They were tapping into signals emitted from nerve cells in a part of the monkey's brain known as F5. This is part of a larger region called the premotor cortex, whose activity is linked to planning and making movements. Some years earlier, the same researchers had discovered that neurons in F5 fired when an animal performed certain goal-oriented motor tasks using its hands or mouth, such as picking things up, holding or biting them.
>
> They wanted to learn more about F5 neurons—how they responded to different objectives with different shapes and sizes, for example. So they presented monkeys with things like raisins, slices of apple, paper clips, cubes and spheres. It wasn't long before they noticed something odd. As the monkey watched the experimenter's hand pick up the object and bring it close, a group of the F5 neurons leaped into action. But when the monkey looked at the same object lying on the tray, nothing happened. When it picked up the object, the same neurons fired again. Clearly their job wasn't just to recognize a particular object.
>
> The neurons turned out to be quite fussy about what [specific

goal-oriented actions] they reacted to. . . . [But] most impor-
tantly, the very same action that made a neuron fire when a
monkey performed it would almost always make the same
neuron fire if the monkey saw the experimenter doing the same
thing. It soon became clear that the motor system in the brain is
not limited to controlling movements. In some way it is also
reading the actions of others.

The identification of mirror neurons in monkeys launched an
immediate effort by neuroscientists to find evidence of them in
humans as well. This was not easy to do because, for ethical reasons, scientists are rarely permitted to implant electrodes in the
brains of human research participants. Consequently, more indirect
evidence had to be sought.

To obtain such evidence, Luciano Fadiga, in collaboration with
other members of the Italian research team, used Transcranic Magnetic Stimulation to test the excitability of the motor cortex in
human subjects. The subjects were tested in four different conditions: watching an experimenter grasp objects; watching the
experimenter make aimless arm movements; watching objects by
themselves; and detecting the dimming of a spot of light. When the
subjects were watching objects being grasped, the evoked poten-
tials measured from their own hand muscles markedly increased. A
similar effect was not observed in the other three conditions. This
was the first evidence that humans have a mirror system similar to
the type found in monkeys—a system in which the same neural circuits are activated while watching someone else perform an act as
when one performs it oneself.

This demonstration is remarkable in its implication that simply
observing another person's acts can elicit incipient imitative acts of
one's own. By creating a neurological isomorphism between the
other's acts and one's own incipient acts, the mirror system might
be responsible for both the physiological synchrony that Levenson
and Ruef have described and for the verbal and nonverbal mimicry

that Hatfield and her colleagues have argued is the basis of emotional contagion. In other words, by generating a partial simulation or "neurological echo" of the other person's experience within our own brain and body, the mirror system might enable us to think and feel for ourselves something of what the other person is currently thinking and feeling.

Interestingly, this view of how the mirror system functions bears some resemblance to one of the two competing theories that have been proposed by psychologists and philosophers to account for our everyday mind reading. According to Vittorio Gallese and Alvin Goldman, the first theory—called *theory theory* by the philosophers—asserts that "ordinary people accomplish mind-reading by acquiring and deploying a commonsense theory of mind, something akin to a scientific theory." This theory assumes that we deduce other people's thoughts and feelings from a set of causal/explanatory laws "that relate external stimuli to certain inner states (e.g. perceptions), certain inner states (e.g. desires and beliefs) to other inner states (e.g. decisions), and certain inner states (e.g. decisions) to behavior."

In contrast, the second theory—called *simulation theory* by the philosophers—asserts that people accomplish mind reading by imagining themselves in the other's place and then experiencing the thoughts and feelings that follow naturally from adopting the other's perspective. This second theory is obviously closer to the view of everyday mind reading suggested by recent thinking about mirror neurons and how they might give rise to phenomena such as physiological synchrony and emotional contagion. Indeed, Gallese and Goldman have proposed that mirror neuron activity "seems to be nature's way of getting the observer into the same 'mental shoes' as the target—exactly what the conjectured simulation heuristic aims to do."

With respect to human mind reading, these two theories are probably not incompatible. Normal humans are cognitively sophisticated enough to reason deductively about other people's thoughts and feelings, but they clearly don't exert the mental effort required to do this all of the time. Instead, they typically revert to the less effortful and more automatic mode of mind reading—the one that depends upon the mirror system and its associated processes of physiological synchrony, emotional contagion, and the incipient simulation of the other's acts in one's own conscious experience. Consistent with this more inclusive view, psychologists Sara Hodges and Daniel Wegner have drawn upon relevant theory and research to make a strong case that people do indeed alternate between using controlled (active and inferential) versus automatic (passive and experiential) modes of everyday mind reading.

Do mirror neurons occupy "ground zero" in both of these modes? It is beginning to look like they do. Once Luciano Fadiga and his colleagues had found evidence that mirror neurons might exist in humans as well as in monkeys, the next big question was where the mirror system might be located within the human brain. To answer this question, research teams led by Giacomo Rizzolatti and Scott Grafton at UCLA conducted PET (Positron Emissions Tomography) scans on human subjects who watched an experimenter pick up and handle objects. The PET scan findings showed activation in areas of the brain that lie above the left temple—a part of the human brain that has traditionally been linked with language production. Interestingly, this region has the same relative location as the F5 area of the monkey's brain in which mirror neurons were first discovered.

This correspondence led Giacomo Rizzolatti and Michael Arbib to speculate that the mirror system that enabled action recognition in the F5 area of the monkey brain was the evolutionary precursor of a mirror system in a corresponding area in the human brain that provided the basis for language development. They argued that the mimetic capacity inherent to the F5 area in the monkey brain and to a region that includes Broca's area in the human brain enabled the gradual evolution of a manual gesture system that eventually "paved the way for the open vocalization system that we know as speech." Because mirror neurons could equate the similar actions of self and other in the brains of each individual, the stage was set for specific hand gestures to evoke the representation of specific acts in the minds of both individuals simultaneously. And once that evolutionary milestone had been reached, the neural structures controlling the vocal apparatus could be similarly exapted (i.e., co-opted through subsequent evolutionary pressures) to enable the coordinated production and mutual comprehension of speech.

With the localization of the mirror system in the area of the human brain that is responsible for language ability, it becomes easy to see how both modes of mind reading—the more effortful and inferential one and the more automatic and experiential one—could have their ultimate origin in the operation of mirror neurons. The more primitive mirror system that controlled physiological synchrony, emotional contagion, and the incipient simulation of another's acts would, over the course of evolution, have eventually been complemented by a coexisting language system that made theory-based inferences possible. If this view is correct, then the experiential mind reading of *simulation theory* can be reconciled with inferential mind reading of *theory theory* in the evolutionarily older and newer structures of the mirror system within the human brain.

In a lecture given to an audience of 6,000 scientists in 1995, V. S. Ramachandran, a neuroscientist at the University of California at San Diego, hailed the discovery of mirror neurons as "the single most important 'unreported' (or at least unpublicized) story of the decade." He went on to predict that "mirror neurons will do for psychology what DNA did for biology: they will provide a unifying framework and help explain a host of mental abilities that have hitherto remained mysterious and inaccessible to experiments."

These are extravagant predictions, and it remains to be seen whether they will be justified by the results of future research.

Meanwhile, there has been no lack of casual theorizing about the kinds of mysteries that mirror neurons might be used to explain. For example, Ramachandran himself has speculated that "a loss of these mirror neurons might explain autism—a cruel disease that afflicts children. Without these neurons the child can no longer understand or empathize with other people . . . and therefore completely withdraws from the world socially."

The question of whether the mindblindness of autistic individuals can traced to a damaged mirror system is clearly important and worthy of study. Perhaps future research will indeed reveal that the most profound cases of autism are found in individuals who have the greatest damage to their mirror system, whereas the mildest cases of autism are found in individuals whose mirror systems are relatively intact. The overall picture might be complicated, however, by cases such as that of Donna Williams, who has reported suffering from an overly *intense* awareness of the stimulation that other people present (see chapter 7). In cases such as hers, is a damaged mirror system accompanied by an inability to restrict or dampen the rushing flood of information from others that threatens to overwhelm the autistic individual? And, if so, are these neurological problems independent or are they related to each other?

In contrast to the case of autistic individuals, we might hypothesize that the mirror system remains undamaged in people who have Williams syndrome—a rare genetic disorder (less than 1 in 20,000 births) that impairs spacial skills and certain intellectual functions but appears to leave everyday mind reading skills intact. The hypothesis of an undamaged mirror system in these individuals is consistent with the fact that they tend to display unique strengths in both their language skills and their social sensitivity—functions that may depend on the same part of the human brain.

Finally, we need to know more about those cases in which the mirror system seems to work *too* well, or—to be more precise— seems to exert too much control over the person's actions. It appears that there are categories of persons whose mirror systems operate without restraint, causing them to mimic compulsively the behaviors of the people around them. Gallese and Goldman have cited one such category in order to make the point that, most of the time, the mirror systems of normal individuals operate within inhibitory constraints that keep them from mimicking other people's responses indiscriminately:

> . . . in so-called "imitation behavior" . . . a group of patients with prefrontal lesions compulsively imitate gestures or even complex actions performed in front of them by an experimenter. This behavior is explained as an impairment of the inhibitory control normally governing motor schemas, or plans. It may be inferred from this that normal humans, when observing someone else performing an action, generate a plan to do the same action, or an image of doing it, themselves. Normally this plan is inhibited so that it does not yield motor output, but such inhibition is impaired in the patient population in question.

The effects of an unrestrained mirror system are even more evident in Oliver Sacks' description of a person afflicted with what he calls "super-Tourette's" syndrome:

> My eye was caught by a grey-haired woman in her sixties, who was apparently the center of a most amazing disturbance, though what was happening, what was so disturbing, was not at first clear to me. Was she having a fit? What on earth was convulsing her— and, by what sort of sympathy or contagion, also convulsing everyone whom she gnashingly, ticcily passed?
>
> As I drew closer I saw what was happening. She was imitating the passers-by—if "imitation" is not too pallid, too passive, a word. Should we say rather, that she was caricaturing everyone she passed? Within a second, a split-second, she "had" them all.
>
> I have seen countless mimes and mimics, clowns and antics, but nothing touched the horrible wonder I now beheld: this virtually instantaneous, automatic and convulsive mirroring of every face and figure. But it was not just an imitation, extraordinary as

this would have been in itself. The woman not only took on, and took in, the features of countless people, she took them off. Every mirroring was also a parody, a mocking, an exaggeration of salient gestures and expressions, but an exaggeration in itself no less convulsive than intentional—a consequence of the violent acceleration and distortion of all her motions. Thus, a slow smile, monstrously accelerated, would become a violent, milliseconds-long grimace; an ample gesture, accelerated, would become a far-cical convulsive movement.

In the course of a short city-block this frantic old woman fre-netically caricatured the features of forty or fifty passers-by, in a quick-fire sequence of kaleidoscopic imitations, each lasting a second or two, sometimes less, and the whole dizzying sequences scarcely more than two minutes.

What we have here is a mirror system that is not just operating unconstrained; it is running completely amok!

So, is empathic intuition our sixth sense? I believe that it is. Of course, there are more than five other senses, with our sense of bal-ance and our "itch perception" being only two of the other recog-nized senses. But empathic intuition might still qualify as our col-loquial "sixth sense" because it is the sense that most enlarges our experience by bringing into our own mind the thoughts and feelings of other people. It is the sense that enables our connection to and commonality with others, the sense that makes it possible for us to incorporate the other into the self. It is the sense that, more than any other, makes our human species unique.

Like Richard Francis Burton, however, I do not believe that this sixth sense is supernatural or paranormal in origin. I believe that its origin lies instead in the long evolutionary history of our species. It remains to be seen whether Rizzolatti and Arbib's account of this history will turn out to be the correct one, but I wouldn't be surprised if an account that strongly resembles theirs will eventually be accepted as more or less correct.

Are mirror neurons the answer to the question of where our sixth sense comes from? Only time will tell. I suspect that mirror neurons are an important part of this answer, perhaps even the most central and essential part. But mirror neurons, by themselves, are not the whole story. Mirror neurons may confer upon us the mindsight that is the opposite of mindblindness, but they must interact with many other neural structures before true empathic intuition can occur. Minimally, they must connect to the five standard senses, which convey to us the necessary information about the target persons' current behavior. They must also connect to our explicit and implicit memory systems, which convey to us to the necessary information about the target persons' past behavior. And they must also connect to the interrelated systems of language, semantic propositions, and cognitive frames—the systems that enable us to theorize and reason analytically about others, to infer their motives and deduce their intentions, and to align our perspectives and interpretations with theirs.

Empathic intuition is indeed our sixth sense, but it depends upon and vastly transcends our other senses. Both familiar and elusive, it is the sense that makes the fullest and most integrated use of our cognitive and perceptual abilities. It is the sense that enables most of us to become apprentices, and a few of us to become masters, in the art of everyday mind reading.

Sources for Chapter 12

Bem, Daryl J., and Charles Honorton. "Does Psi Exist? Replicable Evidence for an Anomalous Process of Information Transfer." *Psychological Bulletin* 115 (1994): 4–18.

Blackmore, Susan J., and Frances Chamberlain. "ESP and Thought Concordance in Twins: A Method of Comparison." *Journal of the Society for Psychical Research* 59 (1993): 89–96.

Brodie, Fawn M. *The Devil Drives: A Life of Sir Richard Burton.* New York: W. W. Norton & Company, 1984.

Derrida, Jacques. "Telepathy," trans. Nicholas Royle. *Oxford Literary Review* 10 (1988): 3–41.

Fadiga, Luciano, Leonardo Fogassi, Giovanni Pavesi, and Giacomo Rizzolatti. "Motor Facilitation During Action Observation: A Magnetic Stimulation Study." *Journal of Neurophysiology* 73 (1995): 2608–11.

Farwell, Byron. *Burton: A Biography of Sir Richard Francis Burton.* London: Penguin Books, Ltd., 1990.

France, Gary A., and Robert A. Hogan. "Thought Concordance in Twins and Siblings and Associated Personality Variables." *Psychological Reports* 32 (1973): 707–10.

Gallese, Vittorio, and Alvin Goldman. "Mirror Neurons and the Simulation Theory of Mind-Reading." *Trends in Cognitive Sciences* 12 (1998): 493–501.

Galton, Francis. *Inquiries into Human Faculty and Its Development.* London: Macmillan, 1883.

Grafton, S. T., Michael Arbib, et al. "Localization of Grasp Representations in Humans by Positron Emissions Tomography: 2. Observation Compared with Imagination." *Experimental Brain Research* 112 (1996): 103–11.

Gurney, Edmund, Frederic W. H. Myers, and Frank Podmore. *Phantasms of the Living.* London: Trübner, 1886 (case nos. 76, 77, 78, 134, and 230).

Hansel, Charles E. M. *ESP and Parapsychology: A Critical Reevaluation.* Amherst, N.Y.: Prometheus Books, 1980.

Hart, Tobin. "Deep Empathy." In *Transpersonal Knowing: Exploring the Horizon of Consciousness*, edited by Tobin Hart, Peter L. Nelson, and Kaisa Puhakka. Albany: State University of New York Press, 2000, pp. 253–70.

Hatfield, Elaine, John T. Cacioppo, and Richard T. Rapson. *Emotional Contagion.* New York: Cambridge University Press, 1994.

Hodges, Sara D., and Daniel M. Wegner. "Automatic and Controlled Empathy." In *Empathic Accuracy*, edited by William Ickes. New York: Guilford Press, 1997, pp. 311–39.

Hyman, Ray, and Charles Honorton. "A Joint Communiqué: The Psi Ganzfeld Controversy." *Journal of Parapsychology* 43 (1986): 205–20.

Kelly, George A. *The Psychology of Personal Constructs*. New York: Norton, 1955.

Levenson, Robert W., and Anna M. Ruef. "Empathy: A Physiological Substrate." *Journal of Personality and Social Psychology* 63 (1992): 234–46.

———. "Physiological Aspects of Emotional Knowledge and Rapport." In *Empathic Accuracy*, edited by William Ickes. New York: Guilford Press, 1997, pp. 44–72.

Lieberman, Matthew D. "Intuition: A Social Cognitive Neuroscience Approach." *Psychological Bulletin* 126 (2000): 109–37.

McClintock, Martha K. "Menstrual Synchrony and Suppression." *Nature* 229 (1971): 244–45.

Motluk, Alison. "Read My Mind." *New Scientist* (January 27, 2001).

Newman, Horatio H. *Twins and Super-Twins*. London: Hutchinson, 1942.

Neyer, Franz J., Rainer Banse, and Jens B. Asendorpf. "The Role of Projection and Empathic Accuracy in Dyadic Perception between Older Twins." *Journal of Social and Personal Relationships* 16 (1999): 419–42.

Playfair, Guy L. "Identical Twins and Telepathy." *Journal for the Society of Psychical Research* 63 (1999): 86–98.

Ramachandran, Vilayanur S. "Mirror Neurons and Imitation Learning as the Driving Force behind 'The Great Leap Forward' in Human Evolution." *Edge* 69 [online]. www.edge.org/documents/archive/edge69.html [June, 2000].

Randi, James. *Flim-Flam!: Psychics, ESP, Unicorns, and Other Delusions*. Amherst, N.Y.: Prometheus Books, 1982.

Rice, Edward. *Captain Sir Richard Francis Burton*. New York: Harper-Perennial, 1990.

Rizzolatti, Giacomo, and Michael A. Arbib. "Language within our Grasp." *Trends in Neuroscience* 21 (1998): 188–94.

Rizzolatti, Giacomo, Luciano Fadiga, et al. "Localization of Grasp Representations in Humans by PET: 1. Observation versus Execution." *Experimental Brain Research* 111 (1996): 246–52.

Rosenthal, Robert. "Meta-Analytic Procedures and the Nature of Replication: The Ganzfeld Debate." *Journal of Parapsychology* 50 (1986): 315–36.

Royle, Nicholas. *Telepathy and Literature*. Oxford, England: Basil Blackwell, 1991.

Sacks, Oliver. *The Man Who Mistook His Wife for a Hat and Other Clinical Tales.* New York: Summit Books, 1985.

Sommer, R., Humphry Osmond, and Lucille Pancyr. "Selection of Twins for ESP Experimentation." *International Journal of Parapsychology* 3 (1961): 55–69.

Strack, Fritz, Leonard L. Martin, and Sabine Stepper. "Inhibiting and Facilitating Conditions of the Human Smile: A Nonobtrusive Test of the Facial Feedback Hypothesis." *Journal of Personality and Social Psychology* 54 (1988): 768–76.

Weller, Leonard, and Aron Weller. "Human Menstrual Synchrony." *Neuroscience and Biobehavioral Reviews* 17 (1993): 427–39.

Zusne, Leonard, and Warren H. Jones. *Anomalistic Psychology.* Hillsdale, N.J.: Erbaum, 1982.

ACKNOWLEDGMENTS

The general shape of this book occurred to me during a conversation with Arthur Aron at a research conference in the summer of 1997. The actual writing began over a year later, however, in anticipation of a summer 1999 visit to the University of Canterbury in Christchurch, New Zealand. With the first two chapters written before that visit, I spent much of my New Zealand stay working on the next three chapters, which benefited from conversations with my host and sponsor, Garth Fletcher. His assistance, and the support of the Erskine Fellowship that I received from the University of Canterbury, are greatly appreciated.

All but one of the remaining chapters were written during the following three summers, with the freedom from teaching that resulted from research grants from the National Science Foundation and the Timberlawn Psychiatric Research Foundation. With the book nearly complete, I benefited from the advice and assistance of

Bruce Holland Rogers, Lansing Hays, Brad Potthoff, and Steve Duck in finding the right publisher for it. That publisher was Prometheus Books, whose editor-in-chief, Steven L. Mitchell, seemed to believe that I really could write a book that might appeal to a general audience as well as an academic one.

Everyday Mind Reading takes the form of a research odyssey, and therefore chronicles a variety of pitfalls, hazards, surprises, and felicitous discoveries. My greatest debt is to the many talented and hardworking colleagues who contributed to the research on empathic accuracy, and who therefore spent considerable time with me on this journey. They include my graduate student colleagues at the University of Texas at Arlington: Vickie Lau Baker, Victor Bissonnette, Jeremy Dugosh, Judith Flury, Stella Garcia, Randy Gesn, Tiffany Graham, Melanie Hancock, Joanna Hutchison, Joli Kelleher, Carol Marangoni, David Mortimer, Hao Pham, Kerri Renshaw-Rivers, Eric Robertson, Linda Stinson, William Schweinle, Gary Teng, and William Tooke. They also include my New Zealand colleagues, Garth Fletcher and Geoff Thomas, and my Belgian colleagues, Ann Buysse and Herbert Roeyers. Last, but by no means least, they include my Texas A&M colleague Jeff Simpson and his graduate student colleagues, who worked so tirelessly with us on our various research collaborations: Tami Blackstone, Lorne Campbell, Jami Grich, Minda Oriña, and Carol Wilson. As a chronicle of the journey that we all took part in, this book belongs to each of you.

My primary source of social support during the time I spent writing was, as always, my loving and patient wife, Mary Jo. I also wish to acknowledge the support, good will, and (in several cases) constructive criticism of many other people, including Cindy Atha-Weldon, Verne Cox, Perry Fuchs, David Funder, Anne Gordon, Judith Hall, Sara Hodges, Lauri Jensen-Campbell, David Kenny, Paul Paulus, Yuan Bo Peng, Greg Pool, Neal Smatresk, and Golden Strader. Finally, I would like to acknowledge the people who did the most to prepare me for this research odyssey: my parents,

William Keith and Shirley Hallman Ickes; and my graduate school mentors, Elliot Aronson and Robert Wicklund. You have been my toughest but most generous critics, and I thank you for it.

INDEX